IRS, TAXES AND THE BEAST
HOW TO SURVIVE IRS' NEW-AGE AUDIT INVASION

Daniel J. Pilla

WINNING Publications, Inc.
White Bear Lake, Minnesota

WINNING Publications, Inc.
2372 Leibel St.
White Bear Lake, MN 55110

First edition: November 1996

Printed in the United States of America

ISBN: 1-884367-01-1

Notice from the Author and Publisher

This book is designed to provide the author's findings and opinions based on research, analysis and experience with the subject matter covered. This information is not provided for purposes of rendering legal, accounting or other professional advice. It is intended purely for educational purposes.

The author and publisher disclaim any responsibility for any liability or loss incurred as a consequence of the use and application, either directly or indirectly, of any information presented herein.

Because the United States currently operates under an evolutionary legal system, the reader bears the burden of assuring the principles of law stated in this work are current and binding at the time of an intended use or application. Caution: the law in this country is subject to change arbitrarily and without prior notice.

DEDICATION

To Joshua

Put on the whole armor of God, that you may be able to stand against the wiles of the devil. For we are not contending against flesh and blood, but against the principalities, against the powers, against the world rules of this present darkness, against the spiritual hosts of wickedness in the heavenly places. Therefore, take the whole armor of God, that you may be able to withstand the evil day, and having done all, to stand.

- Ephesians 6:11-13

There is no crueler tyranny than that which is perpetrated under the shield of law and in the name of justice.

- Montesquieu, 1742

TABLE OF CONTENTS

ABBREVIATIONS

ACS	Automated Collection Site
ADP	Automated Data Processing
BLS	Bureau of Labor Statistics
BMF	Business Master File
CBO	Congressional Budget Office
CD	Certificate of Deposit
CEP	Coordinated Examination Program
CPI	Consumer Price Index
DEA	Drug Enforcement Agency
DIF	Discriminate Function System
FOIA	Freedom of Information Act
GAO	General Accounting Office
GATT	General Agreement on Tariffs and Trade
GNP	Gross National Product
IDR	Information Document Request
IMF	Individual Master File
IRA	Individual Retirement Account
IRMF	Information Returns Master File
ITIN	Individual Taxpayer Identification Number
MSSP	Market Segment Specialization Program
NCPA	National Center for Policy Analysis
NOD	Notice of Deficiency
OCR	Optical Character Recognition
OIC	Offer in Compromise
PLE	Personal Living Expense
PRO	Problems Resolution Office
RAR	Revenue Agent's Report
SFR	Substitute for Return
SSN	Social Security Number
T&E	Travel and Entertainment
TCMP	Taxpayer Compliance Measurement Program
TIN	Taxpayer Identification Number
TSM	Tax Systems Modernization

About the author . . .

For the past twenty years, Daniel J. Pilla has been tremendously successful in his negotiations with the IRS. Nationally regarded as an expert in IRS procedures, Dan has provided people across the country with sound solutions to tax-related financial difficulties. Additionally, Dan's proven techniques effectively prevent IRS problems before they begin.

In 1992, Dan uncovered and subsequently publicized tax-forgiveness programs instituted by Congress but deliberately kept quiet by the IRS. Through Dan's 3000 media appearances and the sale of more than 130,000 copies of his book, How to Get Tax Amnesty, better than three million people have found relief from a tax debt they were unable to pay.

In Dan's latest book, IRS, Taxes & the Beast, the IRS' plan to audit every citizen is exposed. The success of this plan requires the elimination of all deductions and cash, while giving IRS the ability to track all financial transactions. Citing from IRS internal documents, Dan reveals this attack on our freedom, then subsequently demonstrates how you can survive this invasion.

Dan's work has been recognized by the likes of CNN, CNBC, the USA Radio Network and Pat Robertson's 700 Club. His books have been recognized by leading magazines and financial journals such as Money Magazine, Family Circle, Wall Street Journal, Investors Business Daily and many others. Dan has contributed to major articles for Reader's Digest, the National Review and the Family Voice.

Additionally, Dan was a featured speaker at Pat Buchanan's seminar and is an official tax consultant to the US Taxpayer's Party, Howard Phillips' Conservative Caucus, the National Taxpayer's Union and many other taxpayers' groups.

PART I - IDENTIFYING THE BEAST

"The right of the people to be secure in their persons, houses, papers, and effects, against unreasonable searches and seizures, shall not be violated, and no Warrants shall issue, but upon probable cause, supported by Oath or affirmation, and particularly describing the place to be searched, and the persons or things to be seized."

Amendment Four
United States Constitution

Chapter One -
The Face of the Beast
"Meeting the IRS' New Enforcement Tool"

The Story Line

The man sat patiently in his car, watching carefully. He was a safe distance away from the front door of the house but would be sure to notice if anybody came out. He didn't particularly like the waiting, the hours of doing nothing. But hey, it's part of the job.

Suddenly, some action. The door opened and out stepped the object of his curiosity. A tall, middle-aged man walked down the front steps and climbed into his car. He was dressed very casually and carried a cooler.

"This could be it," thought the man. "Here we go!" He started his car and slowly followed the subject.

He was kind of new at this sort of thing. His heart was pounding. He wasn't sure how close to follow. Would he be spotted? But if he dropped back too far, he'd lose him. "Can't let that happen," he thought. "I've been waiting too long for this. Darn! They make it look so easy in the movies."

The subject twisted and turned through traffic, oblivious to his tail. He then headed south, toward the river. The scenic drive along the banks led to the marina. He pulled in and stopped near one of the many piers.

The man followed carefully, but stopped well back of the subject's car. He looked out at row after row of beautiful boats. Even the smaller ones seemed incredible. "How can people afford these things,?" he wondered, more than just a bit rhetorically.

As the subject walked down one of the docks, the man thought, "I've got him now!"

The subject stopped at one of the larger boats, fiddled with lines, hoses and cords, then fired the engines.

The man watched through binoculars as the subject cruised deliberately away from the marina. As the boat turned into the main channel, he mumbled out loud, "Man, that thing musta cost a fortune."

To be sure, he would find out.

What's It All About?

Is this a drug investigation? Is the subject suspected of smuggling? Is the boat part of a cache of illegal booty obtained through underworld activity?

What about the investigator? He must be a police officer, right? Maybe a Drug Enforcement Administration agent. Perhaps an FBI agent tailing a local mafia kingpin.

In fact, the investigation is about none of those things. The subject is not suspected of dealing drugs. In fact, he is not suspected of any illegal activity. He owns a small business in town and has a spotless record. He and his wife have owned the boat for years. Bought it used. It's their only luxury, really.

He's involved with the Chamber of Commerce, is active in his church, and coaches little league every summer. His wife volunteers at the homeless center twice a week and has been the church Sunday School director for going on five years.

What about the investigator? He is not a DEA agent, nor does he work for the FBI. He is not even a local police officer. He's an Internal Revenue agent. That's right. IRS.

He is involved in what he would call a routine tax audit. The subject is not suspected of owing any taxes, necessarily, but the IRS agent is curious about his lifestyle. He is engaged in what the IRS calls an "economic reality" audit.

You Must be Kidding!

No, I am not kidding. The scenario outlined above is fictional, but under the new audit guidelines, I fully expect such investigations to become routine.

In 1994, the IRS introduced an audit program known as the economic reality audit. It is premised upon the notion that every American is cheating on his tax return, but not by overstating deductions. Rather, by underreporting income. In order to verify that the income reported on a given tax return is in fact correct, the IRS' intention is to conduct what could amount to a full scale investigation of the assets and lifestyles of those selected for audit.

There you have it. The IRS believes you are cheating. It believes you earned income you did not report. It intends to use its new audit program to ferret out that income and collect the tax, interest and penalties it is convinced you most certainly owe.

How Did We Get to this Point?

This scenario seems to evidence a radical departure from our system of constitutional limited government where express rights are reserved to the people. One would expect such behavior only from the communist regimes of eastern Europe and the former Soviet Union. Inarguably, it is a departure from our unique system in which the citizen is to be protected from such invasions through a constitution limiting the power of the federal government, and by a Bill of Rights clearly delineating the liberties enjoyed by the inhabitants of our land.

The departure was originally occasioned, and is now exacerbated by the introduction of what I believe to be the grandest public policy mistake of the twentieth century, that being the establishment of an income tax through the 16th Amendment in 1913.

The income tax was the first legislative move imparting to the federal government any claim to direct contact with each individual citizen. Enforcing a law which revolves around what you earn, how you earn it and how you spend it, purports to birth the need of government to know every aspect of your private life.

In 1913, the IRS began as an obscure federal agency. The impact of the tax law at that time was visited upon just one percent of the population, our nation's very richest. But with the passage of time and legislation, the IRS and the pale of the tax law have found their way into the living rooms of every American family. Now, virtually all of us, even underaged children, must contend with the IRS for one reason or another, at one time or another.

With the growth of tax laws comes another phenomenon: tax avoidance. As the income tax sapped more of the emoluments of American productivity, the desire to avoid some or all of the tax grew in proportion. We have reached a point in this country where saving a dollar in taxes carries more benefit than earning a dollar of income. This reality has created a gigantic game of financial cat and mouse between citizens and the tax collector. The IRS perceives the citizens' actions as cheating. The citizens count them necessary just to survive.

The culmination of this game is the economic reality audit, the ultimate inquisition into one's financial standing. This audit is designed to outflank the creative accounting maneuvers, loophole applications, legal gyrations and the other devices of sagacious citizens and tax professionals.

This intrusive audit is certainly not the first of the aggressive acts contrived by IRS to apprehend the non-compliant. It is but one in a long train of moves designed to achieve omnipotence and ubiquity. For without such power, the IRS perceives it cannot win the battle to administer and enforce the income tax laws as they exist.

Chapter 2 -
How the Beast has Grown
"The Growing Power of the IRS"

In Christian literature, the term "beast" is often used to describe a powerful and oppressive entity, person or institution. It is derived primarily from the Revelation of St. John, in which the end of the world and return of Christ are prophesied. The Word foretells of the rise of an ungodly government or governor which oppresses the world until the return of Christ.

More so than other books of the Bible, Revelation is rife with metaphor. It facilitates therefore, not clarity and understanding, but rather, conjecture and supposition. And while the general theme is clear, its specific teachings have been the subject of endless theological debate. At Revelation 13:16-17, we find the following:

> He also forced everyone, small and great, rich and poor, free and slave, to receive a mark on his right hand or his forehead, so that no one could buy or sell unless he had the mark, which is the name of the beast or the number of his name.

The idea of a government or quasi-governmental body controlling the world economy in such a way is, at the very least, chilling. Such a suggestion has made Christian political activists and observers cognizant of public policy proposals which could arguably lead to such control. In evaluating various proposals, a critical eye is inexorably drawn to the IRS.

At the outset, the nature and purpose of the IRS necessarily puts the agency into a position of control over the financial activities of the general public. And because finances are inextricably linked to every other activity, the IRS has staked a claim to at least knowledge, if not control, of all aspects of one's life. To the end of perfecting such knowledge, the IRS has implemented troubling policies over the past score of years. They have awakened the curiosity of those of us concerned about the unreasonable growth of government.

The thrust began in May 1984, when the IRS released Document 6941, the "Internal Revenue Strategic Plan." The plan was much like an army would use to map its invasion strategy. In this case, the invaders are the IRS and the vanquished are American taxpayers. It set forth specific tactics designed to achieve a number of goals. Among these were to, 1) establish a paperless tax return system allowing the IRS to determine your income and expenses, 2) compute your tax liability without the need of your filing an income tax return (a flat tax system), and 3) set up a cashless society in which the transactions of all could be closely monitored for evidence of hidden income.

Perhaps the most chilling of the goals were those pointed at increasing tax law compliance. The IRS set forth the details of a plan to "increase presence" in the lives of all Americans and to make its "computers pervasive" in the cat and mouse game of tax law enforcement.

To achieve these, the IRS proposed a significant hike in its "computer generated contacts" of taxpayers. It also sought to turn up the heat on small businesses, traditionally thought of as licentious lechers when it comes to tax law compliance. It proposed to "modernize" its computer systems to allow it to keep pace with private sector advancements in technology. Its goal here was to build a system to centralize all financial and related information on citizens to guard against tax sinners.

Since 1984, the IRS has traveled a long way down the road mapped out in document 6941. Let us consider just a few of the milestones.

Computer notices. Computer notices are a quick, efficient way for the IRS to make contact with citizens. In most cases, it costs nothing but a postage stamp to collect hundreds in taxes, interest and penalties, whether or not legally owed. The agency knows this well and that is why escalating such contacts was seen as a key toward "increasing presence."

Since 1984, we have witnessed increases in computer notice rates that should boggle the mind of even the most casual observer. In 1984, the IRS issued about 420,000 notices designed to "correct" problems with tax returns. Of course, the correction notices almost always carried with them a concomitant tax bill. By 1986, the number grew to 769,000, an 83 percent increase in just two years. But the IRS was just getting warmed up.

Knowing most people simply paid the bill rather than undertaking the apparent herculean task of challenging the "beast," the IRS stepped up the program in a big way. In her 1991 Annual Report, former IRS commissioner Shirley Peterson declared that service center correction adjustments were responsible for "10 million letters." That is an increase of 1,300 percent from the 1984 numbers.

The worst part of this is not that most of the notices are wrong, but that the IRS knows they are wrong, and yet does little to solve the problems. In 1988, the General Accounting Office (GAO) visited the issue of IRS correspondence. In a report entitled, "IRS Service Centers Need to Improve Handling of Taxpayer Correspondence," the GAO found that 48 percent of all IRS notices were either wrong or incomprehensible. GAO/GGD-88-101, July 1988.

Repeat studies have addressed the question of what has been done to correct the problem. The most recent of these was released in December 1994. There, the GAO examined forty-seven of the most common notices used by IRS to communicate with citizens. The notices accounted for some $190 billion in transactions during tax year 1993. Of those forty-seven notices, thirty-one of them--66 percent of the lot--used inspecific language, unclear references, inconsistent terminology, illogical presentation of ideas, and provided insufficient guidance and information to the recipient. GAO/GGD-95-6, December 1994.

The source of the errors and omissions was pegged as programming glitches. IRS is, according to GAO, fully aware of the problems but claims it cannot free the time and personnel necessary to fix them. In fact, GAO observed that "higher priority demands for computer programming changes lessen the likelihood that notice text changes will be made. While recommended notice text changes remain unprogrammed, the old version of the notice continues to be issued to taxpayers." Ibid, page 9. This does not portent well for a future system in which the IRS computes your liability for you, then simply sends a bill.

During the same period, we have seen a similar explosion in the number of penalties issued by the IRS. With over 140 different penalty provisions in the tax code, the IRS has a smorgasbord of possibilities available to it. Because the IRS makes absolutely no investigation of a given case in the vast majority of penalty assessments, citizens are often improperly yoked with these burdens. Even worse, the citizen has the duty to affirmatively challenge the assessment in the procedurally correct manner before a penalty is forgiven. The level of ignorance of these rights causes most penalties to stick even though they are improper.

In 1980, at the threshold of the decade which brought more than one hundred changes to the tax code, the IRS assessed 19.59 million penalties against individuals and businesses for total revenue of $1.55 billion. The next several years of "tax simplification" culminated in the Tax Reform Act of 1986. It was sold to us as the quintessential simplification measure. The first year the law took effect was 1987.

In 1987, the IRS assessed a total of 26.97 million penalties, worth a total of $9.99 billion in revenue. So, while the tax law was "simplified," the number of penalties grew by 37 percent and penalty revenue exploded by 640 percent.

Penalties continued to grow throughout the 1990s at a similar rate. By 1995, IRS assessed 34.01 million penalties, and penalty revenue grew to $15.6 billion. That represents an increase of 173 percent in penalties and over 1000 percent in penalty revenue compared to 1980.

In these two areas alone, we can safely say the "beast" has made its presence known and felt in the homes and offices of countless millions of American families and businesses.

Tax Systems Modernization (TSM). Tax Systems Modernization is the massive computer rebuilding program the IRS embarked upon in 1984. The program is responsible for well over $3 billion in spending since its inception and Congress had agreed to spend about $20 billion more by the year 2008.

TSM is the IRS' golden calf. The agency believes computer power --hardware and software upgrades--will deliver the tools it needs to become omnipotent and ubiquitous. At the core of TSM is the push toward a paperless return filing system and system of electronic transfer of funds by those who owe taxes. Under the latter system, tax payments are remitted electronically.

Already, IRS has spent a fortune developing optical character recognition (OCR) forms and installing the equipment to read them. OCR-compatible documents are the precursor to eliminating paper entirely.

In 1987, the first full year of electronic filing, some 77,000 returns were filed by sixty-six return preparers in seven metropolitan areas. By 1992, 52,000 participants filed nearly 11 million electronic returns. As of 1994, the number grew to 12.51 million, then dropped slightly in 1995 to 11.14 million.

However impressive this expansion seems, it is not enough for the IRS. Recall that the principle goal of the 1984 plan was to eliminate paper income tax returns and establish a flat tax system. The rate of growth in the voluntary filing of electronic returns from 1986 to the present indicates the IRS is not likely to achieve that goal soon.

Recognizing this, the IRS is moving to achieve the power to force electronic filing. In April 1993, the IRS issued a report entitled, "Final Recommendations of the Service Center Organization Study." The report discusses the IRS' proposals to facilitate TSM. It makes seven specific legislative proposals IRS believes necessary to implement its findings and TSM in general. The recommendations relevant to the question of electronic returns filing are, 1) allowing for tax payments by credit card, and 2) mandate electronic filing by return preparers and business tax returns.

The IRS has seemingly lost patience with the public's lack of acceptance of the electronic filing concept. There is no better way for the IRS to counter the sluggish response than to mandate electronic returns filing. The proposal is to require (initially) return preparers to file electronically. With approximately sixty million citizens using return preparers annually, the IRS, in a single gesture, can increase to about one-half the number of returns submitted by computer.

Look for mandated computer filing to quickly expand to all other areas. Before long, the IRS will require all citizens and businesses to file their returns using electronic media.

A second report on the subject was issued by the IRS on October 20, 1993. That report is entitled, "Internal Revenue Service Legislative Proposals in Support of the National Performance Review" (NPR). In it, the IRS is much more specific on the nature of their legal wish list. In particular, the IRS is seeking "broad regulatory authority to require" that returns be filed electronically.

On November 17, 1993, Leslie B. Samuels, Assistant Treasury Secretary for Tax Policy, testified before the House Subcommittee on Commerce, Consumer and Monetary Affairs, Committee on Government Operations. That testimony emphasized the Treasury's support of the legislative initiatives proposed by NPR. The testimony declared,

> The Service has proposed that the Secretary be given regulatory authority to require that tax returns be filed other

than in paper form, including electronically or by magnetic media. This authority would extend to all tax returns, including income tax returns for individuals, trusts and estates. The Service envisions that the conversion to non-paper filings would be phased in by various groups of taxpayers and returns, taking into account the relative costs and other burdens associated with converting to an electronic filing system.

Thus, we see plainly that the IRS is no longer content to allow electronic filing to remain an elective available to citizens at their option. Because the IRS is plainly intending to force this filing medium upon the public, it is easy to conclude the entire system was never intended to benefit the public in the first place. Proof of this assertion comes from Samuels' testimony. Consider this:

Broad regulatory authority to require that returns be filed other than in paper form is appropriate and *essential to the Service's ability* to modernize its systems, streamline its operations, and in general, deliver quality services at the least cost (emphasis added).

You may be thinking that the process of moving to a paperless system and "modernizing and streamlining its systems" can only save money. Who in their right mind would oppose such a move, especially given the current status of the federal fisc?

If, I repeat--IF--the move were designed to save money by honestly reducing the size of the IRS and its operational budget, I may be inclined to view the proposals in a different light. However, there is adequate proof to support the finding that these plans have nothing whatsoever to do with reducing the size and cost of the IRS.

In a news release issued by the IRS on December 2, 1993, the agency discussed its plans for eliminating five service centers, affecting some 16,000 jobs. A flat tax paperless system eliminates the need for five of the IRS' ten service centers since returns processing work could be cut substantially. But do not think those 16,000 employees will be laid off by the agency. On the contrary.

About this plan, national IRS spokesman Henry Holmes said, "we want the positions to be reinvested for customer service and compliance." In accord with that idea, Robert Tobias, president of the

National Treasury Employees Union, said the IRS' plan "offers employees the opportunity to progress from dead-end jobs of the old tax processing system to jobs with more skills and more direct impact on taxpayers." In other words, look forward to 16,000 more IRS employees turned loose on the streets to harass the public.

This comes on top of the already explosive growth in the IRS' work force. In 1986, the IRS averaged 96,395 employees. By the end of 1995, the total was 114,064, an increase of nearly 20 percent. Of the total employees in 1995, 16,072 were revenue agents charged with the duty of conducting tax audits. From this we see that the Service Center Reorganization Plan could double the number of tax auditors.

As part of the overall plan to eliminate paper tax returns, the IRS is pushing legislation to allow the agency to accept credit cards in payment of taxes due. This was emphasized in the "Service Center Organization Study." However, the public has not been told the truth as to why the agency is pushing this change. We have been led to believe the proposal is designed to make tax payments simpler and less burdensome for taxpayers. Since most citizens own credit cards and since payment with credit cards is more convenient than with checks or money orders, IRS suggests it is merely accommodating those needs. A more in-depth study of the issue, however, reveals a wolf in sheep's clothing.

In testimony to Congress in November 1994, Leslie Samuels shed substantial light upon the issue. The testimony addressed the IRS' desire for legislation allowing it to accept credit cards in payment of tax debts, saying:

> We believe this legislation is an important part of the Service's strategy to shift from a paper-based remittance processing system to an information processing system.

Samuels did not suggest this move is designed to make life easier for any citizen. Rather, it is part of the IRS' overall strategy to eliminate paper returns and cash.

Just as with electronic filing, the measure would begin as a purely optional service. But, as we have seen in the evolution of electronic filing, it will soon become mandatory for all to pay taxes through some form of electronic transfer. And the stage has already been set.

In 1991, IRS established a prototypical electronic funds transfer system for deposits of employment taxes. The system is known as TAXLINK. It did not take long for that to mutate into a mandatory system. Revenue Regulation section 31.6302-1T dictates that beginning in January 1995, employment taxes must be deposited to IRS through electronic funds transfer. As with all such measures, there is a phase-in period set out in subsection (h)(1) of the regulation.

The requirement attaches first to companies depositing at least $78 million in employment taxes during a single twelve-month period. As you can imagine, that certainly does not encompass many businesses. However, the threshold drops steadily. As of January 1, 1996, the level is $47 million. And by January 1, 1999, the amount drops to just $20 thousand (not million, thousand).

Do not be misled. TSM is not intended to help you. It is, in fact, pointed at consolidating IRS' power and extending its reach.

Tracking Citizens and Financial Transactions. IRS consistently laments the lack of what it deems sufficient information on the details of financial transactions. The IRS refers to such deficiencies as holes in the "information reporting safety net." The idea is, the more the agency knows, the more likely it is that individuals will "voluntarily" report all their income and pay all taxes owed. If a particular transaction falls through that safety net, the IRS immediately believes it becomes a source of tax cheating.

The first order of business in plugging the holes is to mandate information reporting on every possible transaction. The second is to eliminate cash.

Since the Tax Reform Act of 1986, there has been an explosion in the requirements for submitting information returns. The rules include real estate transactions, stocks and securities, interest payments and a myriad of others. As of 1986, general cash transactions in excess of $10,000 must be reported to the IRS on Form 8300 by the person receiving the cash in the course of his trade or business. Even payments to babysitters must be reported to enjoy the child care credit available under code section 21. Code section 21(e)(9)(A).

The law requiring reports of cash transactions is said to be designed to track down those engaged in tax evasion by using cash to hide their activities from the IRS. Ironically, the penalty for merely not filing the form can be as serious as the tax evasion penalty itself. Compare Internal Revenue code sections 6721(e)(2)(C) and 7201. The civil penalty is more serious than the criminal fine for failing to file an income tax return altogether. Compare section 7203.

Of course, all the information reporting requirements in the world are feckless if the IRS is unable to assimilate data and tie them back to the individuals in question. For that reason, the IRS is determined to brand all citizens with a peculiar number. The agency has selected the social security number as the mode of preference for this task. In this regard, the number has indeed become the number of your name.

What began as a seemingly innocuous requirement during the 1960s has grown to a heavy burden with pernicious implications. This fact has caused much consternation in the Christian community. It began inauspiciously in the early 1960s when the IRS began implementing rudimentary computer technology. For obvious reasons, it became necessary to organize computer files by number rather than name. Since most working Americans already had a peculiar number assigned to them by the Social Security Administration, the IRS adopted it as the "taxpayer identification number" (TIN). Citizens began filing income tax returns, and businesses filed Forms W-2 and 1099 using social security numbers (SSN) as the identifying link between the individual named and the reported data.

The system operated for decades with nary a hitch. By the late 1970s, however, the IRS became convinced that tax evasion through the use of improper dependent exemptions was on the rise. IRS studies purported to show that between 1965 and 1979, the revenue lost from such exemptions grew from $1.9 billion to $8.2 billion. IRS Publication 1500, "Trend Analysis and Related Statistics," August 1990, page 65.

As early as 1976, the IRS began pressuring Congress for authority to require SSNs for dependent exemptions. However, "[T]his proposal was not pursued at that time because of anticipated concerns of Congress and taxpayers." Ibid, page 64.

But the environment changed substantially by 1984 when the IRS' strategic plan was adopted. Congress became more willing to overlook the privacy and religious concerns of the public so long as it could show that increased revenue would flow to the Treasury. In 1986, the Treasury prepared a report to Congress projecting lost revenue of $4.3 billion in 1987 and $22 billion for years 1987 through 1991 due to illegitimate exemptions. The proposal sought Congress to require citizens to have SSNs for minor children in order to claim them as dependent exemptions. It was adopted in modified form as part of the Tax Reform Act of 1986. Code section 6109(e).

At the time adopted, the requirement applied to dependents age five or older. Shortly thereafter, the IRS surveyed those still lacking SSNs for their dependents. What the agency discovered gave it impetus to push for even stricter requirements. The survey found that,

Of the parents who did not have SSNs for their children in May of 1987, 62 percent had no concerns about getting those SSNs. This figure rose to 66 percent in October and by January 1988 to 73 percent. In January 1988, only 11 percent of those who did not already have SSNs for their children (or 1.2 percent of the total population) were concerned about becoming a 'numbered society' and only about 8 percent of these individuals (0.9 percent of the total population) had privacy worries. Pub 1500, page 68.

Since it seemed precious few cared about the implications of branding their minor children with SSNs, the requirement was soon made to apply to children aged two years or more. It then dropped to one-year olds. And the culmination came on December 8, 1994, when President Clinton signed the Uruguay Round Agreements Act, implementing the much debated General Agreement on Tariffs and Trade (GATT). Public Law 103-465, December 8, 1994.

Because GATT was 1,500 pages of legislation pointed primarily at trade policy, the public's attention never focused upon the few provisions dealing with domestic tax issues. Despite the courage Congress was gathering from the steady and progressive drops in the age threshold, it seemed unwilling to risk any public outcry incident to its next intended move.

Section 742(b) of the GATT legislation set forth a provision requiring SSNs for children at birth. It applies to all tax returns beginning in 1996 and to all dependents claimed on the return, regardless of age.

This provision is the IRS' legislative holy grail. It has been coveted and pursued for twenty years, its passage allows the agency to begin achieving its goal of tracking every move of every citizen. It was buried deep within the 1,500 pages of the GATT agreement expressly to avert any potential outcry.

Despite the requirement to have SSNs for minor children, Congress did recognize that certain citizens holding a religious opposition need not obtain them. Congress specifically wrote that it intends those with a religious opposition be "exempt" from using such numbers for their minor children. In fact, the IRS developed an alternative to the SSN for use in such cases. See *How to Fire the IRS*, pages 68-75.

However, in the 1996 blizzard of tax legislation, Congress attacked even this sanctuary. Buried within the Small Business Job Protection

Act was a law making it mandatory for dependent exemptions to have an SSN--no apparent exceptions. Act section 1615, amending code section 151(e). Whereas once the IRS had no legal authority to deny the exemption so long as its legitimacy could be proven in other ways, now the IRS possesses such authority. Look for the agency to use it with abandon. In chapter three, under the heading, "Guard Your Social Security Number," I discuss what can be done to protect yourself from this invasion.

Here is yet another example of Congress hiding damaging legislation from public view until it is too late. In my mind, this is clear evidence that the IRS is out of control and determined to muscle its way into every aspect of your private life.

The idea of numbering society is not without precedent. In fact, it is that precedent which is part of the reason for the consternation some have about it. In 1 Chronicles 21, we are told that King David did this very thing to Israel. Verse 1 says "Satan stood up against Israel, and incited David to number Israel." David instructed his lieutenants to go throughout the land and number the inhabitants and to "bring me a report." Verse 2.

David was at the peak of his career when this directive was given. His victories in battle were legendary and Israel was prosperous and free under his reign. It seems victory and prosperity went to David's head. Does his will to number the people evidence a desire to be like God?

Throughout Scripture, stories are told of those who fall from grace for this reason. The most compelling example is that of Adam and Eve. Eve was persuaded to eat the forbidden fruit on the premise that when she did, her "eyes will be opened, and you will be like God." Genesis 3:5.

Among the many unique characteristics of God are ubiquity and omnipotence. It seems David's act of numbering the people was carried out for a two-fold purpose. First, it is clear that David wished to pridefully revel in his success governing Israel. By numbering the people, he could quantify that success. A second, more subtle reason is that David, like so many before and after him, wished to consolidate his power, to become like God, ubiquitous and omnipotent. To do that requires knowledge of all that you rule over, especially the people. Numbering them is a key way to achieve such knowledge.

David's chief advisor, the prophet Joab, strongly advised against the plan. Why do such a thing?, he asked. Why "bring guilt upon

Israel?" 1 Chronicles 21:3. But against the advice and warning of Joab, David carried out his plan.

It soon became apparent that David did wrong. David said to God, "I have sinned greatly in that I have done this thing." Verse 8. David referred to his act as "foolishness." And God brought punishment upon Israel for David's act. Verses 9-14. What can America look forward to as a result of what our leaders are now undertaking?

Apart from the Scriptural view of this question, history teaches that numbering society is, at best, a vile affront to individual liberty and at worst, a stepping stone on the road to absolute despotism. Contemporary evidence of this may be more compelling than the example of David's folly.

Prisoners in our penal system are numbered upon entering confinement. The number becomes the "number of their name." As a result of their criminal behavior, they lose their liberty and individuality, becoming nothing more than an article of inventory to be tracked and monitored. And while I do not contend that convicted criminals should be treated any other way, it clearly evidences that "numbering" people is an attack on liberty.

A more outrageous example comes from Nazi Germany. During the zenith of Nazi domination, it operated some thirty concentration camps throughout Europe. The Nazis interned all who posed any threat whatsoever to Hitler's despotic regime. The inmates were stripped of their property, liberty, family, individuality, and for many, eventually their very lives. Upon their arrival in these camps, citizens were physically tattooed on the hand with what became the "number of their name." From that point on, they were no longer considered by their captors to be people. They were merely chattel, often worked to death, experimented upon, or worse. The act of numbering people was that of one of the most horrific tyrants the world has ever known.

Despite new laws, the reporting punch derived from the SSN requirement does not eliminate what has proven to be the IRS' number one nemesis--cash. However, a number is a fundamental prerequisite to eliminating cash. As long as cash circulates freely in the marketplace, those with a will shall find a way to evade payment of some or all of their taxes. Moreover, cash represents privacy and freedom, two concepts antithetical to the income tax. Because the current system is driven by deriving the correct source and true amount of all one's income, it is mandatory the IRS crucify that miscreant.

The elimination of cash, however, is no easy task. The Congressional Budget Office (CBO) reports that as much as 50 to 75 percent of all transactions (by number, not value), are for cash. This is true despite the fact that there has been a rapid increase in the use of checks and credit cards over the past ten years. For example, the use of credit cards has doubled and credit card debt has more than tripled to $350 billion since 1985. CBO, "Emerging Electronic Methods for Making Retail Payments," June 1996, page 17.

To further complicate the matter, much of the cash in circulation is in denominations of $10 or less. The report declares,

> The value of outstanding U.S. coins and bills with a face value of $10 or less is roughly $50 billion. Those coins and bills circulate, and one can be used many times a year. Thus, the total value of the transactions involving the stock of coins and bills in circulation is a multiple of the $50 billion face value. Ibid, pages 16 and 17, footnotes omitted.

Because of the sheer volume of cash transactions and America's reluctance to step away from them, the IRS must approach the elimination of cash in the same way it has ushered in other radical changes to our economic lives--slowly. I believe the process began in earnest in October 1991, when the Treasury began manufacturing currency notes with specialized "anti-counterfeiting devices."

Upon learning of them, I began an investigation into what they were and discovered some curious facts. My investigation took me to the Treasury Department where I spoke with two different officials about the devices. It also took me to the manufacturer of the paper on which currency notes are printed. I spoke with three different people there. I report all the details of my investigation in my book, *How to Fire the IRS*, at pages 19-27.

I learned that U.S. currency notes now contain "covert features" which are in fact encodeable devices intended to carry data imprinted within the note itself. The most significant of these is a "polyester" strip which is imbedded into the very paper on which our currency notes are printed. The strip is located to the left of the portrait, and runs from top to bottom. The strip bears the markings "USA," then a number representing the denomination of the bill. A $10 bill, for example, says "USA 10." The strip is now in all but $1 bills.

The fact is, the term "polyester" is nothing more than the nomenclature assigned to the strip by the manufacturer. It has nothing whatsoever to do with the actual characteristics of the material. We know, for example, the markings on the strips are stamped in aluminum, a fact I discovered after Treasury officials denied there being any metallic traits to the strip.

Since *How to Fire the IRS* was released, I have confirmed through an unimpeachable source that the strip is overcoated with a vacuum deposited aluminum layer and the letters are printed by means of a caustic resistant ink varnish. It is also true that legible printing or bar type optically readable codes are directly stamped onto the metal letters. When I questioned the Treasury about these features, they denied that any were present.

I have questioned whether the bills contained data features which would allow them to be traced through the marketplace. In that fashion, the IRS would conceivably be able to better monitor the exchange of currency and in that way, tighten the screws on the underground economy. The Treasury has flatly denied that the bills are encodeable in this fashion. However, it also denied many other facts which later proved to be true.

Both the Treasury and the paper manufacturer insist the measure is nothing more than an anti-counterfeiting step. Both claim the strip is a security device intended to be used as a means of authenticating U.S. currency notes. A legitimate note contains the strip, verifiable by holding it up to a light source. A bogus bill has no strip.

There are two problems with this. First, the vast majority of the public and certainly the retail community are unaware of the presence of this security device. In fact, the Treasury expressly referred to it as a "covert" device, thereby implying that it would not be widely disclosed. The major retailers I questioned in my investigation knew nothing of the device at the time. How can an anti-counterfeiting device possibly be effective in the protection of retailers if the people it is intended to protect are unaware of its presence?

Secondly, these new bills circulate side by side with existing, uncoded notes. Even if the strip were fully disclosed to the public through a broad based public relations campaign, the protection is of no moment if the old, unsecured bills are not pulled from circulation.

But Treasury officials scoff at the idea of currency traceable through the marketplace. How is it possible to equip all retailers with the necessary tools, then force them to encode currency notes with data about the person who tendered them? And I must confess, this is quite a stretch, even for an agency determined beyond reason to capture the underground economy for tax purposes. That is why I do not believe, and never did, that the device would have any chance of succeeding. In fact, as I have said many times, it is clearly intended to fail. And now, that failure can be evidenced.

In the spring of 1995, the Treasury issued yet another newly designed currency note. The new $100 bill features a greatly enlarged, off-center portrait of Franklin, a serial number with an extra letter, a watermark of Franklin visible when held up to light and color-shifting ink. The numerals appear green when viewed head on and black when viewed from the side.

These changes, sure to appear in other currency notes, are also touted as anti-counterfeiting devices. But wait. Was not the polyester strip supposed to end the problem of counterfeit bills? Apparently, it did not do the job. Be sure that after a time, the Treasury will announce that its new designs have also failed.

Their efforts cannot possibly succeed. The newest bills, just as with bills containing the polyester strip, are to circulate side by side with existing bills. With no effort to remove existing bills from circulation, alleged counterfeiters can continue pirating the old bills without regard to the Treasury's high tech inventions and designs.

The failure to these measures must in turn lead to an announcement that because it is so critical to eliminate counterfeiting, the only solution is to eliminate cash. That, in turn will trigger the systemic replacement of our cash society with one operating purely on an electronic system. Under such a system, each and every transaction in which you engage can be traced and potentially reported to the IRS. Your financial freedom and independence will be a thing of the past.

You may be thinking it is impossible to replace cash because of the tremendous need for coins and small bills in so much of our commerce. But industry is taking care of that problem as I write. In the past several years, we have seen banks and credit card issuers embark upon a major push for more and more credit cards. That, of course, is the first step in eliminating cash. If we all can be convinced to use credit cards rather than cash, the majority of transactions (in value, not number) will be fully recorded and traceable.

Another recent development in electronic money is only now beginning to take shape. Once it grows to fruition and is accepted by the public, it could well eliminate the need for coins and small bills. I speak of the so-called stored value card, sometimes called the "smart card." It is often referred to as an electronic purse, having the same form and appearance as a credit card or ATM card, but functioning much differently.

A stored value card itself contains a reservoir of purchasing power. A consumer buys a card with a pre-set value. To spend the value, the user passes the card through an electronic reader which draws value from the card on the basis of the purchase.

In the past few years, we have seen these cards in various forms. The Washington, DC Metro subway system uses these cards exclusively. To ride the subway, you must first purchase a stored value card. The value is determined solely by the user's needs. For example, say one purchases a card for $20. To take a $1.50 ride on the subway, he passes the card through the reader, which automatically deducts $1.50 from the value of the card. The remaining value is $18.50. When the value is used up, the card is captured by the reader and the customer purchases a new one.

Perhaps the best example of these cards in broad use is pre-paid phone cards. In the same manner as the subway, you buy a card with a pre-set value. The card is passed through the phone in an airport or hotel lobby. The cost of your call is deducted electronically from the card. Once the card is spent, you dispose of it and buy a new one. With such a card in hand, you never need a quarter for a local call. You never need 75 cents to ride the subway. You carry all the change you need in an electronic purse.

Since 1992, businesses, governments and banks have experimented with stored value cards in a big way. The Department of Agriculture's food stamp program replaced coupon books with cards in 1992. In 1994, Chemical Bank in New York City began using the cards for the cafeteria purchases of its employees. The National Football League franchise Jacksonville Jaguars use the cards for stadium purchases of souvenirs. The biggest stored value card program was instituted by Visa in cooperation with several banks. The program was pointed at the one million attendees of the 1996 summer Olympic Games in Atlanta. The cards were used for consumer purchases in restaurants, stores, vending machines, etc. CBO, "Emerging Electronic Methods for Making Retail Payments," June 1996, page 14, Table 1.

The emergence of the stored value card has completed the package of products necessary to sell the idea of eliminating cash. Consider the tools we now have available for completing a transaction. Our wages are paid by check, which we deposit to a bank account. Sometimes, we do not even see the check. It is deposited directly to an account by the employer. From the account, we write specific checks to individual vendors for payment of goods and services. Instead or in combination, we use credit cards to pay for products on a day to day basis, then write a single check to the card issuer at the end of the month. We might also or rather use a debit card, which functions more like an electronic check. When purchasing with a debit card, the funds are drawn directly from a bank account at the time of purchase. Lastly, we can purchase stored value cards from banks and other issuers for such things as phone calls, bus rides, ticket purchases, vending machines and so on. While the stored value card is yet in its infancy, expect it to grow substantially in both acceptance and application very quickly.

With such tools available, what is the further need for cash? In fact, given the problems of lost and stolen cash, counterfeiters, tax cheaters, drug dealers and other criminals with a penchant for using cash, I can plainly see the public relations campaign for eliminating it. The single overriding advantage for the government is, of course, every transaction is now fully traceable and your freedom and privacy is lost in the process.

Tapping Private Databases. The 1984 plan mapped out a very aggressive, and some thought impractical, goal of linking its computers both to all existing government databases and to all private data bases as well. For years, the IRS has had access to the databases of other government agencies. And it should come as no surprise that it obtains data from those agencies for use in administering the laws. What has taken many by surprise is the IRS' announcement of December 20, 1994, regarding its plan to obtain "on-line" access to the nation's private databases including,

> [C]ommercial sources, state and local agencies, construction contract information, license information from state and local agencies, currency and banking reports (CBRS), data regarding assets and financial transactions from state and local agencies, and information on significant financial transactions from reviews of periodicals and newspapers and other media sources. "Notice of Proposed Amendment to Privacy Act System of Records, Federal Register 59, no. 243 (December 20, 1994).

The notice goes on to describe exactly who would be the target of the proposed invasion. The people covered under the aggressive electronic surveillance system are described as,

[A]ny individual who has business and/or financial activities. These may be grouped by industry, occupation, or financial transactions included in commercial databases, or in information provided by state and local licensing agencies. Ibid.

Has anyone been left off the list?

The watershed report. In May 1994, the GAO issued a report which would shake up the IRS like nothing had done in decades. It would cause the IRS to rethink its entire approach to tax law enforcement in general and tax audits in particular. The report would prove to be the genesis of the IRS' economic reality audit program.

The report is entitled, "Tax Gap, Many Actions Taken, But a Cohesive Compliance Strategy Needed." GAO/GGD-94-123, May 1994. The phrase "tax gap" is used to describe the taxes that are owed to the government but not reported on returns and voluntarily paid.

The tax gap figure should not be confused with outstanding tax debts, which are referred to as IRS' accounts receivable. A receivable is a debt which is on the books, but not paid. The IRS knows who owes delinquent taxes. They are assessed but are not collected due to the financial shortcomings of the debtor.

The tax gap, by contrast, is more of a theoretical number. Tax gap research attempts to determine how citizens are avoiding the payment of taxes, either by not reporting income or overstating deductions. As you can imagine, this is not an exact science. Most tax gap findings are derived from audit results, both of a general nature and from the IRS' Taxpayer Compliance Measurement Program (TCMP).

The chief problem with using audit results to project tax gap estimates is the fact that audit results themselves are inaccurate. In a report I wrote for Washington's Cato Institute, entitled, "Why You Can't Trust the IRS," I studied several areas of tax enforcement, including computer notices, penalty assessments and audit results. Based upon a thorough examination of IRS' own internal documents and my own experience, I found the IRS to be wrong about half the time in these and other areas. Cato Institute Policy Analysis No. 222, April 15, 1995.

Drawing exclusively from IRS documents, bulletins, and compliance research analyses, the GAO reported that the lion's share of the tax gap arises from individual citizens' failure to report all income. Specifically, GAO said,

Table 1.1 shows that the tax gap created by individuals' unreported income rose over $22 billion between 1981 and 1992. About half of this increase as well as half of the total $63 billion gap came from unreported sole proprietor (i.e., self-employed individuals) income. Such income is generated by 'informal suppliers' (proprietors who operate their businesses informally, usually on a cash basis), farm proprietors and non-farm proprietors. GAO/GGD-94-123, May 1994, page 15.

The following is Table 1.1, reproduced from the GAO report referenced above.

Exhibit 2-1

Dollars in millions

Source of tax gap	1981 tax gap amount	1992 tax gap amount	Percent Increase
Individual tax gap	$61,900	$93,994	51.8
Unreported income	40,433	62,759	55.2
Sole proprietors	18,714	30,173	61.2
All other income	21,719	32,586	50.0
Overstated deductions[a]	7,449	8,081	8.5
Individual nonfiler	5,231	10,233	95.6
Individual remittance gap	8,300	11,400	37.3
Math errors	487	1,521	212.3
Corporate tax gap	14,066	33,135	135.6
Small corporation	4,461	6,999	56.9
Large corporation	8,638	23,716	174.6
Others[b]	167	420	151.5
Corporate remittance gap	800	2,000	150.0
Total tax gap	**$75,966**	**$127,129**	**67.2[c]**

[a]Includes subtractions for erroneous deductions, exemptions, credits, and other adjustments.

[b]Includes unreported income and overstated deductions for exempt organizations' unrelated business income and for fiduciaries.

[c]As shown in appendix I, table I.2, the gross tax gap in 1992 dollars increased 8.7 percent from $117 million in 1981 to $127 million in 1992.

Source: Income Tax Compliance Research, IRS Publication 1415 (7-88); and Income Tax Compliance Research: Net Tax Gap and Remittance Gap Estimates, IRS Publication 1415 (4-90).

As you see from the chart, the tax gap attributable to overstated deductions rose just 8.5 percent from 1981 to 1992. However, the gap attributable to unreported income increased by more than 55 percent during the same period. This is true of both individual citizens and self-employed persons.

As a result, the IRS has restructured its audit training, redirecting the thrust of its audit activity. Rather than focusing upon the deductions claimed in a return, it now focuses upon the income side of the ledger. This is the heart and soul of the economic reality audit.

As we shall examine in this discourse, the scope of the economic reality audit is far greater than anything the IRS has ever attempted. For reasons we shall explore at length, the economic reality audit promises to be the most invasive and potentially abusive tax enforcement program ever. For these reasons, I have dubbed these audits the "underwear drawer" audits. The IRS intends to rummage through your underwear drawer in search of the $20 it believes you have hidden there.

The IRS and the Beast

The foregoing paints an ominous picture of the IRS and its designs upon the liberty of American citizens. Does it necessarily mean that the IRS is the "beast" spoken of in Revelation? Certainly not. Does it necessarily mean that the government or quasi-governmental agency which is to control the world must spring from the United States? Certainly not. But is it mere coincidence that the goals of the IRS would put the agency in a position to control the buying and selling of all Americans? Is it mere coincidence that the IRS, of all government agencies, has undertaken to number all citizens that it might accomplish the goal of monitoring all buying and selling?

In Search of a Savior

The manifold problems with the IRS and our confusing tax laws have caused a loud cry for changes to our system. The issues were highlighted by the 1996 presidential campaign of businessman Steve Forbes. Forbes called for the elimination of the current system and adoption of a flat tax.

Forbes and other flat tax proponents claim the IRS will be greatly reduced by a flat tax. They claim IRS abuse and misconduct will be eliminated under a flat tax. They claim that for most Americans, the income tax will be nothing more than an April 15 post card mailed once per year to Washington.

The sad reality is the flat tax is simply not the panacea claimed by its proponents. The suggestion that all IRS abuse and misconduct can be eliminated by the flat tax is but the ranting of a monochromatic, casual observer. For example, the economic reality audit system, the most invasive and potentially abusive tactic yet devised by the agency, is designed to operate under a flat tax system. Consider the facts.

The GAO's tax gap report points out that the largest share of the gap is attributable to unreported income, not deductions. The focus of the economic reality audit is, therefore, unreported income, not deductions. Under a flat tax system, one must continue to report income, but deductions are eliminated. What in the world prevents the IRS from auditing a flat tax return in search of hidden income? The answer is nothing! In fact, as I illustrate later, most audits currently attack short form filers. For all practical purposes, short forms are flat tax returns since they report income but no deductions.

More significantly, we must recognize that the majority of people with IRS problems have collection problems. That is, they cannot pay the taxes owed. This leads to penalties, interest and to enforced collection action. Enforcement action consists of, 1) tax liens which encumber property and destroy credit, 2) wage and bank levies which ravage cash flow and make it difficult or impossible to pay living expenses, and 3) property seizures which lead to the loss of one's home, business and other assets. Nothing in a flat tax system addresses this overriding concern.

After careful deliberation of the alternative tax systems available, I have arrived at the conclusion that only a national retail sales tax can eliminate the IRS. A retail sales tax ends the need for the average American to face the IRS in any manner. Because the tax is paid at the point of purchase, no extensive record keeping is required and no returns are needed to report one's income. Because a sales tax has nothing to do with one's earnings, the IRS has no claim to examine the books and private affairs of our people.

Most importantly, the sales tax ends the problems stemming from the IRS' pharisaical enforcement of the labyrinthine tax code. A sales tax is paid at the point of purchase. If a person does not have the money to pay the tax, he cannot make the purchase in question. As a result, there is no such thing as individual citizens faced with enforced collection of delinquent sales tax debts. No more audits, liens, levies or seizures.

Over the past forty years, we have been treated to one tax reform measure after another. All were designed to "fix" certain problems and "simplify" various provisions of the code. This has led to a tax code comprised of 17,000 pages of law and regulation which are more difficult than ever to understand and enforce.

As an agency, the IRS is out of control. This is evidenced by the egregious economic reality audit, as well as a plethora of examples of errors, bureaucratic bungling and outright fraud. Much of this I have documented in my writings over the years. My book, *How to Fire the IRS*, presents this evidence and makes the case more exhaustively for a national sales tax.

If we are going to come to grips with the direction of our nation, if we are going to bring the problems with tax law enforcement and administration under control, if we are to set our nation on a course of economic strength and reliability, we must begin by eliminating the IRS. Only then can all Americans enjoy the level of freedom envisioned by the Spirit-led founders of our nation.

Chapter Three -
Financial Survival in the Era of the Beast
"Simple Techniques for Self-Protection"

What are the potential implications should the IRS achieve its apparent goal of creating a cashless society in which all transactions are either known outright or readily available to prying eyes? What difference does it make if, in fact, you are "unable to buy or sell" without a number inextricably linked to your name? Some people believe it could be a matter of life and death.

The Book of Revelation, chapter fourteen, foretells the ramifications of "receiving the mark" spoken of in the preceding chapter. Revelation 13:9-11 reads,

> And another angel followed them and said in a loud voice: "If anyone worships the beast and his image and receives his mark on the forehead or on the hand, he, too, will drink of the wine of God's fury, which has been poured full strength into the cup of his wrath. He will be tormented with burning sulfur in the presence of the holy angels and of the Lamb. And the smoke of their torment rises for ever and ever. There is no rest, day or night for those who worship the beast and his image, or for anyone who receives the mark of his name."

Apart from the Scriptural view of these matters, there is good reason to be concerned about the growth of government. Total control by government of the economic comings and goings of its citizens portends tyranny. Financial or economic liberty is the touchstone of all other liberty. If you have no freedom to contract for the purchase or sale of goods and services, you have no freedom. What good is the right to vote if financial controls over the marketplace put you at the mercy of government's grace?

Now add to this the fact that IRS is grossly prolific in the errors it makes administering the tax laws. If the billions of transactions in our economy are subject to the scrutiny of the IRS, at what level are people going to be subjected to harassment and enforcement activity due solely to IRS error? You can be sure of one thing. The IRS will be no more able to accurately and reliably assimilate such data than it can the data it presently juggles. And as we know, the IRS is abysmal at best in managing the data it now possesses (more on this later).

As the pincers of economic bondage close around our society, there are practices which hasten its arrival. Conversely, there are those which stave it off, either generally or as to a particular individual. I submit that we should exercise every reasonable, viable option to stave off such bondage, both generally and with regard to our families. Our first earthly responsibility is to our families. He who does not provide for his own family is worse than a thief. By taking reasonable steps now, you increase the chances that later, you will not face the Hobson's choice of taking the mark, or failing to take it and enduring insufferable economic consequences.

It seems clear that those most susceptible to total government control are those totally dependent upon government. While we are told to look to God for our daily bread, more Americans every day cry out to government for their daily bread. People call upon government to fix this problem and resolve that crisis. And government is more than willing to do just that, but always at a price. The price is fixed both economically, with rising taxes, and politically, through the steady and progressive erosion of our liberties. After all, if government is going to be God, should it not have the power of God?

By delegating to government growing responsibilities in all areas of our life, our tax burdens have grown to an all time high. Americans now pay close to 45 percent of every dollar they earn in federal, state and local taxes. The average family is forced to live on just 55 cents of each dollar they earn. Naturally, this makes it increasingly difficult for the average family to sustain a comfortable standard of living. With the tax increases over the past three decades occasioned by government's cradle-to-grave social agenda, Americans now pay more in taxes than they do for housing, household operations, medical care, food, and clothing--combined.

Whereas the average family of the 1950s and 1960s lived a comfortable middle class lifestyle on a single income with a stay-at-home mom, the families of today require two, sometimes two and a half incomes to enjoy the same standard. The difference is solely attributable to taxes. As a percentage of income, taxes consumed about 20 percent of the budget of the 1950s and 1960s family. The same family now pays about 45 percent of its income in taxes, an increase of 2.5 times.

As the tax burden grows and people are less able to provide their needs, ironically, they call out for more, not less government "aid." There is no better example than in the case of health care. Now, there is no question that health care is a matter of great concern which must be addressed, but the fact is, health care consumes about 8 to 10 percent of the budgets of the average family. Compare that with its tax burden, then tell me which should be addressed first.

If government were truly concerned about our ability to provide medical care for our families, it seems plain that the first thing government would do is cut taxes. Yet, all the proposals are just the opposite. More government programs are advocated, which would create more financial burdens for more people on a broader scale. In turn, it makes them less able to provide for themselves. The circle can best be described this way: government taxes the pants off us in order to provide goods and services which we cannot afford to buy--because our taxes are too high!

Make no mistake about it. Growing tax burdens make people poorer. A 1994 study by Gerald W. Scully, professor of economics at the School of Management, University of Texas at Dallas illustrates this point vividly. Professor Scully's analysis finds that if overall tax rates had remained in the 20 percent range as they were in the 1950s and 1960s, real gross national product (GNP, the measure of national production) would have been about $13.6 trillion by 1989. That is about twice what GNP actually was that year. The impact of this on the average family is staggering. It means that the average family would have had twice as much real income as it has today. National Center for Policy Analysis, "What is the Optimal Size of Government in the United States," NCPA Policy Report No. 188, November 1994.

How would your family fare if your income were exactly twice what it is? You have taxes and the growth of government to thank for the fact that you have lost half your potential growth.

Americans must take the responsibility to provide for their families and children in terms of spiritual growth, secular education, medical care, nutrition, basic legal rights, etc. We cannot continue to entrust our constitutional rights, personal health, future financial security and the education of our children to the government or its agencies. In short, to keep the government from imposing draconian economic burdens upon you as contemplated in this treatise, take back your rightful responsibilities. No longer delegate these critical and ever-so-personal functions to an impersonal, one-size-fits-all government agency.

We must defeat the philosophy of total government control at the polls, in both federal and state elections. But you can exercise several reasonable and viable steps at home to begin to make your family less dependent upon government's grace for your daily bread. Let us address just a few which can have tremendous impact.

Get out of debt. The borrower is slave to the lender. Therefore, the single most important step to take in achieving or maintaining any degree of financial independence is to get out of and stay out of debt. Those deep in debt are entirely subject to uncontrollable economic conditions. If interest rates float higher, credit card and other consumer debt payments go with it. As one's interest load grows, the pool of funds available for necessary living expenses drops in direct proportion.

Consumer debt is at an all time high. Since 1985, consumer debt on credit cards, department store purchases, etc., has gone from about $100 billion to $350 billion. At the same time, our national savings rate is barely 2 percent. Western European nations save at about five times our rate and Japan saves at about ten times our rate. High debt and low savings make the individual especially vulnerable to economic vicissitudes. High debt and low savings make you more subject to the whimsical pronouncements of both the lender and the government.

If you have a home mortgage, make every effort to accelerate the process of retiring the debt. It is easy to do and does not take much additional cash. This is one way. Suppose your monthly payment is $750. Divide the payment by twelve, which gives us $62.50. Add that amount to your monthly installment and designate the excess payment to principal. Your new payment is $812.50. Doing this cuts years off a typical thirty-year home mortgage.

Watch the interest rate market closely. Many times throughout economic cycles, interest rates rise and fall, often quickly and sometimes dramatically. Prior to the presidential election of 1992, mortgage rates were at a thirty-year low. Shortly after the election they began to tick upward. By 1995, rates had jumped significantly. By mid 1996, they came down once again, and in rather dramatic fashion.

Each time rates fall, we have a fresh opportunity to consider refinancing mortgage debt. If you can refinance your mortgage debt at 1 1/2 to 2 points lower than its existing rate, you are generally better off. However, there are a few considerations. First, consider how long you will stay in your home. Be sure you can recover any closing costs in the form of savings on the monthly payment, spread over the period of time you expect to stay in the home.

Next, resist the temptation to borrow your equity to purchase depreciating assets. In the refinancing binge which occurred during the 1992 and 1993 low-rate period, millions tapped their hard-won equity and spent it on things that have no lasting value. Banks across the land advertised low-cost and even no-cost equity loans for the "things you've always wanted." They pushed boats, dream vacations, wedding expenses, and so on.

However desirable, none of these things increases wealth over time. Either they depreciate over time (the boat), or they have no intrinsic value at all (the vacation). I am not saying you cannot take a vacation, just that it is foolish to borrow home equity to do it.

If you are going to tap home equity, use the funds to purchase appreciating assets. Home improvements which raise the value of your property, or the purchase of vacation or rental property are just three examples. That way, though you increase debt, you own an appreciating asset to offset it. What is more, as time goes on, if you act wisely, the debt goes down and the value of the asset goes up.

A common mistake of many who refinance is they look upon the savings gained by a lower interest rate as "spendable income." And that is exactly what they do. Their new-found wealth is used to raise their immediate standard of living. They eat more meals in restaurants, take more trips, buy more "things," maybe even a new car.

The savings should not be looked upon as "spendable income." Savings should be looked upon as exactly that, savings. Therefore, save the money. The best way to do it is by continuing to make the old payment. For example, suppose you were paying $812.50 per month on your mortgage, as under our previous example. Your fixed payment was $750, but we accelerated it as illustrated. Suppose further you drop that payment to $600 per month by refinancing. Afterward, do not make a $600 payment. Instead, make the $812.50 payment. Now, rather than accelerating debt retirement by $62.50 per month, debt shrinks by $212.50 per month. And you do it without increasing your monthly expenses. At that rate, you will be amazed at how fast equity grows and debt shrinks.

In my *Smart Tax Special Report*, (Winning Publications, Inc.) in an article entitled, "Protecting Home Equity - A Capital Idea," I give even more ideas and examples on ways to build and protect the equity in your home. A place to live is one of the three indispensable things we need to survive (food and clothing are the others). If your home is paid for, your family is in a very strong position to survive most any financial storm.

Avoid credit card debt. Credit card and consumer debt is growing rapidly. I already cited the rise in such debt over the past ten years. As a result, Americans are paying more interest at higher rates on non-essential items and depreciating assets than at any time before in our history. This is a dangerous pattern and if you struggle with credit card debt, your family may be at risk.

Of course, the card companies do not make it any easier. All you need is a pulse to qualify for this card or that card, with all the benefits and "prestige" that go with it. In fact, one card now uses the marketing slogan, "Because life can't wait."

I submit that life can wait. Resist the buy now, pay later mentality. Too many citizens are buying on credit what they cannot afford, believing they will have the money later. The fact is, if you cannot afford the item now, chances are you will not be able to afford it later. We are not promised tomorrow. We are promised only today. It is therefore unfair and unreasonable to pile up debts today which must be addressed tomorrow, when financial circumstances are uncertain and undefined.

Invest in your own debt. It is not uncommon for families to come into certain amounts of money from time to time. It happens either through savings, inheritances or gifts, winnings, sale of assets, etc. When you come into a sum of money, immediately begin to consider ways to invest it, not spend it.

When you invest money, you put it to work for you. You expect a return from it. The first rule of investing is, do not lose the money! An investment should, 1) increase your net worth, and 2) provide a return commensurate with the risk associated with the investment.

In today's economy, there are a million different types of investments. Literally thousands of mutual funds of every description are available, with new ones being offered every day. We have stocks, corporate and municipal bonds, treasuries, foreign government debt instruments, certificates of deposit, commodities, futures contracts, general and limited partnerships in every venture imaginable, viatical settlements, derivatives, mortgage backed securities, initial public offerings, and on and on and on.

Which is best for you? Which offers a level of risk equal to your tolerance? Which provides ample return or growth of principal? To the novice, the amount of information available on the alternatives only seems to make your head spin.

The average investor screws himself into the ground trying to find a safe investment returning 10 to 12 percent annually. It is certainly not the big score Hillary Clinton managed in cattle futures, but it is safe and it keeps you off the evening news. By the time you pay federal and state income taxes on the gain, you might have between 5 and 8 percent left. Since your capital doubles in ten years at 7 percent interest, that does not seem so bad.

What the small investor overlooks almost every time is the coveted "sure thing" right under his nose. The sure thing is your own debt. Suppose, for example, you have $5,000 in credit card debt and that is your only debt. It bears interest at the annual rate of 18 percent. The monthly interest cost is about $75 of non-deductible personal interest. It is, therefore, a sunk cost.

Now let us imagine you suddenly come into $5,000, which you intend to invest. Remember, your investment should, 1) increase your net worth, and 2) provide a return. Net worth is defined as the difference between assets and liabilities. With $5,000 of debt before receiving the money, your net worth is a negative $5,000.

Suppose you invest the money into a certificate of deposit (CD), paying 5 percent interest. After taxes, the real return is about 3.25 percent, or $13.54 per month. What is the real impact of that investment?

First, you do accomplish the goal of growing your net worth. It goes from a negative $5,000 to zero. That is good. But you do not achieve the second goal of obtaining a return. It is true you realize $13.54 per month in interest income, but when measured against the interest expense of $75, you remain deep in the hole.

Now let us examine what happens when you invest in your own debt by paying off the $5,000 credit card balance. First, you raise your net worth by $5,000. You now have no debt and no asset. That gives you a net worth of zero, just as in the first example. Beyond that, the return on the investment is substantial. Paying off the debt eliminates the sunk cost of $75 per month in debt service. That is a real return on the investment equal to 18 percent, the interest rate charged on the debt. The real rate of return is over five times that of the CD investment. Seventy-five dollars per month is now available for saving and investing elsewhere.

Look around you. What kind of debt are you carrying? What is the interest load on the debt? Home loans range from about 7 to 10 percent, home equity lines, from about 9 to 12 percent. Car loans vary widely. Credit cards and unsecured lines of credit are the worst, with annual rates from 16 to 21 percent, or more. By investing in this debt, your real return is equal to the interest rate and is always higher than all but the riskiest of investments. Next, you accomplish the important goal of reducing total debt, making your family less vulnerable to market fluctuations and the encroachment by government through its monetary and economic policies.

Build a reserve of cash. Nearly one-third of all American families live paycheck to paycheck. These people are but thirty days away from a financial crisis. Without a reserve to fall back on, even for brief periods, they immediately become dependent upon government programs--and demands--should a crisis befall them. When the choice is either adhere to an oppressive demand and feed the family, or ignore the demand and starve, we know reasonable people will opt to feed the family every time.

We see this problem most clearly in the case of those facing present tax debts. As our total tax burden grows, more and more families are thrust into the unenviable position of having to choose between paying their taxes and feeding their families. At present, there are well over twenty million people in this posture.

For these reasons, it is essential to have a reserve of cash savings available to smooth the bumps on the economic road. Ideally, you should have a reserve available to pay six months worth of fixed living expenses. If you can get through such a period, only the worst widespread economic disaster can affect you.

Many people gasp when I suggest amassing such a cash horde. If you are living paycheck to paycheck, how on earth can you save any money? I do not pretend it is easy; I mean only to suggest it is necessary. And the way to begin saving something is to begin saving anything, even if just a few dollars per week.

Carefully examine your lifestyle. I promise you there are things you are doing in your day-to-day activities that cost very little individually, but add up over a period of time. I do not intend to make a list of such items, but suggest you do. Nor is it necessary to eliminate such things from your life, for in most cases, these practices are tiny bits of the "good life." But if you are simply more attentive to how you spend on such things, you quickly find there is room for saving something out of what you thought was a paper-thin budget.

Please understand that it does not matter how much you save. Save something. You shall notice before long that savings accumulate much the same as debts. A little here, a little there. Before you know it, you are faced with a mountain. If you spend regularly--even just a little-- the mountain you face is one of debt. If you save--even just a little--the mountain you face is one of cash. With which would you rather contend?

Get taxes under control. To help your saving potential, take steps to reduce your income tax burdens. As illustrated earlier in this chapter, the largest single expense borne by families is taxes. Not medical care, not housing, not food or clothing--taxes. Therefore, you have the most to gain by controlling that expense.

For the average family, medical expenses and child care take a large chunk of what is left after satisfying tax collectors. It happens that these two areas provide avenues of tax relief overlooked more often than not.

The tax law allows medical expenses and child care costs to be paid with before-tax dollars. It is done through vehicles known as cafeteria plans or flexible spending arrangements. By structuring your expenses to be covered under such programs, you turn non-deductible medical expenses into tax favored expenses, and you double the value--and tax benefit--of the child care credit.

In my *Smart Tax Special Report,* (Winning Publications, Inc.) I have two articles which address themselves to the value of these planning tools. I also explain how to sell the idea to your employer if he does not already provide these benefits. Many employers do. But employees fail to take advantage of them because they overlook their value. Believe me, they can be very helpful when used to their fullest potential.

For most people, it is easier to save a dollar of taxes than it is to earn a dollar of income. That is why you must pay a little attention to managing your tax liability. Even short form filers enjoy many strategies which can reduce their tax bills. The *Smart Tax Special Report* describes many of these.

Own some hard assets. A portion of what you accumulate as your emergency fund should be held in hard, liquid assets. A hard asset is distinguishable from paper assets in this important fashion. Paper assets, such as stocks, bonds, CDs, etc., are simultaneously one person's asset and somebody else's liability. A corporate or government bond, for example, is your asset with a value determined by the terms of the instrument. But, at the same time, it is the liability of the institution which issued it. In the final analysis, the bond is only as good as that institution's ability to fulfill its obligations. If the institution should fail, your paper asset suddenly becomes worthless.

This is not true of hard assets such as gold, silver, real estate, collectibles (art and so forth). However, only gold and silver provide the added advantage of being fully liquid, readily liquidateable, and of indisputable value at any given time. While the value certainly does fluctuate as with all assets, there is never any dispute as to what it is.

For all of recorded history, gold and silver have been money in every civilization throughout the world. Throughout history, the "smart money" always gravitates to gold and silver as a hedge against inflation, political unrest and economic uncertainty. We should follow the lead of the smart money and hold at least a portion of our emergency funds in this form.

You should never invest a dime without professional guidance. This is true of hard asset investments as well. There is no shortage of financial planners available, but not all are attuned to the advantages of hard assets. Kevin DeMeritt, of Meritt Financial Services, does understand them. Kevin has a special report for those seeking more information on accumulating hard assets. The report can be obtained by calling 800-366-7925.

The report shows that too many people are doing the opposite of what they should be doing. Rather than investing, consumer debt is rising sharply. With millions spending borrowed money, it gives the illusion the economy is doing better than it really is. In time, significant adjustments must be made and those holding hard assets will fare better than those who do not.

Stop lending to the IRS. In 1995, the IRS handed out refund checks totaling more than $99 billion to eighty-eight million people. That works out to $1,125 per refund. If you received a refund from the IRS, no doubt you were a happy person. I can tell you, however, that getting a tax refund is bad news, second only to facing a debt you cannot pay.

If you are the average person and received the average refund of $1,125, you paid nearly $94 per month in taxes you did not owe. What is worse, you loaned your money to the IRS for up to eighteen months, without interest! You would never allow your bank to hold your money interest free. Why on earth allow the IRS to do it?

What could you have done with that money? How far along would you be in building your mountain of savings if you stopped lending $94 per month to the IRS? It seems at least some of the difficulty people face saving money can be eliminated with this one step.

There is widespread misconception about income tax withholding obligations. That is why so many people subject themselves to over-withholding, leading to refunds. Withholding for employees is governed by Form W-4, "Employee's Withholding Allowance Certificate." It is the document submitted to your employer declaring the number of "allowances" you are entitled to claim for purposes of computing withholding levels.

Anyone who received a tax refund last year failed to claim a sufficient number of allowances on Form W-4. You may respond by saying, "Wait. I have four kids. I claimed four allowances. What else can I do?"

That is exactly what the misunderstanding is all about. Your children, in fact, all your dependents, including yourself and your spouse, are considered "exemptions" for income tax purposes. They are claimed on line six of Form 1040. You may also claim an equal number on Form W-4. But remember, the W-4 is an "allowance" certificate, not an "exemption" certificate. Allowances include exemptions, but are not limited to them.

The term allowance is defined as any item which operates on the tax return to lower your taxes. That includes not only exemptions, but itemized deductions, a standard deduction, business losses, capital loses, etc. Any one or a combination of these things entitles you to claim allowances on the W-4 in relative proportion.

The rules regarding the W-4 specifically allow citizens to adjust their withholding to match their tax bills. If you have over-withholding, leading to a refund, you may increase allowances to strike a balance. On the other hand, if you are under-withheld, leading to a tax debt, you should decrease the allowances, causing more withholding to balance the two. The goal is to adjust your withholding to match your tax liability.

In my *Smart Tax Special Report*, I have a section which takes you by the hand through the tax code sections permitting the adjustment process. I show you the formula and steps needed to meet your legal obligations without lending the IRS money interest free. By following the steps, you get an extra $94 per month to help get out of debt. Using these and other simple techniques, you will be shocked to learn you can actually double or triple the value of that $94 per month. This helps build an emergency cash reserve or investment base to put you on the road to greater financial independence. The report is guaranteed to help and I strongly recommend it.

Keep an eye on your pension. The federal government has a penchant for attacking untapped revenue sources. In this country today, there are two giant pools of revenue hanging like ripe plumbs before the longing eyes of our debt-ridden Congress.

The first is the vast wealth held in the estates of our aging population. Over the next two decades, we shall witness what could be the largest transfer of wealth from one generation to the next in the history of mankind. The question is, to what extent will such wealth pass intact?

If Congress has its way, very little could pass to succeeding generations. If Congress has its way, the largest share will be gobbled up in estate taxes. It already set the wheels in motion to achieve that by significantly increasing estate tax rates in the 1993 Clinton budget act. Not only were the rates pushed to a top bracket of 55 percent, but the increases were made to apply retroactively in direct violation of the constitution.

The second pool is America's pension and retirement funds. In the past fifteen years, Americans pumped nearly $3 trillion into mutual funds, $2,000 at a time. The mutual fund industry exploded because so many people began taking advantage of IRA and 401(k) retirement programs. These allow for tax deferred investments of up to $2,000 per year, taxed when drawn for retirement. At present, pensions and retirement funds hold more than $4 trillion in untaxed cash. Given the current condition of the federal fisc, how long do you expect the government to keep its hands off that money?

The sad reality is that shortly after taking office, the Clinton administration floated a carefully crafted trial balloon designed to measure the reaction to a tax on pension funds. It was done in such a way as to prevent the matter from being tied directly to the president, but at the same time, get a fix on prevailing attitudes.

In brief, the proposal was, among other things, to impose a 15 percent tax on current pension assets, and a 15 percent tax on future pension contributions. The reaction, as we would have hoped, was vehemently negative. The administration quickly stepped away from the hint, denying it had any intention of taxing pension funds. The whole matter was soon forgotten. For now.

So I repeat my question. How long do you expect our debt-ridden government to keep its mitts off $4 trillion in cash? I cannot myself answer except to say that I do not for a minute believe it will leave the money alone indefinitely. And I can only imagine how and when it will attack. Therefore, I am carefully watching the government's policies and pronouncements regarding pensions, and you should do the same. Be prepared to liquidate your pension and take possession of your money, even incurring a present tax liability, if that means the difference between preserving most of your investment and losing it. However, do not act without professional guidance on any matter concerning pension fund liquidations.

Guard your social security number. For all of its uncertainty, the book of Revelation seems clear on one point. In order to "buy or sell," that is, engage in any economic activity, one must have a number inextricably linked to his name. The number is the presumed means by which to monitor and control your economic comings and goings. Given the progression of the use of the social security number in the past four decades, a case could be made that the SSN is just such a number.

When the social security number was created in the 1930s, it was made clear that it was not to be used for identification purposes. Early social security cards declare right on their face that it is not to be used for identification purposes.

Things changed in the early 1960s with the onset of the computer age. Now the social security number is used for all manner of identification. Banks demand them. Insurance companies seek them. Hospitals and medical clinics want to know. Employers use them for tax reporting. The IRS keeps its files by social security number and is responsible for passing laws requiring one for minor children, even at birth. I explained the idea behind this move in chapter two.

For years, persons harboring a deeply seated, sincerely held religious opposition to the use of social security numbers for minor children could not be forced to obtain or use one. But as we learned in chapter two, Congress has attacked that sanctuary in an all out attempt to defile it. In the same breath, the IRS now offers what appears to be a clear alternative for those with religious proscriptions against the number.

In my book, *How to Fire the IRS*, I talk at length about the fact that for years, the IRS issued what it called an Individual Taxpayer Identification Number (ITIN) to those with religious opposition to SSNs. The number is unique in that it is not used as "the number of your name" in all possible transactions. It is used only for tax purposes.

It is noteworthy that Congress did not specifically repeal the rules regarding the issuance of ITINs to those religiously opposed to SSNs. Indeed, after the Small Business Job Protection Act passed, IRS swung into action and created, for the first time, a form to allow one to expeditiously apply for the ITIN. It is Form W-7, Application for IRS Individual Taxpayer Identification Number. A copy of the form is reproduced on the next page.

The instructions for the W-7 state that the purpose of the form is to obtain a taxpayer identification number for persons "who are required to have a U.S. taxpayer identification number, but who do not have, and are not eligible to obtain a social security number." A person religiously opposed to the SSN for minor children arguably falls into this description.

You must indicate on the W-7 why you are applying for the ITIN. Line 7g of the form gives several options from which to select. Most apply to non-resident aliens. However, the last option says, "Other specify." A space is provided to state your reasons.

Recently, Susan mailed a letter to the Kansas City Service Center asking that they issue an alternative number for her minor child. She explained that she and her husband were religiously opposed to the use of SSNs for minor children, but recognized the need to have a number solely for income tax purposes.

In response, the Chief of the Service Center's Examination Branch wrote to Susan saying, "To receive an ITIN for your son, you must complete Form W-7. Then apply either by mail or in person at some IRS offices."

In the instructions for W-7, the IRS provides the address of the office to mail the application. To obtain the form, contact your local IRS office or call 1-800-TAX-FORM to order from the IRS. You should include sufficient documentation with your W-7 to support your claim of religious exemption. This should include, at a minimum, a detailed affidavit describing your objection, and copies of birth certificates for the children, including perhaps, school records, etc., to prove their existence. For details on the affidavit, see *How to Fire the IRS*, chapter three.

Where other government agencies are concerned, carefully review its authority for demanding production of your number for any reason. You will likely find most have no lawful authority for such a demand. They have merely become accustomed to people caving in without question to each of its demands. Similarly, private sector businesses often have little or no authority to force the release of your number.

Exhibit 3-1

Form **W-7** (June 1996) Department of the Treasury Internal Revenue Service	**Application for IRS Individual Taxpayer Identification Number** ▶ See instructions. ▶ For use by individuals who are not U.S. citizens or nationals.	OMB No 1545-1483

Note: *Do not file this form if you have, or are eligible to obtain, a U.S. social security number (SSN).*

When Completing This Form
- Type or print.
- If you are completing this form for someone else, answer the questions as they apply to that person.

1	**Name**	1a Last name (surname or family name)	First name	Middle name
	Name at birth if different ▶	1b Last name (surname or family name)	First name	Middle name

2	**Address of tax residence** (see instructions)	Street address, apartment number, or rural route number (include postal code where appropriate. Do not use a P.O. box number)
		City or town, state or province, and country

3	**Mailing address** (if different from above)	Street address, apartment number, P.O. box number, or rural route number (include postal code or ZIP code where appropriate)
		City or town, state or province, and country

4	**Birth information**	Date of birth (month, day, year) / /	Place of birth (city or town, state or province, and country)	**5** ☐ Male ☐ Female

6	**Family information** (see instructions)	Father's last name (surname)	First name	Middle name
		Mother's maiden name (surname)	First name	Middle name

7	**Other information**	7a Country(ies) of citizenship	7b Foreign tax identification number	**FOR IRS USE ONLY**
		7c Passport number (if any)	7d Country issuing passport	
		7e Type of U.S. visa (if applicable)	7f U.S. stay limitation, if any (month, day, year) / /	

7g Check the box for the reason you are filing Form W-7. (See instructions.)
☐ Nonresident alien filing a U.S. tax return and not eligible for an SSN
☐ U.S. resident alien filing a U.S. tax return and not eligible for an SSN
☐ Dependent of U.S. person ⎫ Enter name and SSN of U.S. person (see instructions) ▶ ....
☐ Husband or wife of U.S. person ⎬ ....
☐ Other (specify) _____

7h Have you previously received a U.S. temporary Taxpayer Identification Number (TIN) or Employer Identification Number (EIN)?
☐ No/Do not know. Skip line 7i.
☐ Yes. Complete line 7i. If you need more space, list on a sheet and attach to this form. (See instructions.)

7i TIN ☐☐☐-☐☐-☐☐☐☐   EIN ☐☐-☐☐☐☐☐☐☐
Enter the name under which the TIN was issued.   Enter the name under which the EIN was issued.

Sign Here Keep a copy of this form for your records	Under penalties of perjury, I (applicant/delegate/acceptance agent) declare that I have examined this application, including accompanying documentation and statements, and to the best of my knowledge and belief, it is true, correct, and complete. I authorize the IRS to disclose to my acceptance agent returns or return information necessary to resolve matters regarding the assignment of my IRS individual taxpayer identification number (TIN).		
	▶ Signature of applicant or delegate	Date (month, day, year) / /	Phone number
	▶ Name of delegate, if applicable (type or print)	Delegate's relationship to applicant ▶	☐ Parent ☐ Guardian

Acceptance Agent's Use ONLY	Signature	Date (month, day, year) / /
	Name and title (type or print)	U.S. Employer Identification Number

For Paperwork Reduction Act Notice, see page 3.   Cat. No. 10229L   Form **W-7** (6-96)

Unless it has to do specifically with tax considerations, there is often another way to satisfy their need for information controls. Of course, when dealing with private sector businesses, you always enjoy the right to choose to do business with them or not. If a company insists on a number, consider doing business elsewhere.

On this account, the equation is elementary. Government simply cannot track and control your every move without a particular number inextricably linked to your name. The question now is, what can you do about it? Understand that with regard to minor children, the penalty is not death by hanging. The penalty is loss of the exemption, provided you cannot prove the religious exemption.

Perhaps the time has come for us to stop our efforts to side-step these encroachments. Perhaps the time has come for us to face the matter head on, attacking it for the desolate abomination that it is. It is time to rise up and make our views heard by Congress. If our government stands for nothing else, it stands for the notion that we have the unfettered right to the free exercise of religion. For Congress to pass laws it clearly knows invade that sacred sphere is just plain wrong. We must agitate to change the law.

Generally, be aware. Watch what goes on around you. Too often, what is done by government is done in darkness, only because we do not watch. By watching we glean the wisdom to do what is right under the circumstances. My newsletter, *Pilla Talks Taxes* is the vehicle through which I report important law changes affecting taxes and related matters. Trial subscriptions are available from Winning Publications, Inc.

Never forget that "by wisdom a house is built, and through knowledge its rooms are filled with rare and beautiful treasures." Proverbs 24:3-4.

"The Spirit of the Lord is upon me, because he has anointed me to preach good news to the poor. He has sent me to proclaim release to the captives and recovering of sight to the blind, to set at liberty those who are oppressed, to proclaim the acceptable year of the Lord."

Luke 4:18

Chapter Four -
Unmasking the Beast
"Debunking Tax Audit Myths"

One of the most traumatic experiences imaginable by most Americans is an IRS audit. Why are so many Americans terrified of an audit? Is it because they cheat blind on their tax returns? Not Likely. Most Americans do their level best to comply with the tax laws by conscientiously struggling through pages of forms and instructions intended to help them.

They are afraid for two reasons. First, the average citizen does not understand the audit process. And it is not just a matter of lacking information about the procedure. He harbors *misinformation* about it. Americans believe the IRS selects tax returns for examination because it has found an error. When the letter bringing the news of an audit hits the mailbox, the average citizen reacts as though he has just heard from the draft board. He immediately thinks the worst, believing he has made a serious mistake and has "been caught." The mind races from thoughts of what the error may be, to its likely cost. From the start, he adopts a defensive posture premised on the mistaken notion that he did something wrong and will have to pay.

The second problem also stems from misinformation. The public is under the impression that the tax auditor has the power of financial life and death. People believe the tax auditor can disallow deductions at will, effectively increasing their tax bills. They believe the auditor has the authority to use the IRS' potent weapons of lien, levy and seizure. Even worse, people fathom that the auditor can put them in jail. These perceived powers, coupled with the belief that a mistake was made in the first place, makes it difficult or impossible for the uninformed person to survive the audit process.

These facts explain why the IRS has such tremendous success in assessing additional revenue through the audit process. In 1995 alone, the IRS produced more than $27.83 billion in additional assessments through the examination of all classes of tax returns. This includes tax and penalties, but not interest. Interest often doubles or triples a tax bill.

Of the total assessments, $7.75 billion accounted for the audit of individual income tax returns. Tax year 1995 saw the audit of 1.91 million *individual* tax returns. That translates to an average of a bit more than $4,000 in additional tax and penalties *per return audited*. Of the total returns examined during 1995, 89 percent were found to owe additional taxes. Just 11 percent were given a clean bill of health. IRS 1995 Data Book, Publication 55B, page 12.

That means on average, if selected for a face-to-face examination, you have about an 89 percent chance of getting hit with a tax bill of just over four grand, *before interest*. After the interest is added to the injury, expect it to double.

You may be tempted to argue that you are just a "little guy." Because you are not a high powered business tycoon or sophisticated investor, you have little real risk of being hit with such a bill. In fact, you may likely believe you have little chance at all of even being audited. After all, you may suggest, it is only because the IRS fries such big fish that the average cost per audit is driven up. While this certainly is a common and reasonable belief, it *is not* supported by the facts.

In April 1996, the GAO released a detailed report of the IRS' audit activity for the years 1988 through 1995. General Accounting Office, "Audit Trends and Results for Individual Taxpayers," GAO/GGD-96-91, April 1996. The numbers are quite telling. First, it is true that high income citizens have more to lose in a tax audit than do low income citizens. It is not true, however, that low income citizens fare much better, relatively speaking.

The chart found on the next page is reproduced from page 12 of the GAO report. It shows that non-business (individual) tax returns showing less than $25,000 of income, faced additional assessments of $2,400, $2,800, and $3,100 during 1992, 1993, and 1994 respectively. During the same periods, high income citizens, those with more than

Exhibit 4-1

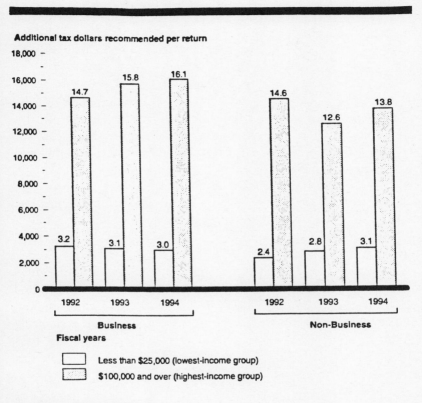

Additional tax dollars recommended per return

Business

Fiscal years	1992	1993	1994
Less than $25,000 (lowest-income group)	3.2	3.1	3.0
$100,000 and over (highest-income group)	14.7	15.8	16.1

Non-Business

Fiscal years	1992	1993	1994
Less than $25,000 (lowest-income group)	2.4	2.8	3.1
$100,000 and over (highest-income group)	14.6	12.6	13.8

☐ Less than $25,000 (lowest-income group)
▦ $100,000 and over (highest-income group)

Source: GAO analysis of IRS data

$100,000 of income, were clobbered with assessments of $14,600, $12,600, and $13,800.

I notice a disturbing trend, at least for low income citizens. Do you see it? While the overall tax assessment rate for high income citizens is *down*, the assessment rate for low income citizens is *up*. In fact, not only are the assessed dollar amounts down for high income citizens, but the GAO's analysis revealed that audit rates for such citizens are also down. Consider this:

IRS reported audit rates from fiscal years 1988 to 1995 (1) *increased* in the last two fiscal years among those in the lowest- income group (less than $25,000), particularly for business individuals, *for whom the rate more than doubled,* and (2) *decreased* among those in the highest-income group ($100,000 or more), particularly for nonbusiness individuals, *for whom the fiscal year 1995 rate dropped to about one-fourth of what it had been in fiscal year 1988.* Ibid, page 10; emphasis added.

In 1994, a whopping 38 percent of all returns examined were 1040A, *short forms,* reporting income of less than $25,000. That is up from 28 percent in 1992, and 30 percent in 1993. By contrast, the rate for returns reporting $100,000 of income or more, was just 9 percent in 1994, down from 14 percent in 1992, and 13 percent in 1993. The chart below shows the audit rates for all classes of returns for 1992 through 1994.

Exhibit 4-2

Table II.1: Number of Individual Returns Audited by Audit Class, FYs 1992 Through 1994

| Audit class | Number and percentage of returns | | | | | |
| | Fiscal year 1992 | | Fiscal year 1993 | | Fiscal year 1994 | |
	Number	Percent	Number	Percent	Number	Percent
1040A, TPI < $25,000	338,683	28%	315,469	30%	470,723	38%
Non 1040A, TPI < $25,000	172,557	14	125,697	12	129,132	11
TPI $25,000 < $50,000	191,166	16	159,070	15	143,243	12
TPI $50,000 < $100,000	150,905	13	127,484	12	110,193	9
TPI $100,000 and over	167,394	14	136,908	13	110,004	9
C-TGR < $25,000	41,293	3	51,934	5	106,169	9
C-TGR $25,000 < $100,000	64,070	5	69,253	7	87,561	7
C-TGR $100,000 and over	65,939	5	61,768	6	57,766	5
F-TGR < $100,000	7,333	1	5,980	1	6,203	1
F-TGR $100,000 and over	6,679	1	5,403	1	4,713	0
Total	1,206,019	100%	1,058,966	102%	1,225,707	101%

Legend

1040A = nonbusiness returns filed by individuals
TPI = total positive income (income from positive sources only)
C-TGR = Form 1040 Schedule C (Profit or Loss from Business) total gross receipts
F-TGR = Form 1040 Schedule F (Profit or Loss from Farming) total gross receipts

Note: Percentages are the percent of total individual audits for the year and have been rounded to the nearest whole percent

Source: GAO analysis of IRS data

Why pick on the low income citizen? Is there not more to be gained from attacking the rich folk? In a word? No. Low income citizens are easier to audit. As a result, more can be accomplished in less time. In fact, the GAO's study revealed that the amount of tax dollars netted by the IRS per "direct hour" of audit work grew steadily for low income citizens from 1992 through 1994, while it fell for high income citizens during the same period. Today, the IRS expects to retrieve $983 *for every hour* spent auditing the return of a low income citizen. In short, rich people can afford to fight back; poor people cannot.

The foregoing facts teach us it is fundamentally necessary to understand the basics of the tax audit process if we are ever to survive the ordeal. Let us start by debunking the two myths identified earlier.

The first relates to how returns are selected for audit. A tax return is not necessarily targeted because it contains an error. It is true that certain correspondence is generated by errors in the return, either real or imagined. In the face-to-face confrontation, however, most returns are selected by nothing more than a computer analysis of its claims. As I shall explain at length later in this chapter, the computer compares entries in your return with industry averages. If any line of your return is out of sync with those averages, the difference is scored. The higher the score, the more likely it is to be audited.

That is not to say that differences in your entries versus the national averages mean your return is in error. On the contrary, averages are nothing more than a balanced high and low for a given category. It only means that those sufficiently in excess of (or in some cases, below) the national average may be called upon to prove their claims. Assuming you understand this *and are able to prove your claim*, you will owe nothing as a result of an audit.

The second myth relates to the power of the tax auditor. Too many people succumb to pressure from the IRS to accept what they know are improper results because they wrongfully believe the agent has the power to make their life miserable. We must realize that the tax auditor has no power to put people in jail.

Revenue agents, those who conduct the tax audit we speak of, are examiners only, working under the Examination Division. Their sole function is to determine the "correct tax liability." They are not the arbiters of whether laws were violated. In fact, the investigation of possible tax crimes is not within the scope of their jurisdiction. Such is done by Special Agents, working under the authority of the Criminal Investigation Division.

Nor do tax auditors have the legal authority to use the IRS' enforced collection tools of lien, levy and seizure. Those tools are within the sole province of the Collection Division, under the operation of Revenue Officers. Before any such weapon may be trained upon or executed against a citizen, there must first be in place a valid "assessment" of tax. An assessment arises *after* the tax has been determined, either by the citizen signing a tax return, or through administrative procedures, such as an audit. Once an assessment is in place, the case is transferred to the Collection Division (out of the hands of the tax auditor) for collection of the tax.

Tax auditors do not even possess the power to change your return, i.e., disallow deductions, without your consent. Rather, tax auditors make *recommendations* that certain deductions be disallowed or other changes be made to the return which lead to an increase in taxes. However, you must assent to those recommendations before the auditor's report becomes binding. Should you refuse, various rights of appeal develop. When used properly and to their fullest extent, these rights ensure you will never pay taxes you do not owe. These rights are the subject of chapter eleven.

What is a Tax Audit?

Even the most basic element of the tax audit is misunderstood. Many look upon the audit as a form of punishment in and of itself. To some extent that may be true, given the amount of time and effort often needed to complete the task. However, the true premise is much different.

The tax audit is nothing more or less than the process by which the IRS ascertains the correctness of a given tax return. Going into an audit, the IRS has no clue whether, for example, your claimed $5,000 deduction for charitable contributions is correct. The fact that your return may have been selected on the basis of this claim does not signal an error. It says only that the IRS questions the claim and is calling upon you to verify it.

Each tax return contains two general categories of claims. The return states an amount of income alleged to have been earned during the year and it alleges reductions to that income which operate to lower the tax. Such reductions might include, alone or in combination, personal dependent exemptions, a standard deduction, itemized deductions, business expense deductions, capital losses, operating losses, tax credits, etc. The IRS has the authority to require a person to prove any or all such claims.

The new Economic Reality audit focuses upon income. As stated earlier, the IRS is of the opinion that most of the perceived cheating occurs with regard to income, not deductions. And while Congress further narrows the scope of deductions allowable in the first place, it broadens the net by which income is gathered in. Therefore, the more fruitful approach for the IRS is fast becoming a challenge to your income, not your deductions. That helps to explain why the agency is spending more time on low income tax returns.

While the stated purpose of the tax audit is to ascertain the correctness of one's return, the IRS looks upon the audit as a revenue enhancement tool. Stated another way, it uses the audit as a means to "get the money." My years of experience dealing with the IRS in the audit environment has taught many sobering lessons. The most troubling is the IRS cares little about whether your return is correct or not. Its intention is to "get the money" regardless.

Tax auditors use carefully orchestrated and well rehearsed tactics to persuade citizens to part with money they do not owe. In July 1995, I presented testimony to the House subcommittee on IRS Oversight, Committee on Ways and Means, concerning these problems. In my testimony, I referred to the deliberate acts of tax auditors to bluff and intimidate citizens into accepting audit results which are just plain wrong. I identified nine specific duplicitous tactics used to accomplish that goal. Quoting directly from my testimony, they are:

1. Where examiners wrongfully claim a citizen has insufficient proof to support an otherwise legitimate deduction and therefore the deduction is disallowed;

2. Where examiners wrongfully give an incorrect statement of the law to a citizen regarding a particular tax deduction or tax treatment of an item, leading to the disallowance of such item;

3. Where amounts of money transferred from one of the citizen's bank accounts to another (transactions known as redeposits) are double and triple counted by examiners, and therefore a citizen is said to have earned income he did not report on his return;

4. Where tax examiners falsely claim that citizens have no, or limited appeal rights from the decision of tax examiners, and therefore have no choice but to accept audit results which are clearly in error;

5. Where tax examiners falsely claim that citizens will suffer other or greater penalties if they pursue their right of appeal, and therefore accept audit results which are clearly in error;

6. Where tax examiners explain to citizens that the avenue of appeal is lengthy, costly, time consuming and the IRS wins its cases anyway, all the while additional accumulations of interest and penalties stack up against the citizen;

7. Where, in certain unusual cases but nevertheless prevalent, tax examiners claim a citizen can be put into jail if he does not sign and accept audit results which are clearly wrong;

8. Where, as very commonly happens, tax examiners threaten citizens with lien, levy and seizure of bank accounts and property if they refuse to sign and accept audit results which are clearly wrong;

9. Probably the single most common reason erroneous audit assessments are recorded against citizens is most citizens are simply unaware of their right of appeal.

Upon completion of a tax audit, the IRS mails to the citizen a so-called 30-day letter. The letter contains the Revenue Agent's Report (RAR) which details the changes proposed to the citizen's return. Citizens commonly mistake the RAR for a bill, which it is not. They do not understand that it is a proposed change to their tax, which they can appeal. But with lack of understanding of the appeal right or process, and lack of funds to hire a professional, many do nothing. This leads to the issuance of a notice of deficiency, which requires the filing of a petition in the Tax Court within 90 days. If the petition is not filed, the amount of tax claimed becomes assessed without further action necessary on the part of the IRS. In effect, the citizen loses his tax audit case by default. Testimony of Daniel J. Pilla, Hearing before the subcommittee on IRS Oversight, House committee on Ways and Means, "Taxpayer Compliance Measurement Program," Serial 104-30, July 18, 1995, page 146.

As I explained to the subcommittee, this is not an exhaustive list of the things that commonly happen to honest, law abiding citizens during the course of face-to-face examinations. They are, however, a few of the more common examples of what takes place on a daily basis within the realm of tax law administration.

Now let us add to this the fact that auditors are poorly trained in a constantly changing law. In testimony to that same subcommittee in an earlier hearing, Lynda D. Willis, associate director of tax policy at the General Accounting Office, described many problems businesses face in complying with the tax laws. She described the results of a survey GAO conducted to determine the compliance burden faced by small businesses. Among other things, she said,

> The complexity of the code has a direct impact on IRS' ability to administer the code. The volume and complexity of information in the code make it difficult for IRS to ensure that its tax auditors are knowledgeable about the tax code and that their knowledge is current. Some business officials and tax experts said that IRS auditors lack sufficient knowledge about federal tax requirements, and in their opinion this deficiency has caused IRS audits to take more time than they otherwise might. General Accounting Office, "Tax System Burden, Tax Compliance Burden Faced by Business Taxpayers," GAO/T-GGD-95-42, December 9, 1994, page 3.

The audits not only take more time, leading to more cost for both the agency and the private sector, but they often result in incorrect conclusions. This leads to the assessment of taxes, penalties, interest which are simply not owed.

In 1994, the GAO released the result of a study of the IRS' Coordinated Examination Program (CEP). CEP is designed to audit the largest, most complex corporations. Despite having spent 1,700 staff years to examine 1,700 such corporations, GAO was able to confirm that only 22 percent of the amount of tax proposed through audit was ever collected. General Accounting Office, "Compliance Measures and Audits of Large Corporations Need Improvement," GAO/GGD-94-70, September 1, 1994.

GAO generally cites two reasons for the tremendous difference in the amounts of tax recommended by examination, versus that assessed and collected. First is the complexity of the tax laws. This factor gives rise to "opportunities for different interpretations" of complex tax law issues. Secondly, IRS encourages CEP teams to "recommend more taxes in the shortest time possible." This not only makes it difficult to do a complete audit, it makes it impossible to do a correct audit.

How Returns are Selected for Audit

Let us now turn our attention to the question every citizen asks. "How are returns selected for audit?" Let us start by identifying the two general types of tax audits. First is the correspondence audit, the second is the face-to-face audit. As their titles imply, the former is conducted through letter writing, while the latter takes place "in person." Let us address each in turn.

The correspondence audit. Every tax return filed is scrutinized by IRS computers. The computers perform a number of review and comparison tasks leading to millions of notices demanding increased taxes and penalties. The notices explain that IRS reviewed the return and found an error. It declares that you owe additional tax and penalties as a result and demands payment.

Computers review returns for mathematical correctness to determine whether all necessary supporting schedules are included and to determine that entries are properly carried from one form or schedule to another. The computers also compare all information returns filed, such as Forms W-2 and 1099, with tax returns. The cross-checking is designed to ensure that all income is reported on the return and that those required to file in fact do file their returns. In 1995, nearly 4.5 million notices were issued claiming citizens either failed to file or did not report all their income.

Often these letters are unclear or incomplete, providing little detail as to what citizens are to do. In half the cases, the letters are dead wrong. A 1994 GAO examination of the IRS' correspondence process found serious problems throughout the system. The GAO looked at forty-seven of the IRS' most common notices regarding citizens' accounts. It found that thirty-one of the notices--66 percent of those examined--used inspecific language, unclear references, inconsistent terminology, illogical presentation of material, and insufficient information and guidance. General Accounting Office, "IRS Notices Can be Improved," GAO/GGD-95-6, December 1994, page 8.

Some notices provide no information regarding the errors allegedly made. I have come to refer to these notices as "arbitrary notices." They merely claim a mistake was made and demand payment. Because people are unaware of how to handle these letters and are intimidated by the IRS, most end up just paying the bill.

If there is just one reason to understand your rights as a citizens, this is it. The IRS issues tens of millions of computer notices each year and the high error rates are well-documented. Any citizen, however honest and forthright he may be, can be victimized by such errors. As I said earlier, it is simply not enough to be honest. You must be prepared to back your honesty with action. The action must take the form of proper and timely responses to IRS attacks.

My repeated complaints about this serious problem forced Congress to at least partially address it. With the passage of the Taxpayers' Bill of Rights Act 2 in early 1996, Congress amended code section 7522. The law requires that notices mailed to citizens set forth "the basis for" any tax, interest or penalty demanded. However, Congress failed to build any teeth into the measure. The law states that the lack of an adequate description, "shall not invalidate such notice." Section 7522(a). As a result, we cannot expect the IRS' practices of sending bogus bills to the public to end anytime soon.

My book, *41 Ways to Lick the IRS with a Postage Stamp* (Winning Publications, Inc.) takes the reader step-by-step through these and other notices. I illustrate what the notices are and how to respond properly to keep the IRS from collecting money you do not owe. I discuss the process briefly in chapter thirteen.

The face-to-face audit. The IRS conducts face-to-face audits of approximately 1 to 2 percent of the returns filed in a given year. The decision to conduct a face-to-face examination is based upon several selection criteria. However, the most prevalent is the so-called Discriminate Function System (DIF). Nearly one-third of all returns audited are selected through the DIF scoring process.

DIF is a sophisticated computer program which compares every line of your return with national and regional statistical averages for a person in your same income category and profession. If any line of your return is out of balance with those averages, the difference is scored. The higher the DIF score, the more likely you are to be selected for examination.

The DIF scores are built through a research audit program known as the Taxpayer Compliance Measurement Program (TCMP). The TCMP audit is a grueling line-by-line examination of your return. You are asked to prove your name, address, marital status and so on, throughout the entire return. The results of TCMP audits are assimilated into the DIF parameters. TCMP audit victims are selected on a purely random basis, without regard to any particular claim whatsoever. The last TCMP study was conducted in 1988.

In 1995, the IRS proposed the most far-reaching TCMP audit ever. It was to spend $240 million and three years examining 153,000 individual and small business tax returns. This would have been the largest universe ever examined in a TCMP sweep.

The good news is Congress stalled the audits by defunding them, and it did so as a result of my testimony to the Ways and Means IRS Oversight subcommittee. I showed Congress that because of the significant error rates in the audit process, TCMP results are simply unreliable. To in turn use those results as the means by which to subject more than one million citizens per year to a face-to-face audit is simply unreasonable.

The bad news is that Congress did not *kill* the TCMP audit. By merely defunding it for the time being, it left itself the option of resurrecting the program at some later date.

While the DIF score continues to be the most widely used audit selection process, the IRS uses many other means as well. In 1993, the IRS began an audit research program directed squarely at businesses. The program is known as the Market Segment Specialization Program (MSSP).

MSSP is to businesses what the Economic Reality audit is to individuals. It is designed to examine and evaluate every single aspect of how a business operates. The MSSP program is pointed at certain types of businesses within a given market place.

For example, one MSSP project focuses upon gasoline retailers. Let us say the marketplace is Philadelphia. IRS selects for audit a number of gas retailers within that area, perhaps dozens or more. To build a profile of how gas retailers operate, it audits every element of the business. The audit includes not only an examination of income and expenses, assets and liabilities, but delves deeply into the industry itself. Auditors may contact manufacturers, wholesalers, distributors, trade associations, and others directly or indirectly connected.

The results of the audits lead to the production of an MSSP handbook. The handbook is a working model for the audit of such a business in other areas of the nation. To date, the IRS has issued twenty-nine MSSP handbooks and include the following businesses:

- Attorneys
- Ministers
- The Wine Industry
- Gasoline Retailers
- Alaskan Commercial Fishing
- Bars and Restaurants
- Beauty and Barber Shops
- Auto Body and Repair
- Grain Farmers
- Taxicabs
- Pizza Restaurants
- Bed and Breakfast
- Trucking Industry
- Mobile Food Vendors, and
- Entertainment Industry

Other audit selection criteria include the general nature of the return and its specific claims. These are referred to as compliance projects. For example, since the early 1980s, the IRS has targeted tax sheltered investments. Any return revealing tax shelter attributes is subject to review. Such specialized selection classes include trusts, tax protesters, and multi-level or direct marketers and others.

Compliance projects are responsible for a great number of audits. For example, the IRS has targeted multi-level marketers in general, and Amway distributors in particular. The IRS claims most Amway distributors are not engaged in legitimate business operations. Rather, it contends the endeavors are merely hobbies undertaken for the benefit of pursuing lavish travel and opulent entertainment.

In the rare instance where the agency concedes the legitimacy of one's distributorship, it attacks the travel and entertainment as purely personal, non-deductible expenses. Many other deductions find themselves on the chopping block as well. The IRS has leveled its guns at the mileage claimed by Amway distributors, their home office deductions, long distance telephone charges, and so on. When the agency's computer screening mechanism identifies one or more areas of curiosity, the chances of a face-to-face audit grow significantly.

Now that we have debunked the basic misconceptions about the tax audit process, let us move to the next level. We shall examine the manner in which the IRS attacks a return during the course of a typical tax audit.

Chapter Five -
Facing the Beast
"How the IRS Attacks a Tax Return"

As we examined at length in chapter four, the IRS is successful in tax audits largely due to the misinformation people harbor about the process. The IRS makes matters worse with its steady campaign of disinformation. We have already debunked many myths about the audit process. It is now time to turn our attention to some basic truths concerning it.

We learned that the IRS attacks returns on two general grounds. First, is the question of income. Second, is the question of deductions. The IRS may claim you earned income but failed to report it on the return. Or, it may claim one or more of your deductions is invalid for various reasons. Through either or a combination of such tactics, the IRS acts to increase taxable income, leading in turn to a higher tax bill.

To win a tax audit, it is important to understand this great truth about the process. *You have the burden of proof* on the question of the veracity of items claimed in your return. You must prove you reported all income. You must prove your deductions are not only accurate in terms of amount claimed, but are allowed by law in the year claimed. Generally speaking, the IRS need prove *nothing* to extract more money from you. (There are a few exceptions to the general rule which we address in chapter nine.)

If you are confused about this, the results of your audit are entirely predictable. If you fail to understand how to prove the correctness of your return, again, the results are fully predictable. Simply review once more the GAO statistics on audit results shown in the previous chapter. On the other hand, when you know exactly how the IRS is likely to attack your return, and precisely how to defend it, your success is just as predictable.

How the IRS attacks a return

With 17,000 pages of law and regulation, we can safely say there are countless *possible* ways the IRS could attack a given return. The limits are dependent upon the actual claim in a given return. If, for example, you did not claim a deduction for charitable contributions, you cannot expect trouble in that regard. That does not mean, however, the IRS cannot scrutinize other itemized deductions.

But for all the code's breath and complexity, for all of the millions of audits raising countless potential tax law questions, you might be amazed to know that there are just a handful which arise over and over, year after year. In 1993, the GAO released a report identifying the most common audit issues resulting in disputes with citizens. The GAO found that of the 12,000 cases before the Appeals Division in 1992, just fourteen tax code sections accounted for 45 percent of the pending issues and 57 percent of the proposed tax dollars at stake. General Accounting Office, "Recurring Tax Issues Tracked by IRS' Office of Appeals," GAO/GGD-93-101, May 1993.

It appears, therefore, the IRS tends to hone in on specific areas for two reasons. First, there is no question that people make mistakes in recordkeeping, return preparation and applying the complex tax law. Second, and more importantly, when the IRS finds an easy mark, it works the angle for all it is worth. It seems these fourteen tax code sections tagged by GAO are, at least in about half the cases, an easy way to find more income, disallow deductions, and in general, increase tax bills.

These are the fourteen code sections identified in the report, listed in the order of frequency:

Code section	Subject matter
162	Business expense deductions
61	Gross income
167	Depreciation of business equipment
482	Allocating income to proper taxpayer
461	Proper tax year of deduction
263	Capital expenditures
166	Bad debts

Code Section	Subject Matter
165	Deductions for losses
2031	Definition of gross estate (estate tax matters)
451	Proper year for claiming income
172	Net operating losses
901	Foreign taxes
472	Inventories
311	Taxability of corporate distributions

As you can surmise from the list, most of these issues involve businesses. However, there is one overriding issue pointed squarely at both businesses and individuals. It is code section 61, gross income. When the IRS makes a determination that you failed to report all your income, the adjustment made in the course of the audit invokes the authority of section 61. Being second on the list, it accounts for nearly 20 percent of all disputed cases in 1993. It is critical, therefore, that you understand how the IRS attacks income and how to prove yours is correctly reported.

The first item on the list relates to business expenses. Code section 162 allows a deduction for any "ordinary and necessary" expense incurred for the purposes of "earning income." As a business, whether a small corporation or sole proprietor, you are entitled to deduct any expense you incur that is necessary to generate income for your business.

The list of such deductions is broad and variable, depending upon the nature of the business. What is ordinary and necessary for one business may not be for another. What generates income in one business may not for another. This very broad brush is what accounts for the fact that over 21 percent of all audit disputes with the IRS involve section 162 deductions.

In a separate 1995 analysis of only section 162 deductions, the GAO shed light on this specific area of concern. GAO found six recurring themes in the IRS' practice of disallowing business deductions under section 162. General Accounting Office, "Recurring Issues in Tax Disputes Over Business Expense Deductions," GAO/GGD-95-232, September 1995. They are:

•*Inadequate documentation* - citizens either did not provide documentation or documentation was inadequate to prove the expense,

•*Unreasonable compensation* - closely held corporations deduct more than is "reasonable" for officer's salary,

•*Not a trade or business* - IRS claims citizen is not involved in a business for profit, but rather, is engaged in a non-deductible hobby,

•*Personal expenses* - IRS claims expense was not business related, but a non-deductible personal expense,

•*Capital expenditures* - IRS claims expenses are capital in nature and must be depreciated rather than fully deducted in the year incurred, and

•*Miscellaneous* - involves a number of general areas.

Sole proprietors face the highest risk of all business taxpayers that the IRS will in some way tamper with their return. Of the cases reviewed by GAO for its 1995 report, 51 percent involved sole proprietors, more than any other category. The chart reproduced at the top of the next page illustrates the percentage breakdown of issues in sole proprietor disputes.

As you can see from the chart, two specific issues of the six identified pose the most problems. First is the question of documentation of the deduction. Two-thirds of all disputes with IRS involve inadequate documentation. Next is the hobby versus business question. Twenty one percent of the cases involve a claim by the IRS that the business is not legitimate, but rather, is a hobby. If you are to survive an audit as a sole proprietor, you better know how to document your deductions and prove your business is legitimate.

The next chart, reproduced at the bottom of the next page, illustrates the same data relative to small corporations. Small corporations are also attacked on the basis of documentation, but to a lesser extent. At 36 percent, inadequate documentation is still the number one problem corporations have, but at half the rate of sole proprietors. Two other major problems present themselves for small corporations.

Exhibit 5-1

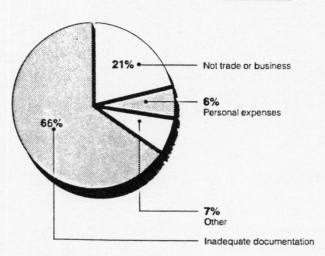

Source: GAO analysis of petitions filed with the U.S. Tax Court.

Exhibit 5-2

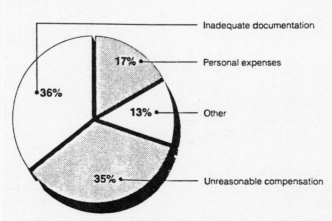

Source: GAO analysis of petitions filed with the U.S. Tax Court.

One is the question of reasonable compensation. Since corporations are entitled to a deduction for salary but not for dividends paid to shareholders, the IRS is wont to claim that officers' salary is "unreasonably high." By reducing the salary, it decreases the corresponding deduction. The risk of such an attack is on par with the risk associated with inadequate records.

The second involves personal expenses. Seventeen percent of all small corporation cases involve a claim that one or more deductions were in fact non-deductible personal expenses.

One Problem with the Tax Code

We just saw that most audit issues spring from what the IRS claims are inadequate records. One must wonder why so many people face such problems. It is especially curious given that more than half of us use tax professionals for our recordkeeping and return preparation needs. The problem can be traced to the lack of clear guidance or specific definitions as to exactly what constitutes adequate records.

Under section 446(a) of the code, a citizen is required to compute his income using "a method of accounting on the basis of which the taxpayer regularly computes his income in keeping his books." If that statement is not confusing enough, consider this: The code provides precious little guidance as to the "books" one must keep.

Consequently, each citizen and business may have, and often does have, an entirely different method of keeping track of income and expenditures for tax purposes. Add to this the great "discretion" the IRS has under section 446(b), and the potential for abuse is staggering. Section 446(b) reads,

> (b) If no method of accounting has been regularly used by the taxpayer, or if the method used does not clearly reflect income, the computation of taxable income shall be made under such method as, in *the opinion of the Secretary,* does clearly reflect income (emphasis added).

I have already demonstrated that the "opinion of the Secretary" is most individuals have income beyond what they report on their tax returns. "In the opinion of the Secretary," then, they are to have their incomes "adjusted" under such method "as does clearly reflect income." To translate, the IRS adds taxable income, and hence, tax liability, in almost every audit situation. Expect these problems to grow worse in years to come due to the new economic reality audit.

How the IRS Attacks Income

The IRS uses several techniques for flushing out evidence of additional income. Most of the techniques are concealed in the camouflage of seemingly meaningless questions and exercises. Next we examine seven of the most common methods IRS uses to attack income.

1. The Bank Deposits Method. The IRS regularly reviews the records of one's bank accounts. It is quite common for the IRS to request all personal and business bank records, including duplicate deposit slips, monthly bank statements, canceled checks and loan documents for a given year.

What do they learn from all of this? A lot! For example, most people are under the impression their bank transactions are sacred. This is not true. The IRS has ready access to bank records through the use of IRS Form 2039, Summons. Records are obtained with or without your cooperation. You would be *shocked* to learn just how free-wheeling banks are with supposedly private information.

But believing the account is private, money or receipts which may not be reported on the tax return are nevertheless deposited to the bank account. This creates a discrepancy in the amount of the "apparent income" shown on the tax return versus bank deposits. Let me illustrate:

Suppose you work for a large corporation during 1995. At the end of the year, the corporation issues a Form W-2, Wage and Tax Statement. The statement, also filed with the IRS, reports total wages earned during the year. When you prepare your return, you overlook the fact that you sold that old riding lawn mower to your neighbor. That money, along with all of the garage sale proceeds, were deposited to your bank account with a paycheck one month.

When the auditor totals the deposits to the account, taken from the duplicate deposit slips and monthly statements you provide, he finds that, for example, $1,200 more appeared in the bank account than was reported as income on your tax return. The difference is determined to be unreported income.

Only in the case of criminals is the failure to report the added income a deliberate act. Most do not believe every dime that comes into their possession must be reported to the government. And in fact, not every dime is required to be reported. Even for those highly conscientious about reporting everything, truthfully, who remembers to write down *every dime?* Yet, the IRS believes these "underreporters" are hiding income intentionally, and when the new tax liability is computed, penalties are naturally included.

Another common ploy is to double count re-deposits. It is easy to do when a person has more than one bank account and does not see it coming. This is how it works.

Suppose you earn W-2 wages of $40,000 and deposit all your paychecks to a checking account. Suppose further you run a small business on the side, which needs operating capital from time to time. As a result, you write checks from your personal account to your business account to cover periodic cash crunches. Of course, all your business income is deposited to the business account as well.

When the business tax return is prepared, the income figures are taken from the income journal. The journal is the daily log book reflecting income from all sources. The log may be nothing more than your bank deposit records. If there is a separate journal, it does not show the deposits of cash from your personal account because, simply, that is not income to the business. Naturally, they are shown in the bank account.

When the auditor reviews the business checking account, he adds all deposits to the account, assuming they are income. If you re-deposited $2,500 from your personal account to your business account, those deposits are picked up as income. The result is the auditor assumes you have $2,500 more income than is shown on your business return.

However simple this may sound, however simple it may be to prove the matter, take note of something very important. Tax auditors do this *all the time.* They do it *knowing* it is wrong and they do it *knowing* they will get away with it a fair percentage of the time.

2. Information returns. Information returns are a rapidly growing source of data for the IRS. The returns I speak of are Form W-2, "Wage and Tax Statement" and Form 1099, "Miscellaneous Income."

Every wage earner is well aware of the W-2. Prepared by the employer and provided to both the employee and the IRS, it reflects wage income paid, as well as federal, state and social security taxes withheld. It may also provide other miscellaneous data on payments to employees.

Form 1099 covers a wide range of non-employee payments. For example, 1099-R reports royalty income, 1099-INT reports interest income, and so on. The 1099-MISC is used to report non-specific payments, such as those to independent contractors.

The law requires a W-2 on every employee reporting the first dollar of wages. A 1099 is required when payments during the course of a year exceed $600. For some time, the IRS has been working to have the threshold lowered. Before long, look for it to drop to $100 or less.

As I explained earlier, the IRS' computers cross-check information returns with tax returns. They look for unreported income. Suppose, for example, the IRS shows two Forms W-2 reporting total wages of $35,000. However, the return reports income of just $20,000 from one source. Such a discrepancy leads to the assumption that you had income you did not report on the return.

Most of the cases turned up through this process are handled by correspondence, but not all of them. It is not unusual for cases to be assigned for face-to-face examination when other factors justify it.

3. Net Worth Increases. Another method, used less commonly, is the "Net Worth Increase" method. Under this system, the IRS makes a determination of any substantial increase in one's net worth (the value of his assets less liabilities) during a particular year. Once a year-end net worth is established, it is compared with the net worth as it existed at the beginning of the same year. The difference is then calculated. The difference is compared to the income shown on the tax return. The IRS asks itself whether the after-tax income is sufficient to account for the increases in net worth. If not, it claims additional income was earned.

Let me illustrate. Suppose on January 1, 1994, you have a $75,000 mortgage on your home. The home is worth $100,000. If that is your only asset and liability, your net worth is $25,000. Let us further suppose that by December 31, 1994, your home mortgage is paid in full. Without any debt on the home, your net worth, assuming no other assets or liabilities, is now $100,000. Your net worth *increased* by $75,000 in one year.

Now let us suppose that your 1994 tax return discloses wage income of $50,000. Based on all deductions and exemptions shown in the return, let us further suppose your after-tax income, that left after paying federal, state and social security taxes, is $33,000. This is the amount of money you have available to spend on all personal living expenses, recreation, investments, etc.

As anyone can plainly see, and *so would the IRS,* it is impossible with that amount of money to have paid off the $75,000 mortgage balance on your house. Obviously, the government quickly concludes you had additional income. Equally obvious is the fact that such income was not reported on your return.

The example I just gave is exaggerated and simplified. This is because *all* assets and liabilities must be taken into consideration before any increases can be assumed. Furthermore, the IRS must *correctly* fix the net worth at the beginning of the year in question before it can say the net worth *increased* by the end of the year.

A thorough investigation would likely reveal the information necessary to accomplish this. For example, all real estate transactions are recorded and in most cases, *reported* to the IRS. Similarly, motor vehicle acquisitions are recorded. As we already know, the IRS has speedy access to your bank account and the information which can be mined there.

4. Cash Expenditures. Code section 6050I requires all cash transactions in excess of $10,000 be reported to the IRS. The law stipulates that if any person engaged in "a trade or business receives more than $10,000 in cash in one transaction (or two or more related transactions)," that person must provide Form 8300 to the IRS. The form reveals the payer's name, social security number and the date and nature of the transaction.

The IRS uses this information to make evaluations of unreported income in much the same way it does with net worth assessments. Using the same example as above, suppose, rather than paying off the house, information reveals you purchased several expensive furs and diamonds during the course of the year. While these assets are not "title" assets as an automobile or house, they are just as easily traceable through the reporting requirements of code section 6050I and Form 8300.

In addition, the IRS regularly uses Form 4822, "Estimate of Annual Personal and Family Living Expenses," to redetermine income. The form, discussed in detail in chapter ten, asks the citizen to list all personal expenses paid during the year, either by check or with cash. If the expenses seem to exceed the disposable income available, the IRS assumes you earned additional income and increases the tax accordingly.

5. Bureau of Labor Statistics Estimates. The Bureau of Labor publishes statistics on the average earnings of persons in the United

States. The statistics cover individuals in virtually every walk of life. They also take into account the level of disposable income necessary to exist in a given community in the United States.

These data are typically enlisted by the IRS if one fails to file a tax return. In the absence of any adequate information, the IRS makes an estimate of income based upon Bureau of Labor Statistics (BLS). Using employment and geographic location as a starting point, the IRS refers to the myriad of tables in BLS publications to fix an amount of income you "must have received" in order to exist under the conditions apparent. The statistics consider whether you are a homeowner, whether married and with children, and other factors either known or readily ascertainable.

Despite the fact that they are in actuality nothing more than guesses, BLS estimates often stand up unless the citizen can demonstrate the figures are incorrect. See chapter nine for exceptions.

6. *Consumer Price Index Estimates.* The Consumer Price Index (CPI) marks increases in the cost of living in the United States from year to year. Moreover, like the BLS tables, these figures are broken into specific geographic locations. A person in St. Louis, for example, may not be faced with the same cost of living increases as, say, a person in San Francisco. The differences are reflected in the particular tables compiled within the CPI.

Like BLS tables, CPI tables provide the IRS with a fruitful source of information upon which to base a tax assessment in the absence of more accurate data or a tax return. Commonly, when CPI tables are employed, the IRS pulls the last tax return available for the taxpayer, determines his gross income as shown on that return, and merely increases it year to year by multiplying the appropriate CPI ratio to the last known income figure. Let me illustrate.

Suppose your last federal income tax return, filed in 1991, discloses income of $38,000. Suppose also that you live in Atlanta, Georgia. Let us further suppose that the CPI for Atlanta increased each year by 4 percent. The IRS simply multiplies $38,000 (your 1991 income) by 1.04 to determine that your 1992 income is $39,520. That latter figure is again multiplied by the 1.04 factor to arrive at 1993 income of $41,000. The procedure is repeated until each year is accounted for.

7. *Weighted Averages.* The weighted average is a mathematical computation performed when partial or incomplete records are available. It works this way: Suppose you have a bank account for eighteen months during 1991 and 1992. In July 1992, the account is closed and you have no further transactions with any bank. As a consequence, the IRS has records of income through bank deposits for all of 1991, just half of 1992, but none at all for 1993.

To determine income for the last six months of 1992 and the entirety of 1993, the IRS averages the deposits shown in the first eighteen months of the period in question. That average is then projected over the balance of the eighteen month period, taking into account the increases anticipated from the CPI tables. These averages form the foundation for IRS' claim of income for the eighteen month period in which no bank records exist.

New Tools for Determining Income

As the years roll by, Congress is faithful in cutting the number of deductions legally allowed. As fewer deductions are available, there are fewer to audit. At the same time, the IRS is concerned about the growing underground economy. It has therefore employed new weapons in the fight against unreported income. These new tools are embodied within the economic reality audit. As we shall learn in Part III of this discourse, the economic reality audit is based upon one or more of the seven techniques outlined above. However, it goes much, much further, as we shall soon see.

Chapter Six -
Staring Down the Beast
"How to Counter the Attack"

All face-to-face audits begin at the same point, with a notice from the IRS. The notice says that your return for a stated year has been selected for "examination" and establishes a time and a place for the meeting. Accompanying the notice is a form known as an "Information Document Request" (IDR). There was a time when these documents were pre-printed form letters, but with the advent of word processors, they seem more tailored to specific cases.

The IDR presents a list of items the auditor wishes to inspect. These are the documents relating to the items claimed in the return. In many cases, the IDR makes a specific request for production of documents relative to a particular claim, such as evidence to support a mortgage interest deduction. In other cases, the IDR is more general. It may seek "all records relative to your claim of deductible items in the return."

In step-by-step fashion, we examine the phases of preparation you must undertake to negotiate successfully in the tax audit.

Step One. Audit defense preparations must begin with a careful analysis of the IDR. Ascertain the issues in question, whether income, specific deductions, etc. Do not be intimidated if the IDR demands you produce a laundry list of records. You will quickly notice that much of the material asked for does not exist. The IRS generally paints with a broad brush when seeking records. You can narrow the list in a hurry after recognizing that most do not apply to you and your return.

Step Two. After reviewing the notice and IDR, you may now begin to determine two essential facts with respect to each return item in question. First, what in fact was claimed on the return with regard to that item? And second, are you in possession of sufficient proof to verify that the entry is correct?

Settling on what in fact was claimed on the return is a simple matter. Just look to the 1040 form or supporting schedule bearing the entry in question and note the amount shown. An example is the amount claimed as mortgage interest. If you claimed $5,000 in mortgage interest as an itemized deduction on Schedule A, that is the amount you must prove in the audit. If you used a return preparer, meet with the preparer and go over the return to be sure you understand each of the entries.

Do not proceed to an audit without reviewing the tax return in this manner. If you do, you will have no idea whatsoever as to your burden of proof. You will be completely at the mercy of the auditor.

Step Three. The next step is to match your documentary proof to each item to be sure the two figures coincide. This answers the factual question whether you indeed incurred the expense claimed.

Exactly what type of documentation is considered "sufficient proof" is addressed later as the main subject of this chapter. Preliminary preparation must satisfy this question: Do existing documents, that is, documents currently in your possession or under your control, support the amount of income, deductions or credits claimed on the return? If the answer is "no," then you must, using one of the methods expounded upon later in this chapter, supplement your proof so that it is sufficient. If the answer is "yes," then you may proceed to Step Four.

Step Four. Now you must determine whether the proof is sufficient from a legal standpoint. This usually involves slightly more effort than just adding receipts and checks with a calculator. It necessitates, unless you own a copy of the current tax law, a trip to the library.

Most public libraries, and certainly every law library, has a copy of the United States Code. The United States Code is a compilation of all the acts of Congress currently in effect in the United States. It is the body of American law known as "statutes." The statutes are organized within the United States Code by topic. Each topic is assigned a number, known as a "Title."

All tax laws are found within Title 26 of the United States Code, commonly referred to as "the Internal Revenue Code." Within Title 26, each separate statute (and there are thousands) is numbered individually, beginning with "1." The statute is then referred to as a "section." Hence, the citation "26 USC 6511" is a reference to Title 26 of the United States Code (the Internal Revenue Code), at section 6511.

Paperback copies of the Internal Revenue Code are available from several publishers. They are inexpensive and quite handy. Two companies in particular focus upon publishing materials relative to income taxes and are practiced with regard to the Internal Revenue Code. These companies are Commerce Clearing House, 4024 West Peterson Avenue, Chicago, IL 60646, and Prentice Hall, Englewood Cliffs, NJ 07632.

The purpose of referring to the code is simple, yet important. Expect revenue agents to assume one of two stances with regard to a given deduction. The first and most common is where the citizen's proof does not meet or exceed the numbers shown on the return. "Without further substantiation," you will be told, "I cannot allow the item you have claimed. You are unable to prove satisfactorily that you in fact spent the amount claimed." Hence, down the drain goes the deduction, in whole or in part. Remember the GAO study on documentation? Of all disputed cases, 66 percent have this problem.

When the proof matches the amount claimed, the revenue agent shifts gears. Reverting to Plan B, he claims that while you did indeed spend the amount of money claimed, the law does not allow the deduction. "The law is clear," begins the refrain. "A deduction is just not permitted for money spent in this fashion. I am sorry, but I just cannot allow it."

In anticipation of the two-pronged attack, proper preparation for the audit must address both the factual (how much was spent, for what, and when) and the legal (what the statutes say about money spent in this fashion) aspects of a given deduction.

As we have already seen, even IRS agents know little about the law given that so many sweeping changes have occurred. They can, however, bluff and intimidate citizens on these points. That is why I recommend everyone have my library of IRS defense materials. The books address your rights and IRS procedures in nearly every kind of tax dispute.

How to Use the Tax Code

Using the code, particularly in paperback form, is very simple. Just refer to the index, under the "key word" in question. For example, suppose you wish to determine the circumstances under which "entertainment" expenses may be deducted. Under the general heading of "Entertainment," the index points you in several directions. Review the list to see which sub-entry is applicable.

Look for the number printed to the right of the index entry. That number is a reference to a code *section*, not page number. Next to the heading "Entertainment," you will find the reference "274." This is the specific section of the code where the legal authority to deduct entertainment expenses is found.

We must now read and analyze the pertinent statute. Section 274(a) reads, in part,

> (a) Entertainment, amusement, or recreation (1) In general
> No deduction otherwise allowable under this chapter shall be allowed for any item--
> (A) Activity
> With respect to an activity which is of a type generally considered to constitute entertainment, amusement, or recreation, *unless the taxpayer establishes that the item was directly related to*, or, in the case of an item directly preceding or following a substantial and bona fide business discussion (including business meetings at a convention or otherwise), that such item was associated with, the active conduct of the taxpayer's trade or business. Code sec. 274 (a), (emphasis added).

At first blush, it appears that someone is trying to confuse you. This is probably because they are! It appears that no deduction is allowed. However, upon reading more carefully, we find in subparagraph(a)(1)(A) that an exception is created by the words *"unless the taxpayer establishes . . ."* The statute goes on to describe what must be "established."

Specifically, if one can demonstrate that any such expense was "directly related to or associated with the active conduct of the taxpayer's trade or business," then the entertainment expense is deductible under the general terms of 274(a). Only by actually reviewing the particular statute in question is one capable of accurately stating "what the law is" in a given case.

In addition to the Internal Revenue Code where we find the statutes, the body of tax law is made up of other sources of authority. These sources include:

1) Tax Regulations. Regulations are passed into being by the IRS. An IRS regulation becomes effective when Congress *fails* to act upon it by expressly voting against its enactment. Through this system of law by default, thousands of requirements are heaped upon us by unelected bureaucrats.

2) Court Decisions. Court decisions interpret the statutes and regulations on a case by case basis.

3) Revenue Rulings. Revenue Rulings are the *IRS' written* opinion as to how the law should be applied in a given set of hypothetical facts and circumstances.

Each of these sources of authority on the law can be helpful to provide support to any single claim made by a citizen.

How to Prove Income

In anticipation of the IRS' attack upon your tax return's income revelation, be prepared to counter by rallying one of the proven methods used to verify that your disclosure is correct. This is particularly important in the age of the economic reality audit. As Congress eliminates more deductions, the IRS is, to a greater and greater extent, left with only your income to challenge.

I have distilled four primary techniques which, if used alone or in concert with one another, allow you to ensure that the income portion of your return remains intact. Each of the techniques, together with a true to life example of how it is used, follows.

1. Ledgers. My many years of experience with the IRS has taught me that the most effective way to verify one's income is with records made personally and contemporaneously with earning the income. Records which reflect income are commonly referred to as ledgers, logs or journals. These records are, in the absence of patently contradictory evidence, most persuasive in an income dispute.

A case comes to mind where logs were the difference between paying tens of thousands of dollars in illegitimate taxes and a just conclusion that such was not owed. Dennis went through a tax audit in which he presented to the auditor his bank records and evidence to support his business deductions. Unaware that the auditor was fishing for evidence of unreported income, Dennis candidly answered a barrage of questions about the manner in which he operates his business.

As a piano tuner, Dennis made house calls to his many customers. Some of the customers paid by check. Many paid in cash. Naturally, all of the checks were deposited to Dennis' bank account, but the cash was not. When the IRS audited Dennis' tax return, they reviewed his bank records. The auditor, a self-styled Sherlock Holmes, believed he stumbled upon a major discrepancy in Dennis' finances.

The discrepancy was Dennis wrote off many thousands of dollars in business expenses on his Schedule C. But deposits to his bank account did not come close to matching those amounts, not to mention other deductions claimed on Schedule A. Even though Dennis declared sufficient income to account for these expenditures, it was obvious he was doing a large part of his business in cash. This caused the auditor to jump to the erroneous and unfounded conclusion that Dennis significantly underreported his income.

The auditor did all of this gum shoeing without Dennis' knowledge. Had the agent simply asked, Dennis could have provided ample verification of his income. Instead, soon after the audit was complete, the agent mailed Dennis an examination report with a cover letter. The cover letter explained that Dennis was expected to pay the additional tax and penalties promptly in order to avoid further interest. Upon reviewing the examination report, Dennis was shocked to find that the agent included thousands of dollars in "unreported income." Flabbergasted by the report, we immediately drafted the necessary paperwork to carry out an appeal.

During the Appeals conference, we presented the ledgers Dennis maintained. They were used as the source of information for the income declaration in his return. Not being an accountant, the ledgers were rudimentary by professional standards, but quite functional for his needs. As it happened, they were also more than adequate to establish that Dennis' income was reported correctly. Remember, the law does not require that you keep records in a "professional" manner. The law requires only that records be kept such as are sufficient to "clearly reflect income." Code section 446(b).

In form, Dennis' ledgers looked something like this:

MONTH/YEAR	Date	Name/Address	Job	Paid

Beneath the heading in each column Dennis recorded the data called for. Next to the amounts shown in the "Paid" column, Dennis indicated with a check mark whether the amount was paid at the time of rendering service, or whether he had to bill the customer. At the end of the month, statements were mailed to any person whose name did not bear a check mark in the "Paid" column. The eventual payment was then recorded in the month it was received. At the end of the year, it was a simple matter of adding the amounts in the ledgers bearing a check mark. The total amount was reflected as the gross income on the tax return.

Verifying income at the Appeals level was a less-than formidable task. We provided copies of Dennis' ledgers together with an explanation as to how they were maintained. Dennis' testimony that these ledgers were made contemporaneously with earning the income was critical. That is to say, they were not concocted in a desperate hope to avoid the additional taxes occasioned by the auditor's zeal.

In the absence of any specific evidence to the contrary and given the fact that Dennis' explanation was *plausible,* reasonable and Dennis was an *honest* person and clearly *projected* that, the appeals officer accepted his proof and recalculated the audit changes. In the process, he dropped all of the phantom income "found" by the revenue agent.

Many businesses use professional accountants or bookkeepers to establish ledgers or journals which accurately and neatly reflect the company's daily business. Those without the benefit of experts should take a lesson from Dennis. Be careful not to fall into the trap of creating ledgers too complex and difficult to follow. Unless supervised by an accountant, ledgers should be simple and to the point. Most importantly, make them at the same time the events being recorded occur. It is important to be able to testify believably that your ledgers were made at the time the income *was earned and* not on the way to the courthouse.

2. Bank Records. Just as the IRS uses bank records to *increase* income, a knowledgeable citizen can use them to *cast aside* IRS' erroneous estimates. Useful tools include monthly bank statements and duplicate deposit slips. Between the two, a person can fix his income quite accurately. In fact, I maintain that the best and most accurate ledger or journal a person can have is his business bank account.

When you receive money in the course of your affairs and deposit it to an account, a permanent record is made of the amount and date it was received. When the IRS questions income, reliance on the bank records as the full and complete record of one's receipts is virtually unassailable. This of course assumes the IRS cannot point to large cash expenditures or net worth increases which betray bank account information.

To illustrate this, I point to a case where the IRS made an estimate of a man's income for two years in the early 1980s. Don did not file income tax returns for the two years in question. Using the BLS tables mentioned earlier, the IRS estimated his income based upon the town he lived in and his business. Don was a plumber, but not a very successful one. Personal circumstances caused his business to dwindle and he was working odd jobs to generate money on which to live.

BLS statistics, unfortunately, do not take into consideration whether one is successful in business or not. They are, by admission, mere *averages.* In order to have an average, there must of course be a high and low. Don's income was at the low end of the scale. But the BLS tables put his income over five times higher. With penalties and interest included, the IRS wanted Don to pay more in taxes for the two years than he earned in income.

Using bank records as the starting point, we set out to determine the *accurate* amount of gross income Don earned. The bank account in question was in fact owned by Don's wife, Linda. Linda was employed in a job of her own and earned her own money. She also filed her own tax returns and paid her own taxes. But Don was depositing his money into *her* account. As she had no obligation to report his income, she reported only her own.

We knew how much Linda earned from her job each month and we knew that she was paid twice each month. A monthly bank statement reflected each deposit and withdrawal transacted in a given month. We carefully reviewed the bank statements and with a red pen, drew a line through those deposits which were identified as Linda's paycheck. In some cases however, a deposit larger than a single paycheck was shown. In that case, we went back to the deposit slip. A deposit slip *identifies* each of the individual items which make up a deposit. By referring to the deposit slips, we were able to focus upon and mark out each of Linda's paychecks.

The remaining deposits represented money Don earned. Having isolated Don's income on each of the bank statements, it was just a matter of adding the deposits which we could accurately say were his. The total of each of the twelve months was Don's income for the years. Our tally was presented to the Appeals officer together with *testimony* to the effect that all of Don's receipts were deposited to the account. We also proved that Linda's wages were responsible for the other funds deposited to the account, and showed that Linda had already filed her own return.

With no other evidence that Don earned the income claimed by the IRS, it was forced to accept the facts as presented. As in the previous example, credible testimony from Don to the effect that all of his income was deposited to Linda's bank account spelled the end for the BLS estimates.

Not all solutions are that simple. Sometimes, bank account analysis is much more laborious. Further effort is necessary when the IRS skews figures taken from two or more separate accounts. As I explained earlier, it happens all the time. In my judgment, the IRS' acts are deliberate and therefore reprehensible. The typical plot unfolds this way.

A small businessman has two (or more) bank accounts. One account functions as a business account, to which he deposits his receipts and from which he pays business bills. The other is a personal account. The personal account is funded by periodic payments from the business account. From the personal account he pays personal living expenses.

During the course of an examination, the IRS reviews the records of both accounts. The deposits to the business account are totaled. Then the deposits to the personal account are totaled. The two figures are then *added together,* and the sum called "corrected income." It happens too often to be called an error. Unfortunately, this process just as often handcuffs the citizen.

Let us look at what such a trick does to one's gross income. Suppose total deposits to the business account are $200,000. Suppose further the owner of the business takes a "draw" or self-imposed salary of $3,000 per month, which he pays to himself with a check drawn on the company account. In the typical sole-proprietor business, all business income as well as expenses are reported on Schedule C. The difference between company receipts and expenses is considered personal income to the owner. With very few exceptions, that difference is manifested by the "draw" or salary.

Under our example, the yearly income of our hypothetical proprietor is $36,000 ($3,000 per month). The $36,000 is subtracted from the $200,000 gross, yet when the IRS adds together the total deposits of *each* account, it concludes that the gross was $236,000, not $200,000. Worse than that, since there appears to be no additional *expenses* to offset the apparent unreported income, the net income to the proprietor is figured at $72,000, exactly *twice* what he earned.

So, what is the cure? In one very similar case, we explained to the agent that the funds he called "unreported income" were in fact re-deposits from the business account. We further explained that the money was already accounted for on the Schedule C. Sitting back in his swivel chair, he cracked a devilish smile and glibly said, "prove it." So we did.

Beginning with the canceled checks written on the *business* account, we shuffled through them individually. Anytime we happened upon a check written to the citizen or his wife, we set it aside. After unearthing each such check, we unfolded the bank statements from the *personal* account. We compared the specific deposits to the personal account with the checks written on the business account. In this manner, we traced the money from its source in the one account to its destination in the other. A yellow highlighter marked the particular line of the statement where one could find a "re-deposit." Thus, we traced each personal deposit to its origin in the *business* account. The conclusion is no money came into the personal account from any source other than the business.

At the same time, we tallied the deposits to the business account by reference to the monthly statements. That number was then compared to the one shown on the Schedule C as gross receipts. As anticipated, the two matched.

Back for a second meeting with the examiner with proof in hand, I traced these steps. Pointing first to the canceled checks drawn on the business account, then to the monthly statements for the personal account, I insisted that the evidence plainly showed the sole source of funds in the personal account were re-deposits from the business account.

Next, I waved the business account's monthly statements in the air together with a calculator tape depicting the total deposits. Gesturing then to the Schedule C, I made the point that there was no "unreported income" as originally alleged by the agent. In the face of this presentation, the agent was forced to alter his posture. He assented to the proposition that all income was correctly reported.

Bank records do not lie. For that reason, they are often extremely helpful in verifying one's income. This is particularly true where bank records are the only source of certifiable intelligence on the question.

3. Information Returns. Information returns reflect data compiled by a third party and transmitted to the IRS. The information, usually in the nature of a Form W-2 or 1099, communicates to the IRS how much a person was paid by an employer, a bank, etc. In the absence of any contradictory evidence, an information return can be the last word on the question of income.

An Appeals officer once told me that in his experience, information returns were incorrect about 30 percent of the time. My personal experience shows an error rate at least that high. Usually, they *overstate* income. As a result, the IRS "adjusts" one's tax return to match the income shown on the information return. For that reason, it is always a good idea to compare paycheck stubs with the W-2 or 1099 to ensure the latter's correctness.

Assuming however, that the information return is indeed correct, it is a helpful tool when the IRS attempts to increase income for some reason. Though they should, many people who receive wages or are commissioned salespersons do not necessarily keep a journal reflecting their periodic receipts. For this reason, until the Form W-2 or 1099 is received, they have no idea what they have earned. This makes them prime targets for the IRS to arbitrarily increase their income. This precise thing occurred in the case of a commissioned jewelry salesman.

Paul was audited for tax year 1985. His return claimed income from sales in the amount of $18,300. The auditor could not believe Paul could survive on that "little amount of money." Agreeing with the auditor, Paul said, "I couldn't! That's why I had to find a new job!" But in her mind, the auditor was convinced Paul's income as stated in the form was "just too low."

"That is all I made," he assured her.

"Well, then I would like to see your bank account statements for the year" she replied.

"I didn't have a bank account," Paul popped. "There is nothing to show you."

In her audit report, the agent included extra income determined by "using the cash transactions method." She arbitrarily assumed that Paul needed an additional $3,900 in which to live (ignoring his paltry living habits and expenses) and thus, *added that much to his declared income.*

Later, we presented a statement in the form of a 1099 from the person for whom Paul worked. The form verified Paul's claimed income. In addition to the form, Paul submitted a statement from the employer to the effect that such was all he earned during the year. Furthermore, Paul provided *his own testimony* to the effect that he did not earn any more than was claimed. As there was no bank account for the year, these uncontradicted statements were, as they had to be, accepted as the true reflection of Paul's income.

The new economic reality audits and the corresponding attitudes of examiners force us to be mindful of the limitations of information returns. In Part III, I discuss at length what these limitations are and how to effectively and conclusively overcome them.

4. *Testimony*. The area of testimony is the most misunderstood aspect of the audit process. Is testimony acceptable? If so, under what conditions? Who may provide the testimony? These questions are often unanswered by tax professionals and ignored by the IRS. In fact, in twenty years of experience with the IRS, I have never met an agent who fully understands the role testimony plays in the tax audit.

Contrary to popular belief, testimony is a useful adjunct to the other methods of verifying income. In some cases, it is the only method. The IRS has, over the years, become quite adept at putting citizens on the defensive with regard to their tax returns. Indeed, the IRS is practiced at painting people into corners from which there is no apparent escape.

Let me offer an example. Earlier, I related a case where the IRS arbitrarily increased Paul's earnings by $3,900 on the theory that "he could not live very well on what he earned." Nobody suggested he could. In fact, he pointed out the details of his limited lifestyle.

But without bank records, Paul was not in a position to prove with extrinsic evidence that he did not earn the additional $3,900. Furthermore, the auditor chose to ignore the Form 1099 from the employer on the topic. So what was Paul left with in the way of proof? His only remaining option was to provide testimony to shed light on the subject. Still, is the IRS bound to accept "his word" on such an important issue? I submit it is, and over the years, several court decisions have agreed.

Let us first understand the posture into which the taxpayer is thrust. Under these circumstances, one must "prove a negative." Since the IRS' changes to a tax return are "presumed to be correct," the burden rests with the citizen to prove that such determination is incorrect. You must therefore prove *you did not* earn the income the IRS attributes to you. You must, in essence, prove you cannot fly, something we all know is difficult, if not impossible to do.

The IRS does not make this task any simpler. It usually maintains that whatever testimony you may offer to support your "negative" position is "inadequate" or (and this is their favorite phrase) "self-serving." Without corroborating documentation, suggests the con, testimony is unacceptable.

However, this concept has been expressly rejected by the courts. These are just a few of the relevant court decisions, *Portillo v. Commissioner*, 91-1 USTC 50,304 (5th Cir. 1991); *Carson v. Commissioner*, 560 F.2d 692 (5th Cir. 1977); *Demkowicz v. Commissioner*, 551 F.2d 929 (3rd Cir. 1977), *Adams v. Commissioner*, 71 TC 477 (Tax Court 1978).

When the IRS makes an affirmative claim with regard to income, that claim must be supported by some "foundation of substantive evidence" before the burden shifts to the citizen to disprove receipt of phantom income. *Weimerskirch v. Commissioner*, 596 F.2d 358 (9th Cir. 1979). (This is *not true* of deductions.) Stated another way, without the IRS itself presenting tangible proof of the additional income, your testimony that you did not have such income is completely sufficient to defeat the claim.

One court put it this way, "So long as the taxpayer found himself unable to prove a negative," the IRS could not rely upon the "presumption of correctness" in connection with its claim. *Carson v. Commissioner*, Ibid. The *IRS,* not the citizen, is forced to present evidence to prove the receipt of unreported income. Without such evidence, the court must "readily reject" the IRS' claim.

Thus we see that the IRS, not the citizen, has the burden to present "extrinsic" evidence on the question of income. Without it, one may fully and legally rely upon testimony to combat such a claim.

Still, there is great confusion on this point and the IRS uses it to its unfair advantage. The very premise of the economic reality audit is based on the idea of putting the burden on the citizen or face an increase in taxes. The IRS almost always demands "records" to prove whatever may be your stated position. But what happens when no records are kept? As you may recall, Paul did not keep a bank account. Was he therefore stuck with the determination, albeit arbitrary, that he in fact had additional unreported income? Certainly not.

In one Tax Court case, the citizens explained the absence of records most suitably. The IRS maintained that two ministers had substantial unreported income for several years. To justify its estimate, the IRS pointed to the BLS tables. Both men lived exclusively upon gifts from their family and members of their congregation. Under the tax code, gifts are expressly delineated as *non-taxable*. As such, neither man filed a tax return or kept records of how much they received.

The government argued the two failed to prove that they did not have sufficient income to require a tax return. In its brief to the court, the IRS attorney stated that the two,

> [D]id not place in evidence any books and records that reflected that they did not receive taxable income during the years at issue.

This obviously ridiculous argument was countered with the following diatribe:

> First of all, why would one keep records to prove there was no need to keep records? Section 6001 of the Code provides in part:
>
> "Every person liable for any tax imposed by this title, or for the collection thereof, *shall keep such records,* render such statements, make such returns, and comply with such rules and regulations as the Secretary may from time to time prescribe."
>
> If one is not 'liable for any tax imposed' by the Code, one is not required, by virtue of that very Code, to keep records. We have seen that sections 102 and 107 specifically exclude from 'income' the only two types of payments received by the Petitioners during the years in question. Why should they keep records of these payments when the law imposed no tax upon such payments, and thus, no duty exists to record them?
>
> The idea that one would record a negative is superfluous. When was the last time this Court saw a contract written by two parties solely for the purposes of proving there was no contract between them? What would such a document say?
>
> If there is no contract, then there would be no written instrument between the parties. Similarly, if there is no income, there naturally and logically would be no records. A record, by its nature, evidences a happening, an event, an historical occurrence. One cannot record that which does not occur. We do not record the fact that no children were born to a family. We record those that are. We do not record automobiles that *are* not purchased, we record those that are. And we do not record the home that *is not* purchased, we record the one that is purchased. So too, we do not record income which is *not* received, we record only the income which

is received. The Petitioners had nothing to record. Hence, no recording was carried out (emphasis in original).

As argued, it is utter nonsense to suggest that one should create and maintain records to prove a negative. Yet the IRS makes you believe that without such proof, you are stuck with whatever wild conclusion the agent may wish to concoct. As we have already seen, such is not the law.

What then must one's testimony consist of in order that the IRS' arbitrary decisions may be overcome? Court cases cited earlier provide substantial guidance in this regard. They teach three things.

1. Testimony must be very particular as to the issue. In this regard, "unequivocal denials" of having received the additional income are quite compelling. Any testimony which tends to be unclear or somehow without conviction as to the subject matter will not dissuade the court from the IRS' point of view.

2. Testimony must be believable and reasonable, not "improbable, unreasonable or questionable." *Lovell & Hart, Inc. v. Commissioner*, 456 F.2d 145 (6th Cir. 1972). To this end, whether one's testimony is credible and believable depends to a large extent upon his personality, his attitude and demeanor. A person who "appears" to be lying may communicate that his testimony is unbelievable. On the other hand, one who testifies with a knowledge of the facts and is not vague or evasive with his testimony, and who is capable of explaining the details of any transaction in question, will generally be held up as credible and believable.

3. Testimony should be "uncontroverted." If not uncontroverted, one should be able to cast such doubt upon the contrary evidence that the court finds the *contradiction,* and not your *testimony,* to be lacking in credibility. In this respect, if one insists he did not have the additional income alleged, he would do well to be sure the IRS cannot present bank records or substantial purchases with cash to controvert the testimony. Similarly, "surprise witnesses" who appear at the last minute to testify that one was skimming large amounts of cash from a business tend to discredit oral testimony. That is not to say that such contrary evidence is the last nail in your testimonial coffin. If a reasonable and plausible explanation, or an outright impeachment of the witness disarms the impact of the damaging "evidence," the court could very well elect to disregard the contrary evidence. This result is more likely if your testimony is otherwise believable and convincing.

Perhaps the most important lesson from the case law is this: "we believe that the taxpayer was not required to 'corroborate' his testimony in order to meet his burden." *Demkowicz*, Ibid. Stated another way, you need not keep records to prove a negative.

If the courts have ever "come clean" on anything, it is the notion that it is impossible to "document" a negative. Even more difficult is the task of anticipating the negatives one may be called upon to prove at some time in the future, then undertaking a recordkeeping sojourn to satisfy those unknowns. The very idea is not only preposterous, but thinking about how one would accomplish it gives me a headache.

Now that citizens have been taken advantage of for years in this regard, Congress has finally enacted rules to help us hold the IRS' feet to the fire on this question. As part of the Taxpayers' Bill of Rights Act 2, passed in June 1996, Congress enacted a rule to require the IRS to do more than baldly allege unreported income. See chapter nine.

How to Prove Deductions

In the case of deductions, the burden of proof is always on the citizen. The courts are fond of pointing out that "deductions are a matter of legislative grace." The one claiming the benefits of a deduction bears the burden to "point to some specific statute to justify his deduction and establish that he comes within its terms." *Roberts v. Commissioner*, 62 TC 834 (Tax Court 1974). One is not "inherently entitled" to claim deductions. Without sufficient proof, the deduction is simply not allowed.

To this end, the earlier section of this chapter entitled, "How to Use the Code" is quite valuable. Many people are bluffed out of deductions because revenue agents tell them their proof is legally insufficient, or because certain language in the law renders the deduction improper. This is taken by the ignorant citizen at face value, since precious few have even seen a copy of the Internal Revenue Code, much less actually read a provision or two.

It can be said that certain standards apply in proving deductions. Without exception, one must be prepared to prove the following four elements with regard to any payment claimed as a deduction:

1) that the money was paid in the year claimed,

2) that the amount claimed on the return was in fact paid,

3) that the character of the payment is recognized by the code as a deductible expense, and

4) that the amount claimed does not exceed any statutory limits.

Let us now examine six ways to prove deductions.

1. Canceled checks. Some people deal exclusively with banks and checkbooks. I have known persons who, rather than carry any cash at all, write checks for such minuscule sums as $1.58. As this is a routine practice, all their evidence is in the form of canceled checks.

This is not all bad. Canceled checks provide a most handy tool to prove deductions. On the face of one document an auditor finds the date the bill was paid, the amount paid, to whom paid, and if the check writer is careful, a notation showing the purpose. All of this information is necessary if one is to establish his entitlement to a deduction.

The difficulty with canceled checks is that people have a tendency to be lazy. For example, one may write a check payable to William Jones, rather than to Dr. William Jones. The check written to William Jones contains no proof on its face that William Jones is a physician and that the payment is a deductible medical expense. Because of the omission, additional evidence must be submitted to prove that William Jones is indeed a practicing physician and the expense is deductible.

The lower left corner of the check blank contains a space for recording bits of information relative to the payment. Use it! This space helps to establish the nature of the payment and the fact that such payment meets the requirements of a deductible expense. This is especially true with small businesses. Many times, the proprietor of a small business writes checks appearing from their face to be for personal purposes. Checks to "Bill's Supermarket," or "Stan's Repair" may be for purely business purposes and fully deductible. However, without supplemental data, they may be classified as a personal expense and disallowed by the auditor. A notation in the memo portion of the blank helps put any such questions to rest.

2. Cash receipts or invoices. The cash receipt or invoice functions in much the same way as the canceled check, but is susceptible to much more looseness. The reason is that store and shop proprietors who make out receipts generally are even more harried than those writing checks. In the interests of time, the operator scribbles the amount and sometimes a description of the item purchased. As often as not, the date is missing and usually, the description of what is purchased is so sketchy as to defy a third party to figure it out.

When making cash purchases, be careful to have the receipt completed in a manner sufficient to plainly communicate what is purchased, the date, and the amount paid. It is not improper for you as the purchaser to make your own notes on the back of the receipt. Notes made contemporaneously with the purchase are quite helpful to trigger one's recall during an audit several years later.

You may wish to note in your own terms, rather than in the retailer's product number, the item purchased. You may also note how the item is put to use. This information is most helpful to establish the deductible nature of your purchase.

It is not uncommon or improper to combine a canceled check with the cash receipt or invoice. This is very helpful for the simple reason that between the two documents, you find all necessary information.

A word of caution about the invoice. An invoice is a bill mailed or presented to one for payment on goods or services. Unlike a statement, the invoice is not by itself proof that anything was paid. For example, telephone bills are invoices. The bill contains no independent proof that you in fact paid the amount demanded. Be careful that such proof *does* accompany an invoice when presented to the IRS.

3. Year-end statements. A year-end statement communicates information compiled by a third party. The most common example of a year-end statement comes from your mortgage company. The document states how much of the payment was applied to interest, principal and taxes during a given year. The statement is indispensable because even though a person can prove that payments were made to the mortgage company each month, he generally cannot prove how the payment is applied to interest and principal. Of course, only the interest and real estate taxes portion of such a payment is deductible. For these reasons, proving these items is difficult without the statement.

In many cases, year-end statements are the only available method to prove your entitlement to certain deductions. This is often the case where one has invested in a limited partnership or other investment arrangement managed by a third party. An example is the audit of Larry's 1985 income tax return. On Schedule E he showed gross royalty income from a limited partnership. On the same schedule he reported his expenses associated with the business. The profit was computed and carried over to Form 1040.

The company sent Larry a statement which spread on a month by month basis the income and expenses associated with his share of the investment. Totals were shown in two areas. They were identified as "Gross" and "Expenses." These two totals were placed upon the appropriate lines of the Schedule E.

During the audit, Larry was asked to provide support for the expenses claimed on Schedule E. He mailed the auditor a copy of the year-end statement. After reviewing the statement, the auditor wrote asking for further proof that these expenses were incurred by Larry. I responded to the letter and explained that, "The year-end statement was prepared by the authorities of the company based upon their own records. As you can see, most of Larry's share of the proceeds were applied to the expenses of earning the income. The specific records are not available to Larry, as he did not keep them. The company was responsible for keeping the records, which they did; and to report to Larry at the end of the year, which they did. His return is based upon these reports. All documentation in his possession proves that he incurred the expenses claimed."

The agent replied by asking for a copy of the company's tax return. "We do not have the return," I wrote. "Furthermore, we do not have access to the return. We have a statement prepared by the company reflecting Larry's expenses. We are entitled to rely upon that as proof of his expenses."

In Larry's case, the IRS accepted the year-end statement as proof of the expenses. We were careful to point out the statement was prepared by the company based upon company records. That forced the agency to the conclusion that the proof was valid with respect to those expenses.

To the greatest extent possible, year-end statements are a good habit to develop from the standpoint of a citizen. The reason is they take all of the guess-work out of proving deductions. All of the information necessary to prove a deduction is contained in one document prepared by a third party, not the citizen himself.

For example, a year-end statement from a church or other charitable organization is prepared by the secretary or treasurer of the organization, not the citizen. It is presented on the letterhead or similar document of the organization. It states the year the sums were paid, and the total amount paid. With such a statement, it becomes unnecessary to sift through the hundreds of canceled checks in an effort to segregate those paid to the organization.

Moreover, the statement of a third party tends to be more credible in the eyes of the auditor than one's own records. I do not mean to suggest that one's own records are inadequate. They of course, are not. I mean only to suggest ways to simplify the task.

4. Log books. A log book is a ledger or diary made by the citizen as the event being recorded occurs. Examples of common logs are automobile mileage and related costs, and travel and entertainment (T&E) expenses. The log is either a separate book or is incorporated into an appointment calendar or similar device.

The law is rigid on the type of information required to substantiate travel and entertainment expenses. For this reason, logs are quite helpful. For example, code section 274(d) requires that in order to prove entitlement to such a deduction, one must show:

1) the amount of the expense,

2) the time and place of the travel or entertainment, etc.,

3) the *business purpose* of the expense, and

4) the *business relationship* to the persons entertained.

It is easy to see that such detailed information is most readily kept in a log made contemporaneously with the travel, etc. Anytime you engage in regular activity, use a log to record your actions. Without a log book, one must go back to reconstruct all of the necessary information needed to fit through the eye of the needle.

CAUTION: IRS Agents Lie! One of the most common bluffs used on unsuspecting citizens rears its ugly head in this very area of logs and T&E expenses. IRS auditors often say that unless your logs are made *contemporaneously* with having incurred the expenses, the deduction absolutely is not allowable. And that is absolutely *not true!* Logs are *helpful* to organize and prove T&E expenses, but they are not mandated by law.

With the Tax Reform Act of 1984, a provision was placed in the law declaring that all T&E expenses must be substantiated with a contemporaneous log. This provision was expressly *repealed* in 1985 when President Reagan signed Public Law 99-44. The 1985 legislation did, among other things, the following:

1) revoked the contemporaneous substantiation requirement *as though it had never been enacted,*

2) provides that T&E claims may be supported by "adequate records" or by other "sufficient evidence" *which does not* have to be written to corroborate one's claims of entitlement to the deduction, (274(d)(4)),

3) repealed the IRS's regulations implementing the contemporaneous record-keeping rules,

4) eliminates the requirement that tax return preparers tell their clients that all T&E expenses must be verified by contemporaneous records, and

5) repealed the so-called "no fault negligence penalty" imposed if the contemporaneous record-keeping requirement was not met.

I like logs because they make the job easier. But in the absence of logs, you are still in a very strong position to verify deductions using any one or more of the other methods. *Do not be misled!* Revenue Regulation 1.274-5(c)(1).

5. Reconstructions. Reconstructions are used where there are no supporting documents upon which a claimed deduction is based. It is perhaps the least known method of proving deductions. The reason is that the IRS has its prey convinced that without a piece of paper supporting the claimed expense, the expense is not allowable. This is just not true. Reconstructions are done all the time and when done correctly, are every bit as valid as the other methods of proof. In fact, you have a duty to reconstruct records if they are lost or destroyed. Your burden of proof is not extinguished merely because you have lost records through no fault of your own. *Robbins v. Commissioner*, 42 TCM 809 (1981).

Revenue Regulation 1.274-5(c)(5) provides, in part, as follows:

> Where the taxpayer establishes that the failure to produce adequate records is due to the loss of such records through circumstances beyond the taxpayer's control, such as destruction by fire, flood, earthquake, or other casualty, the taxpayer *shall have a right* to substantiate a deduction by reasonable reconstruction of his expenditures (emphasis added).

The following history demonstrates how reconstructions are useful. Kathy was a traveling sales representative for a clothing firm. She traveled all across five midwestern states and did so for three years. Often using her American Express card, she went from town to town peddling her wares. As an independent contractor, she was responsible for paying her own costs of doing business, including travel and related expenses. These expenses climbed into the tens of thousands of dollars for each year she was on the road.

Due to a series of residential moves during a traumatic period of her life, she lost her personal records. When called for an audit of the tax returns claiming the greatest amount of travel and related business expenses, she did not have one scrap of paper to document a trip around the block, much less across the region several times. Without sympathy for her hard luck story, all of the business expenses were disallowed.

IRS issued a notice of deficiency and Kathy appealed to the Tax Court. The case was assigned to an attorney for litigation and we began the process of reconstructing three years of her life. As a starting point, we had her address book in which she recorded the names and addresses of the various retailers who purchased her wares and upon whom she called, whether or not they ultimately purchased. We also knew Kathy used her American Express card quite often while on the road.

She mailed a letter to American Express requesting copies of the monthly bills for the three years. As you may know, charge card slips are itemized with the name, address and date of the item charged. Most hotel and meal charges, we reasoned, could be shown on the slips. More importantly, IRS procedures expressly allow one to prove deductions with the records kept by such institutions when originals are lost. Revenue Procedure 92-71, 1992-2 C.B. 437.

When the American Express material arrived, the long process of retracing Kathy's steps was undertaken. The first charge slip showed Kathy spent a night in Fargo, North Dakota. Looking to her list of actual and prospective customers, she ascertained, then listed on a separate sheet, each of the retailers she called upon in Fargo and its immediate area. When we were able to pin down the specific amounts spent on food and fuel, they were noted. When we were unable to do so, the amounts were estimated on the basis of reason and common sense.

We followed this process for each of the thirty-six months at issue. When we completed the painstaking task, Kathy was able to document most, if not all of the expenses incurred. Where there was a gap in time or place due to the incompleteness of the American Express records (the card was not used 100 percent of the time), we supplemented the estimates with testimony. Testimony, in conjunction with the address book, proved the likelihood Kathy indeed was where she said she was, at the time she said she was there. The reconstructions were allowed-- to the penny.

By their nature, reconstructions are estimates and to the best extent possible, attempt to recreate a picture of reality as it was in years past.

Because they are not "self-contained" as are canceled checks or cash receipts, they must be supported with oral testimony. For example, in many cases, Kathy's charge slips showed a hotel expense evidencing that she spent the night in a distant town, but did not show any cost of food. Common sense dictates that one must eat on a daily basis, but the IRS does not always fly with common sense alone. For that reason, we were careful to provide *testimony* to the effect that food was purchased on those days when no food charges were shown.

When used in conjunction with oral testimony, which is "credible, consistent and uncontroverted," reconstructions are as valid a method of proving deductions as exists. *Mantell v. Commissioner*, T.C. Memo 1993-420 (Tax Court 1993).

6. *Oral testimony*. Testimony is nothing more than the oral representations and assurances by the citizen to the effect that the amounts claimed were in fact paid. When such proof is offered to a revenue agent, the most common response is something such as, "Well, I am sure you are telling the truth, but I cannot take your word for it. I must have some kind of proof."

This statement assumes that your word is not "proof." The courts have taken a completely different view of your word, however. Courts regularly allow deductions when the only proof offered is testimony-- your word. How is that so? When the testimony is plausible, believable and credible, the court cannot refuse to consider it. Testimony which meets these criteria is just as valid as any piece of paper I can name. *Mantell v. Commissioner*, T.C. Memo 1993-420 (Tax Court 1993).

Let me prove it. Tom was a regular churchgoer. Every Sunday, he and his family attended weekly services at the local church. Every Sunday, Tom put money in the collection plate. For spiritual reasons, Tom did not put the money in an envelope or otherwise associate his name with the contribution. He gave cash, usually $40, each Sunday.

At the end of the year, Tom deducted $1,980 from his income tax return as a charitable contribution. He was later audited. As you may have guessed, the auditor requested to see substantiation for the charitable contribution deduction. He did not have any written substantiation as he gave only cash. But he did explain to the agent what his practices were, why he engaged in the practices and that without a doubt, he did give the money.

The auditor was not impressed. After resolution of all other issues, Tom took an appeal on the question of his deductions. His case ended up before the Tax Court. During the trial, Tom testified to the judge as to his practices and the reasons for them. The judge kindly asked Tom questions about his habits and how he was able to determine how much money he gave. Tom's answers were direct and to the point. His answers were sensible and believable. All in all, Tom was honest and forthright with the judge during the trial.

In addition to his own testimony, Tom presented the testimony of the church pastor who corroborated the fact that Tom was present at church each Sunday. The pastor backed up Tom's position that he always tithed with cash rather than by check. The pastor's attitude and demeanor reflected the same attributes as Tom's.

At the conclusion of the trial the court ruled in Tom's favor. Specifically, the court held that the deduction was supported by his testimony and that of the church's pastor.

You may be thinking that a trip to court probably is not worth the few dollars in additional tax liability one would incur if the measly $1,980 were disallowed. That is subjective. Each person will answer differently. My answer is that the IRS' rules and regulations, and even statutes recognize that testimony is an acceptable means of proving deductions. For example, code section 274(d), the travel and entertainment section we discussed above, contains the following language:

> No deduction or credit will be allowed . . . unless the taxpayer substantiates by adequate records or by sufficient evidence corroborating *the taxpayer's own statement.*

The express language of the law allows one to prove these touchy deductions with oral testimony. Furthermore, an Internal Revenue News Release issued in 1986 states that, with respect to the business use of a motor vehicle, the IRS would not require contemporaneous logs to prove the deduction. Rather, the citizen could substantiate such use "with any type of evidence, including the taxpayer's own oral statements corroborated with no more than circumstantial evidence." Announcement IR-86-37 (March 28, 1986).

Circumstantial evidence is evidence which tends to make a particular fact more (or less) probable. It is not direct evidence such as that of an eyewitness, or in this case, a canceled check. Circumstantial evidence may consist of countless different types of proof which, when considered as a whole, make your claim of expenses more probable.

To be effective, oral testimony must be specific. Qualified claims and vague recollections will not carry the day. Be sure that all explanations are seasoned with as many hard facts as humanly possible. Specificity leads to believability. To illustrate, one citizen recently provided testimony to an auditor on the issue of church contributions sufficient to justify the amounts claimed in the absence of records. The auditor asked several questions about how much money was put into the collection plate and how often.

As people generally do, Tammy's initial answers were not sufficiently specific to satisfy the auditor's curiosity. But the auditor was not making this known to Tammy. I could see it, so I cut in and began the questioning. I asked, "How often do you go to church?" She answered, "Every week." That information gave us the multiplier to use in computing her total contributions.

Next I asked, "If you had to state an *exact* figure which you gave *each* week, what would that figure be?" Tammy quickly replied, "$15 per week." That answer *completed* the equation: $15 per week multiplied by fifty-two weeks per year; total: $780. Tammy claimed $750 on her return. Thus, the figure was plausible under the circumstances.

Lastly, I asked how it was that she always seemed to have cash on Sunday. She answered that she receives her check on Friday and takes it to the bank. She deposits half the check and takes the balance in cash. She then goes to the grocery store to stock up for the next week. That way, she has spending money for the weekend, including money for the church collection plate.

As before, this information was direct, to the point and made sense. Clearly it was not a concocted line one could smell coming a mile away. On the basis of this showing, her contributions were allowed at the audit level without a single scrap of paper to support them!

A Final Word on Testimony

I hope it is clear that testimony plays a key role, both in establishing your income and proving deductions. The question now is, how do you present the testimony without going to court? The process is surprisingly simple.

Testimony is presented in writing through a tool known as an affidavit. An affidavit is nothing more than a detailed letter of explanation which you have notarized. This makes it a sworn statement carrying the same weight as testimony presented under oath in a courtroom.

Affidavits are needed not only to augment reconstructions, but are necessary any time a claimed deduction involves an "intangible" issue. An intangible issue is one for which, under no circumstances, will you have documentation to support your claim. Let me give three examples.

When claiming an office in your home, the law requires you to prove a number of things, including that the space in the home is not used for any purpose other than business. This is the so-called "exclusive use" test. Code section 280A.

There is no piece of paper I can imagine that will prove the exclusive use test. Only your own testimony, and perhaps that of others such as a spouse, can establish the fact that the home office is not used for any personal purpose whatsoever. More details on the home office deduction are found in my *Smart Tax Special Report*.

The second example involves mileage expenses. As you may know, to be deductible, auto mileage must have a legitimate business purpose. You will likely never receive a slip of paper showing your auto mileage was racked up for a given purpose. Only your testimony can establish the business purpose of your auto mileage.

Lastly, is an area of major concern for small businesses. As I stated in the previous chapter, one of the IRS' primary attacks on small businesses is to claim they are not businesses at all, but rather hobbies. To prove your business is legitimate and entitled to all the deductions of any other business, you must prove a "profit motive." Code section 183.

While the IRS looks to several factors to determine a profit motive, your own testimony as to the nature of your business, goals, objectives, and profit potential are important. These can only be presented in the form of testimony. Details on the hobby rules are presented in my *Smart Tax Special Report*.

Affidavits should be complete, detailed and specific. When making reference to particular documents, attach copies whenever possible. Affidavits are quite useful in settling a number of IRS disputes, audits being just one example. For that reason, I included a lengthy chapter on affidavits in my book, *41 Ways to Lick the IRS with a Postage Stamp* (Winning Publications, Inc.). Because that chapter is so thorough, I do not restate the material here. When making an affidavit to help in your audit, refer to chapter four of *41 Ways* for more guidance.

Looking to the Future

As we learned in chapter five, adequate records are the key to settling most audit disputes. While this certainly comes as no surprise to most, the reality is most have no idea how to keep such records in the first place. This topic is the focus of much work in my book *How to Fire the IRS*. I dedicate two chapters of that book to showing you how to set up a recordkeeping system necessary to prove your claims. You also learn how to use those records, and IRS-approved procedures, to audit-proof and penalty-proof your tax return so future filings are beyond reproach.

Chapter Seven -
Bruising the Heel of the Beast
Understanding Your Rights in an Audit

In chapter four we identified many of the myths that allow the IRS to take advantage of people in the tax audit process. Recognizing those myths puts you in a strong position to defend yourself. However, you are made even stronger when you know the *specific rights* you have to prevent being run over in the process. In no particular order, let us examine some of the important rights you have in the tax audit environment.

The time and place of the audit. One of the most common complaints I hear is the IRS is insensitive and inconsiderate when it comes to setting the time for an audit. Audit notices dictate that the examination must be conducted on "Thursday, at 9:00 A.M." Or an arrogant phone message exclaims that if you are not in the office by "the 20th, enforcement action will be taken."

Citizens are deliberately left with the impression that they have no say in determining the date or time of their audit. More times than not, they are bullied into believing they must jump through whatever hoop happens to be hoisted by the tax examiner.

"To every thing there is a season, and time to every purpose under the heaven" says King Solomon in Ecclesiastes 3:1. The tax audit is no exception.

One right the IRS does not want you to recognize is you indeed have a say in determining the time of your audit. Section 7605 of the Internal Revenue code states in part,

The time and place of examination pursuant to the provisions (of the code) shall be such time and place as may be fixed by the Secretary *and as are reasonable* under the circumstances (emphasis added).

Historically, there has been a tremendous amount of abuse by the IRS on the question of what is "reasonable under the circumstances." In 1988, Congress passed the first Taxpayers' Bill of Rights Act, requiring the IRS to schedule audits at a time and place convenient to the citizen. The IRS' response was to draft a regulation directing employees to "balance the convenience of the taxpayer" with the needs of the IRS when scheduling the audit. Revenue Regulation section 301.7605-1(a)(1).

This is not a bright line so there remains much abuse. However, the gray language of section 7605(a) actually works to the advantage of the citizen. On a regular basis I have made it my business to insist that pre-scheduled audits be re-set to accommodate either calendar concerns, or to facilitate further preparation and record-gathering.

To claim your right under section 7605(a) and have a voice in determining what is "reasonable," you must be assertive. Failure to be assertive means the IRS alone dictates where and when you meet, without regard to your needs.

Consider the case of Paul, who knew, if not in form then in substance, of his right under section 7605(a). The IRS notified him of the pending audit of his 1985 income tax return. The auditor set up a meeting, sent a document request, and awaited the appointed date. Two factors, of which the agent was unaware, prevented the audit from coming off as she might have hoped.

First of all, Paul was an independent salesman on the road almost four full weeks per month. He worked in a season-sensitive business and had to travel from early March through October's end to reap his industry's harvest. Any time off during that period seriously impacted his ability to earn commissions. Secondly, Paul moved subsequent to filing his 1985 tax return and most of his records were lost. Those that were available were in a state of disarray, at best.

Time was needed to either locate the lost records or reconstruct them if they could not be located. We also had to organize and make sense of those which were on hand. This had to be achieved during the industry's few off-peak months if Paul were to earn any kind of respectable living. The agent was notified, not asked, that circumstances dictated the scheduled meeting be postponed. An explanation of the facts was given to demonstrate that the request for additional time was "reasonable under the circumstances." The date originally set was ignored and Paul went about his business.

Finally, only after the records were located and the peak season had come and gone, did Paul attend the audit. During the audit, the agent made the remark that she had been handed, but did not want to delve into, the man's 1986 tax return. "I just want to get '85 finished and off my desk," she said. "You're just too hard to get a hold of."

Had Paul sheepishly appeared on the date first set, two undesirable consequences would have been certain. First, his records were not in order so it is a given that many, if not all deductions would have been disallowed. Secondly, since the auditor did not seem to understand that appeal rights exist (a right discussed later in this chapter), she may well have convinced him to sign a waiver and accept the disallowances. The outcome would have been the payment of taxes, interest and penalties not owed.

Do not be forced to attend an audit for which you are ill-prepared. Furthermore, the IRS has no authority to force you to attend an audit at a time which would prove costly or otherwise inconvenient to you.

Assistance of professional counsel. The right of representation before the IRS is absolute. Publication 1, "Your Rights as a Taxpayer," states, "You may either represent yourself, or with proper written authorization, have someone else represent you in your place." Section IV. This derives from section 7521(c), which holds, in part,

> Any attorney, certified public accountant, enrolled agent, enrolled actuary, or any other person permitted to represent the taxpayer before the Internal Revenue Service who is not disbarred or suspended from practice before the Internal Revenue Service and who has a written power of attorney executed by the taxpayer may be authorized by such taxpayer to represent the taxpayer in any interview.

IRS Form 2848, Power of Attorney, is used to provide written authorization to a professional to represent you. Without the 2848 properly prepared and executed, the IRS will not talk to your representative. The 2848 should be submitted to the tax auditor prior to any meetings.

Once the 2848 is properly executed and delivered to the agent, the agent is not authorized to contact you directly. All contacts, whether verbal or written, must be channeled through the representative. Furthermore, the IRS agent "may not require a taxpayer to accompany the representative" to any meeting or conference in the absence of a summons. Code section 7521(c).

Even if you began an audit without counsel, you have the right to stop the proceedings in mid-stream to obtain help. Section 7521(b)(2) states clearly that even while an interview is pending, if you express a desire to consult counsel, the auditor "*shall suspend such interview* regardless of whether the taxpayer may have answered one or more questions" (emphasis added).

Abuse of the right of counsel by the IRS is not unheard of. It grows from a provision within section 7521(c) which allows the agent to contact the citizen directly, without regard to a properly filed power of attorney, when the agent and his immediate supervisor are of the opinion that your representative "is responsible for unreasonable delay or hindrance of an Internal Revenue Service examination or investigation of the taxpayer."

In some cases, letters to this effect are mailed to a citizen when his representative does not allow the client to turn out his pockets. It is an intimidation tactic designed to create distrust between the client and the tax pro. It is also intended to bluff the representative into caving in on whatever matters he has been holding out on. In one case, Tom represented a corporate taxpayer and refused to allow the agent to enter the company's premises. Since there was absolutely nothing in the corporation return which could be verified by a site inspection of the company's premises, there was no need for a visit. It would serve only to disrupt the work environment and Tom would have no part of it.

The agent huffed and puffed, then mailed a letter to both the client and Tom, saying it was his opinion Tom was guilty of unreasonably delaying the examination. The agent put the demand for a site inspection directly on the corporation. The corporate officer responded with a simple letter saying, "take it up with my lawyer." Tom issued another letter, citing chapter and verse from the IRS' regulations about site inspections, saying if the agent could justify his request in accordance with the regulations, he was welcome to view the premises. The agent could not and that was the end of the matter.

The correspondence audit. Are you good under pressure? Do you talk too much? Or do you have a propensity to freeze up or even worse, to babble when presented with questions and demands by an authority figure? Many people fall apart at the seams when confronted by authority, and most assuredly, the IRS. When I suggest one has the ability to deal with the IRS without the need of an expensive professional, the typical response is, "There is no way I can confront those sharks and win. They will trap me and that will be the end of it."

Without a doubt, much of the IRS' audit techniques revolve around asking questions and seeking information designed to "trap" you. The agent knows in advance the purpose of a particular line of questioning, but does not reveal it. Instead, he asks the questions without providing any answers of his own. This is especially pronounced in the economic reality audit in which the agent probes for hidden income.

Not only is this practice unfair, but it has the effect of rattling an ignorant citizen. If you are easily rattled or intimidated, or afraid that you might "talk too much," staying out of danger is simple. Just stay away from the audit!

I am not suggesting you should refuse to be audited. On the contrary. As I illustrated earlier, you have the obligation to prove the claims of income and deductions in your return are true and correct. I am suggesting there is an alternative to your physical presence at the audit. It allows you to comply with your legal requirements *without* subjecting yourself to a painful and intimidating confrontation.

Larry was the kind of person just described. He was naturally nervous at the very thought of dealing with the IRS and the last thing he wanted to do was face an auditor, even if he did not have to take time off work. Consequently, when he received an audit notice, he was adamant that he did not want to personally appear. Under these circumstances, Larry demanded that his examination be handled via correspondence.

The so-called "correspondence examination" is very common and the IRS routinely uses it to verify returns. The right grows from Revenue Regulation section 601.105(b)(2)(ii), which states in part,

> Examinations are conducted by correspondence only when warranted by the nature of the questionable items and by the *convenience and characteristics of the taxpayer*. In a correspondence examination, the taxpayer is asked to explain or send supporting evidence by mail (emphasis added).

In its description to the public of the correspondence audit, the IRS says in Publication 1, *Your Rights as a Taxpayer*, the following:

> We handle many examinations and inquiries by mail. We will send you a letter with either a request for more information or a reason why we believe a change needs to be made to your return. If you give us the requested information or provide an explanation, we may or may not agree with you and we will explain the reasons for any changes. You should not hesitate to write to us about anything you do not understand. If you cannot resolve any questions through the mail, you can request a personal interview.

To assert his right to a correspondence audit, Larry mailed a letter to the agent. It pointed out that he did not wish to appear personally. He further explained that he would answer all questions presented in writing and would provide copies, with written explanations, of all documents and receipts necessary to verify the correctness of his return.

As the audit progressed, Larry was called upon to present copies of bank statements, canceled checks and other data relevant to the examination. Each time, he responded in writing by submitting the applicable material with any needed explanations. When all was said and done, Larry never set foot in an IRS office. He never laid eyes on a tax examiner, and never lost one hour of work. Most importantly, Larry never placed himself in an environment where his own fear and ignorance might come back to haunt him.

The right to record the audit. In every court hearing, a record of the proceeding is made. This is to provide proof later of what was said. This is not a bad idea for tax audits. The problem is the IRS provides no court reporter to take dictation. At the same time, however, it cannot refuse to allow you to make your own audio recording.

Code section 7521(a)(1) provides specifically that IRS personnel conducting interviews with a citizen must allow one to make an "audio recording of such interview at the taxpayer's own expense and with the taxpayer's own equipment." The proviso is that the citizen must make an "advance request" to make the recording.

The term "request" as used in the statute is misplaced. You need not ask permission to make the recording. You need only give notice, in writing, at least ten days in advance of the meeting. You must also bring your own recording equipment.

Similarly, the IRS has the right to make a record of the hearing. The agent must tell you beforehand of his intent to record and you have the right to obtain a copy of the transcript of the recording. Code section 7521(a)(2).

The success in an audit from the IRS' perspective is dependent upon bluff and intimidation by the agent and the fear and ignorance of the citizen. When an audit conference is recorded, you can be sure the overt incidents of such tactics diminish substantially.

The repetitive audit. "I've been audited four years in row now. Each time, they pick on the same deduction. And each time, I end up owing no taxes. This is getting old. What can I do to stop it?"

There is good news and bad news. The bad news is the IRS has the right to examine any return for any year provided the assessment statute of limitations has not expired. The fact that it may have examined a prior return and found no taxes owed does not preclude the examination of a subsequent year, even on the same issue. For example, just because you proved your claim of charitable contributions for 1993 does not mean you can prove the claim for 1994. Each year stands alone.

The good news is the IRS has an examination policy designed to guard against unnecessary repetitive audits. The policy is expressed in Internal Revenue Manual section 4241. It states, 1) if an audit has been performed for either of the two preceding tax years, 2) the issues raised in the current audit are the same as those in the prior audit, and 3) the prior audit resulted in no change or small tax change, the case can be closed. The repetitive audit rules generally do not apply to Schedule C (small business) or Schedule F (farmer) returns. However, your local IRS district office may have adopted policies on repetitive audits for these returns. If you file such a return, request a copy of the repetitive audit policy for the local district if in need.

To argue the repetitive audit defense, respond to the IRS' initial contact in writing. Explain you have been audited for one or more of the previous two years. Assert the repetitive audit guidelines of the manual and suggest the audit should be closed. To prove the repetitive audit guidelines apply, send the auditor a copy of the initial contact letter for the prior audit, the audit report issued by the previous examiner, and the final letter explaining there was no change (or small change) to your tax bill.

The defense can also be asserted during your first meeting with the agent. This might be necessary if the initial contact letter did not specifically describe the issues in question in the current audit. However, it is best to have these issues established in writing beforehand, then make your repetitive audit defense in writing, before meeting the agent. Though the IRS is not required by law to close a repetitive audit, its manual definitely suggests it do so under the appropriate circumstances.

The right to present evidence. Tax auditors can be fickle about the burden of proof question. On the one hand, they pound you on the fact that you have the burden of proof on all matters in the return. On the other hand, they try to limit your ability to present evidence. They do this two ways.

The first is the effort to cram the presentation process into an unreasonably constrictive time envelope. "You must have the material to me by Monday or I will not allow it." The second is the effort to prevent witnesses from attending the audit conference who can testify to relevant issues. "No one is allowed at the audit except an attorney, accountant or enrolled agent."

Since acceptance of your return as filed is dependent upon proving the correctness of all its elements, you must not let this happen. You must take care to ensure that all necessary evidence is submitted to the auditor so a correct decision can be made.

Neither the tax code nor its many regulations hand the auditor the authority to arbitrarily set unreasonable or unrealistic time constraints on your ability to present evidence. The one time period which governs in this situation is the assessment statute of limitations. This is the law preventing the IRS from assessing taxes on returns beyond a stated period of time. More on that later in this chapter.

When the IRS is up against the assessment statute, it has the right to demand records within sufficient time to allow it to evaluate the records and pass on the correctness of the return. However, the assessment statute is generally three years from the date the return is filed. In the garden variety audit, the IRS selects the return well in advance of the statute expiring. Therefore, it does not risk missing the statute by affording you extra time to collect records, gather facts and otherwise present your case.

Presentation of facts includes the presentation of testimony on material matters which cannot be proven by documentation. I outlined just a few examples of these items at the end of chapter six. I refer to them as the "intangible" elements of a deduction. Ideally, the presentation of testimony should be done in writing, through an affidavit. However, there are times when presenting the facts live may have more impact.

You have the right to present live witnesses and the IRS cannot refuse to allow the presence of such a person merely because he is not an attorney, etc. The argument used to keep such people away is that they are not "authorized to obtain confidential tax information about you." As a result, the agent asserts he cannot possibly discuss the issues in the presence of someone who is not an attorney authorized to receive such information through a valid power of attorney.

The argument, like so many made by the IRS, is based on partial truth. It is true that without proper authorization, no person can obtain your confidential tax information. It is also true that it is not enough for you to "tell the agent" that it is okay to talk about your tax matters in the presence of another person. The authorization must be in writing.

It is not true, however, that only an attorney, accountant or enrolled agent can obtain such authorization. Any person can be authorized to receive your confidential tax information *if you deem it necessary*. Furthermore, the IRS created a form for doing just that. It is Form 8821, Tax Information Authorization. Use it expressly for the purposes of authorizing disclosure of tax information to a person *not* intended to represent you before the IRS. Such a person could be a witness needed to present material facts to the agent. With a signed 8821 in hand, the agent cannot preclude that witness's presence at the audit.

Assert tax advantages not claimed in the return. One of the most common defense mechanisms used to combat audits is the fact that people often do not claim all the deductions the law allows. In the event of an audit, additional receipts are presented as a means of offsetting any disallowance which may result.

While I question the wisdom of this approach for a number of reasons, the IRS has developed a response of its own. It is to *ignore* the additional items. In one case, a citizen was told that in order for the additional deductions to be considered, he would have to file an amended return. This created a distinct disadvantage. He was under audit now. The amended return would first have to be filed with the service center for processing, and then, *maybe*, it would be accepted.

In the meantime, the audit of the present return was progressing with dispatch. "I'll wait to see what happens," he reasoned. "After all, if I come out of this with a clean slate, there is no reason to spend money just to get back a few extra dollars." Unfortunately, he ended up with a small tax bill, which, after paying, he rationalized the same way. "It's just a few dollars. No big deal."

Contrary to my friend's logic, it was a "big deal." The reason is he held a pearl in his hand which he did not recognize, and which the agent bluffed him into casting before swine. The claim that additional deductions can be claimed only on an amended return is just flat wrong. In fact, revenue regulations expressly provide that any additional deductions which a citizen may have overlooked may rightfully be claimed at an audit. Regulation section 601.105(b)(2)(ii) reads in part as follows:

> During the interview examination, the taxpayer has the right to point out to the examining officer *any amounts* included in the return which are not taxable, or any deductions which the taxpayer failed to claim on the return (emphasis added).

This regulation gives the citizen two specific rights. The first is the right to change the "income" shown on the return by demonstrating that certain amounts claimed as income were in fact, not taxable for whatever reason. This has the effect of reducing taxable income. Secondly, the citizen has the right to assert entitlement to any additional "deductions" not claimed on the return. We all understand the effect of this.

A conference with a supervisor. You always have the right to request a meeting with the agent's supervisor in order to discuss issues in the case. Generally, a meeting with the agent's manager is reserved for discussion of the final report if you disagree with the agent's findings. However, this is certainly not the only reason to request such a conference.

Anytime you face an impasse, ask to see the manager. This might happen if there is a scheduling conflict. Suppose you cannot appear at the time set by the agent, or you are unable to fully prepare in time. If the agent is unreasonable, appeal the matter to the manager. Such an appeal is helpful in the event of a procedural dispute. Suppose, for example, the agent refuses to allow a witness to appear, or will not accept for filing an affidavit. Appeal the matter to the manager.

When the examination is complete, expect the agent to issue his examination report. The report is often referred to as a thirty-day letter, because it provides thirty days in which to act. Three optional courses of action are presented in the letter. First, submit more information on the issues resolved against you. Second, request a conference with the agent's manager. And third, request a conference with the Appeals Division.

Always exhaust the remedy of meeting with a manager, but do not be deluded. Be ever mindful of the function of the Examination Division. We summarized it in three words earlier in this discourse: get the money! For that reason, it is usually necessary to bring the matter to the Appeals division. We explore the appeals process more fully in chapter eleven.

The right of appeal. The right to appeal the decision of tax examiners is absolute. Revenue Regulation 601.105(b)(4) provides, in part:

> At the conclusion of an office or field examination, the taxpayer is given an opportunity to agree with the findings of the examiner. If the taxpayer does not agree, the examiner will inform the taxpayer of the appeal rights.

To describe the process in more detail, the IRS offers Publication 556, Examination of Returns, Appeal Rights, and Claims for Refund. Pub 556 explains,

> You may appeal an IRS tax decision to a regional Appeals Office, which is independent of your local District Director or Service Center Director. The regional Appeals Office is the only level of appeal within the IRS. Appeals conferences are conducted in an informal manner.

The cost of an appeal is a postage stamp and the brief time it takes to fashion the protest letter necessary to commence the process. As we have seen in chapter four, the audit process is fraught with errors and the appeals function is intended to correct them.

Freedom from the tax audit--the statute of limitations. "The IRS can chase me 'til I'm dead." This is the belief most have about the agency's power. As I already stated, the IRS is governed by a statute of limitations in all its actions, including the power to audit a return.

Under code section 6501, the IRS must make assessments of tax within three years of the date the return is filed. Thereafter, the agency's ability to assess taxes evaporates. It is therefore precluded from examining a tax return after three years from the date of its filing.

For example, suppose your 1992 tax return was filed on time on April 15, 1993. The IRS has until April 15, 1996, in which to make an examination and assessment of taxes with respect to that return. After April 15, 1996, the return is considered a "closed year." It can be examined only under especially extenuating circumstances. We consider some of those later.

But first, let us examine important rules which apply when determining the starting point of the three-year period of limitations.

1. *The return must be complete.* To commence the running of the statute of limitations, the return must be complete. It must disclose gross income, deductions and taxable income in such a manner as to enable the IRS to determine its correctness. A return that does not disclose information from which a tax can be computed is not a return. That does not mean the return must be "perfect" (as if that is possible). The return need only evidence an honest and genuine attempt to comply with the law. Inadvertent omissions or inaccuracies do not suspend the statute of limitations.

2. *Returns filed early.* Code section 6501(b)(1)provides that returns filed *before* the April 15 filing deadline do not trigger the three-year period on the date filed. Rather, it begins to run on the *due date* of the return. Even though you may have filed your 1990 return on January 31, 1991, the statute of limitations did not begin to tick until April 15, 1991.

3. *Returns filed late.* Conversely, returns filed *after* the due date trigger the statute of limitations as of the date of filing. This is true even if you were under a valid extension of time to file. Thus, if your 1990 return was filed on July 15, 1991, the statute of limitations expires on July 15, 1994.

Let us now turn our attention to the various exceptions to the general three-year period of limitations. In some circumstances, the period is merely extended. In other situations, the period of limitations is suspended.

1. *Certain amended returns.* Section 6501(c)(7) *extends* the statute of limitations when certain amended returns are filed. An amended return filed during the sixty-day period immediately before the

expiration of the statute of limitations extends the statute for sixty days from the date the amended return is received.

For example, suppose the statute covering your 1987 tax return was set to expire on April 15, 1991, (three years from the due date of the return). Suppose further that on March 15, 1991, (during the sixty-day period immediately before the expiration of the statute) you file an amended return. The statute of limitations is extended to May 15, 1991, sixty days from the date of filing the amended return.

2. *Substantial omission of income.* Section 6501(e) provides that when one omits "in excess of 25 percent of the amount of gross income stated in the return" the assessment period *extends* to six years.

There is an important restriction on this rule. As you now know, the citizen generally bears the burden of proof on all items claimed in the return. When the IRS asserts the 25 percent omission rule, however, *the agency* bears a two-pronged burden. It must prove both that you had more income than reported, and the amount omitted should have been included in gross income.

For purposes of determining whether 25 percent of gross income is omitted, the calculation is made without respect to any deductions or credits which may be taken against such income.

3. *Loss and credit carry backs.* Under certain circumstances, operating losses incurred in connection with a business, capital losses incurred in connection with investments, and unused credits may be carried back to previous years. This operates to reduce taxes for the previous years, usually resulting in a refund.

Sections 6501(i) and (j) provide that when a loss or credit is carried back to a prior year, the statute of limitations on that year is *held open* as long as the year in which loss or credit was generated is open.

To illustrate, suppose you incur a capital loss in 1990. Suppose you carry back a portion of that loss to tax year 1989, resulting in a refund for 1989. The normal statute of limitations for 1989 expires on April 15, 1993. The loss was incurred in 1990 and the statute of limitations on 1990 expires April 15, 1994. Therefore, tax year 1989 (the year to which the loss was carried) remains open until April 15, 1994.

4. *False or fraudulent return.* Code sections 6501(c)(1) and (2) *suspend* the assessment statute of limitations in either of two circumstances. The first is when a return is filed which is false or fraudulent "with the intent to evade the tax." The second is where the citizen attempts "in any manner to defeat or evade tax." These are the

so-called fraud exceptions to the statute of limitations. When invoked by the IRS, it may assess taxes for the year it proves fraud, regardless of age.

However, the fraud exception carries the same burden for the government as the 25 percent understatement rule. The IRS shoulders the burden to prove with clear and convincing evidence, one of two facts. Either, the citizen filed a false or fraudulent return with the intent to evade taxes, or, he committed an affirmative act calculated to deceive or mislead the IRS, all in an effort to evade or defeat payment of the tax. Unless the IRS can prove fraud, it cannot assess taxes beyond the normal three-year statute unless some other exception applies.

I must point out here that the "no statute" rule for fraud applies only in civil cases. Criminal prosecutions for fraud are governed by a separate rule.

5. *No Return filed.* The normal rules governing the assessment of taxes *do not apply* when no return is filed. Thus, if you failed to file a tax return for 1985, the IRS may move to assess and collect taxes despite the passage of time.

As with the fraud rule, the "no statute" rule for failing to file applies only in civil cases. Separate rules govern criminal prosecutions for failure to file tax returns.

6. *Commissioner filed returns.* When the IRS believes a false return was filed, or a citizen failed to file, the agency is authorized by code section 6020(b) to make a return for him based upon "available information."

The normal statute of limitations on assessment does not apply to Commissioner filed returns. Because the returns are made only in cases where the citizen filed a false return or failed to file entirely, the statute of limitations on assessment is *suspended.*

7. *Judicial actions.* Under some circumstances, judicial actions undertaken by a citizen can *toll* the assessment statute of limitations. Two examples are:

a. Tax Court. If a citizen cannot reach agreement with the IRS in an audit, the agency mails a notice of deficiency asserting additional tax. In response, he may petition the Tax Court within ninety days of the notice of deficiency. The IRS may not assess the tax while the ninety-day grace period is pending. Furthermore, it may not assess the tax if the citizen files a timely petition. The tax may be assessed after the grace period expires if no petition is filed. It may also assess after the Tax Court rules in favor of the IRS. Code section 6215.

At the time of mailing the notice of deficiency, the statute of limitations on assessment is *tolled*. The statute remains tolled until the earlier of, 1) the expiration of the ninety-day grace period, or 2) a ruling from the Tax Court. In either case, the statute begins running sixty days after the occurrence of either event. Code section 6503(a)(1).

b. Summons enforcement. The IRS has authority under code sections 7601 and 7602 to issue summonses to third parties, such as banks, etc. The summons requires a party to produce records or give testimony. Code section 7609 affords the right to ask a federal court to "quash," or prevent the summons from being enforced.

When the citizen moves to judicially quash a summons, all applicable statutes of limitation are *suspended* during the time the proceeding is pending. Code section 7609(e)(1). Additionally, if the summoned party does not release the records sought within six months of service with the summons, all applicable statutes of limitations are suspended. The suspension begins with the date six months after service with the summons. It ends on the date of compliance or resolution of the summoned party's response. Code section 7609(e)(2).

8. *Voluntary Extensions*. The statute of limitations on assessment may be *suspended* if both parties agree in writing to a suspension. The agreement is formalized on Form 872. Once executed, the agreement extends the assessment statute until the date shown in the form.

As hard as it may be to believe, the IRS is not always honest about the operation of the assessment statute of limitations. It has attempted to audit citizens in cases when the assessment statute has expired. In such a case, the IRS has no legal authority to force you to produce records, attend an audit or pay any taxes not assessed within the proper time period.

Required Reading. While I have often accused the IRS of not telling the whole truth to citizens in its information publications, there are some worth reading. When it comes to the tax audit process, review two in particular. Both have been mentioned already, and you can pick up a copy of each at your local IRS office. The first is Publication 1, Your Rights as a Taxpayer. The second is Publication 556, Examination of Returns, Appeal Rights, and Claims for Refund. These will help in your quest to understand the tax audit process.

*"But you, O God, are my king from of old;
you bring salvation upon the earth. It was
you who split open the sea by your power;
you broke the heads of the [beast] in the
waters. It was you who crushed the heads of
Leviathan and gave him as food to the
creatures of the desert. It was you who
opened up springs and streams; you dried up
the ever flowing rivers. The day is yours, and
yours also the night; you established the sun
and moon. It was you who set all the
boundaries of the earth; you made both
summer and winter."*

Psalm 74:12-17

Chapter 8 -
In the Beast's Cauldron
"Dangers of the Economic Reality Audit"

Stirring the Pot

Keith sat at the table with his wife. He fidgeted nervously as the agent poured over bank statements. With each notation the auditor made, Keith's heart pounded a little harder. His obvious concern was not lost on the agent. "Sure wish I could see what he's writing," he thought. Looking at his wife, he knew she was thinking the same thing.

When they were notified that their tax return was to be audited, Keith and Nancy were naturally concerned, but confident too. As the owner of a small construction business, Keith used a downtown accounting firm to do his returns and was convinced there could be no real problems. After all, he's honest. Reports all his income. Doesn't do anything under the table. He has nothing to hide.

But none of that changed the fact that his stomach knotted up like a phone cord when he saw the letter in the mailbox. And reading it floored him! He expected questions about his business expenses, interest payments, things like that. Instead, they wanted to know about every dime he spent and how he spent it.

"Look at this," Keith said to Nancy. "I can't believe it. They want us to list how much money we spent on food and clothes during the year."

"What is that?," Nancy asked.

"It's a laundry list of things we're suppose to come up with," Keith said, handing it over.

Nancy read the sheet accompanying the audit notice. Entitled "Statement of Annual Estimated Personal and Family Living Expenses," IRS Form 4822, it asked them to classify by cash, check or credit, how much they paid for things such as groceries, clothing, laundry, barber, beauty shop and cosmetics, mortgage payments and utilities, recreation, club dues, contributions, gifts and allowances, even reading materials and smoking supplies. The list went on and on, covering every possible aspect of their life. To Keith's amazement, none of it had anything to do with his tax return.

"This will take weeks to organize," Nancy moaned.

To make matters worse, the letter demanded the material within two weeks, and set a meeting in three weeks--at their home!

Keith and Nancy did their best to gather the material. The accountant was little help. Since all the items were non-deductible personal expenses, he hadn't asked for or used any of the data in the tax return.

After burning the midnight oil for an impressive string of evenings, Keith and Nancy assembled a package they believed was responsive to the demands. "The only people who will make out on this deal is the paper company," he said sarcastically while dropping the package in the mail.

Now that the agent was in his kitchen looking over everything imaginable, Keith couldn't help thinking he did something wrong somewhere. But what? He could only guess--and wait.

The agent was especially concerned about their lifestyle, the boat in particular. He asked an awful lot of questions about it, questions Keith would never have thought possible in a tax audit. Funny thing is, Keith never claimed the boat as a deduction. The accountant said it was a gray area. Even though he entertained plenty of customers, why take a chance?

Wasn't an audit supposed to be about your tax return? Instead, he wanted to know when Keith bought the boat, how much he paid for it, whether he made any substantial repairs or improvements to it, how much it costs to operate, how much he spent on accessories, and, get this, how often--*and who*--he entertains on the boat.

"What's that got to do with our tax bill,?" Keith asked just a little indignant.

"It's important for us to construct a full picture of your economic activity to determine the accuracy of your tax return," the agent replied in a stoic but well rehearsed way.

"I can certainly understand the financial part," Nancy said, puzzled, "but why does it matter who our friends are and how often we have them on our boat?"

Without answering, the agent just fired another question. "Now you keep your boat at the Hidden Bay Marina, right?"

"Yes," Keith answered, wondering how he knew that.

"It costs about $2,000 a summer to rent a slip in that marina, doesn't it?"

"Well it depends on the size of the boat, but that's about right for what we have."

Shuffling through the heaving pile of checks and work papers, the agent picked up the personal living expense statement Keith and Nancy worked on so carefully. "I'm curious," he said. "You didn't show that expense on your 4822. Why not?"

"We don't actually pay the bill," Keith explained. "My company did some remodeling work at the marina. The owner paid for the materials and I provided the labor. I worked on it during the winter months, while both of us had spare time. He helped too. He agreed to give me three years worth of free slip rental."

"I see. So you got three years free rental, worth about $2,000 per year."

"Yea. That's about right," said Keith, wondering about the significance. He was afraid to ask.

As the agent was making notes, Keith felt pressure to offer more details on the marina arrangement. He didn't want the agent to think he was getting away with something there. "We still have to pay for pump outs, pulling the boat out for service, things like that."

The agent looked up from his work and slowly nodded his understanding. After making more of the notes that were driving Keith and Nancy mad, he came back with another question. "You mentioned pump outs and pulling the boat for service. What's that all about?"

Cautious, Keith said, "Well, the holding tank for the toilet has to be pumped out when it gets full and they charge for that. And sometimes the boat needs to be taken out of the water for service, like fixing the prop, and they charge for that too."

"How often do you have to do that?"

"It depends. If we use the boat a lot, then it has to be pumped more often. And with repairs, you never know. Last year we never had a problem, but this year I've gone through two props already, plus a bilge pump. They had to pull the boat to get to the props."

"I notice those costs don't show up on your personal living expense statement either. You'll have to itemize those and get them to me."

"Sure," murmured Keith, dreading more midnight labor.

"I also notice from your property tax statement that the assessed value of your home went up quite a bit. Did you make substantial improvements on your home?"

"Yes. We finished the basement and converted a large closet upstairs into an extra bathroom," Keith explained.

Nancy joined in. "My mother is getting up in years and she stays with us most of the time now. We needed the space, so we put in two bedrooms downstairs and moved the boys down there. The extra bathroom is for mother. She needs special equipment like grab bars around the toilet, things like that."

"Do you provide food and other living expenses for your mother when she's here?"

"Why, of course," replied Nancy. "She's my mother, but she helps too. She chips in for groceries, watches over the kids while I'm gone in the afternoon and does light housework. She can't really do that much, but it's important to her to help. And we don't have to pay babysitters. That saves a lot right there."

"How much time did she spend here last year,?" the agent asked.

"In all, about six or seven months."

"And how much do you suppose she contributes each month?"

Looking at one another and wondering out loud, the two figured mother must kick in about $300 to the family fisc. And the baby-sitting? That probably saves $100 a month or so.

The agent made more notes, then turning to Keith he inquired, "How much did you spend on the remodeling?"

"Well, counting the stall we added to the garage, about ten, maybe twelve thousand. I haven't added it all up. I did the work myself, the boys helped. Some friends helped with the trade work. My neighbor is a plumber. He did the bathroom. Nancy's brother did the electrical work. It really saved us a lot. And I helped them in return, you know.

Nancy's brother built a garage and I installed the siding and roofed it for him. Sort of a pay back."

"But your checking account doesn't show anywhere near that amount for home improvement expenditures. Where did you get the money?," the agent asked with more than a bit of accusation in his tone.

"We used some savings," Keith pleaded, exasperated.

"But I don't see any evidence of that in the documents you sent me," the agent rebuffed. "By the way," he continued, "Would Nancy's brother be willing to confirm that he did work for you?"

"Of course he will," barked Nancy. "Bill's completely honest and we have nothing to hide." Before they knew it, Keith and Nancy were providing the names of all who helped in exchange for a return favor. The agent made even more of the notes that were really starting to get on Keith's nerves.

All at once, the agent put his pencil down, organized his papers, then looked up, first at Keith, then Nancy. "It appears from my preliminary analysis that you had income you did not report on your return. You had barter income from the marina of at least $2,000 in one year alone, and that appears to carry into other years. I will be picking up the returns for those other years. That doesn't include the barter income from the plumber or Nancy's brother. Also, you spent thousands on your home with no apparent means of paying for it. You're paying expenses for the operation of a boat which don't show up anywhere. And, you're providing support for your mother. Not only that, but your mother pays rent to you worth about $4,800 a year in the form of groceries, housework and babysitting. On the basis of this information, you must have had at least $15,000 to $20,000 more in income than you reported on your return. There is no other way to support those activities."

Keith and Nancy sat stunned, staring back in utter disbelief. They would never dream of hiding income from the IRS. And how can taking care of your mother count as income anyway? Even if Keith didn't want to, his accountant was adamant about reporting all income. "You don't want any fraud problems," he would say. Boy, is that the truth!

"That's not right," Keith protested. "That just can't be. I've always reported every dime."

"You didn't report the barter income," the agent popped. Gesturing to the tax return in front of him, the agent asked pointedly, "Did you claim $6,000 worth of free slip rental as income on your returns?"

Keith, surprised and confused, said, "Um, well, no. We never actually got $6,000. I mean, he never gave us any money. Just the use of the slip."

The agent quipped, "What you got was barter income and it's taxable. You should have reported it and paid taxes on it just as if it were cash. The same is true of the electrical and plumbing services you received while remodeling the house."

Keith's heart sank. Instantly he began to realize why he felt so awkward throughout the entire audit process. He had no idea where this guy was coming from and now was sure this wouldn't be the last time he got blindsided. Then his mind began to race. "If I got barter income from Bill, then *he* must have gotten barter income from *me*." He suddenly grew sick at the idea that he just unknowingly and certainly unwillingly turned his own brother-in-law into the IRS.

He barely heard the agent say, "I'll expect the additional information I've asked for so I can complete my report."

Keith snapped back to the moment as the agent handed him a sheet of paper. "This is an Information Document Request," he explained. "I've listed the items I want you to provide by the date indicated on the top of the form, right there. If you have any questions, you can feel free to call me. Otherwise, get that material to me by the deadline." The agent then unceremoniously packed his briefcase and got up from the table.

Before he reached the door, his attention was grabbed by the wall on which Nancy lovingly hung dozens of family photos. "That's a nice shot," he said, in a tone more personable than he used to that point. "Where was it taken?"

Nancy, suddenly collecting herself if just a bit, said, "Florida. We took the kids there last year. Visited Disney World and Tampa. My sister lives in Tampa. That was at the beach. We had a wonderful time."

Turning to face the couple, the agent very calmly announced, "You didn't include the vacation costs on your living expense statement. Please add them to the list."

He turned and walked out the door.

Economic Reality Audits Explained

Economic reality is an aggressive audit program pointed squarely at the income reported on a return. With the steady decline in the deductions available, the IRS is less able to generate enforcement revenue by focusing audit activities on deductions. It can be more productive attacking income. This is true even with those who claim relatively low income. Since the premise is that all hide income, those with low incomes are more likely to be skimming.

The IRS has always had the authority to question income. That is not new. In chapter five, we spend a good deal of time discussing the "traditional" ways it does so. It is plain to see, however, that the economic reality approach goes far beyond anything the IRS has ever done before.

Historically, the audit called upon the citizen to prove only that his various tax return entries were correct. If the IRS questioned, say, a $2,000 charitable contribution, the citizen was asked to prove the claim. This is known as a "verification" audit.

In the context of economic reality, the IRS asks the question, "How can the citizen afford to give $2,000 to charity in the first place?" In this way, audits have been transformed into "investigative" audits.

In the over six hundred pages of IRS documentation on economic reality audits, they are defined as one "whereby the financial status of an individual taxpayer, as measured by his/her standard of living and operating in the community, is evaluated in relation to information reported on the return." "Examining for Economic Reality," Facilitator's Guide to Workshops 1 through 6, Training Aid 3302-127, page i.

Is it an exaggeration to refer to this process as a full scale investigation? Certainly not. In many ways, it resembles a criminal investigation. The IRS itself refers to economic reality as an "investigative" audit and here is how it describes the "objectives of economic reality:"

> Evaluate the whole taxpayer (including consideration of related tax entities) from an economic reality point of view instead of only focusing the audit on some narrow aspect of tax consequence.
>
> Perform *investigative* audits instead of *verification* audits. Ibid. (emphasis added).

To build the economic profile of the citizen, the IRS focuses upon five questions. They are:

• *What is the standard of living?*

What does the citizen and "dependent family" consume? How much does it cost to "maintain this consumption pattern?" Is reported *net income* sufficient to "support the standard of living?" Facilitator's Guide, Training Aid 3302-101, page T1-6a.

• *What is the citizen's accumulated wealth?*

How much has the citizen expended in the "acquisition of capital assets?" When and how was this wealth accumulated? Is reported income "sufficient to fund the accumulations?" Ibid, page T1-6b.

• *What is the citizen's economic history?*

What is the "long term pattern" of profits and return on investment in the citizen's business? Is it "expanding or contracting?" Does the reported business activity "match with the changes" to the citizen's "standard of living and wealth accumulation?" Ibid, page T1-6c.

• *What is the business environment*?

What is the "typical profitability and return on investment" for the nature of the business, given its location? What are the "typical patterns of non-compliance" in that business? What are the "competitive pressures and economic health" of the business? Ibid, page T1-6d.

• *Has the citizen made assertions to receipt of funds considered non-taxable?*

Do such claims "make economic sense?" How credit worthy is the citizen in view of his "assertion that funding was secured from loans?" If the citizen claims funds were received from sources other than conventional lenders, "what was the lenders source of the funds?" Ibid, page T1-6e.

You may have wondered why, in our fictional account of Keith and Nancy's interview, the agent spent so much time on matters not relating directly to the return. The boat and its operation are critical elements of their lifestyle, spending patterns and asset acquisitions.

Remodeling the house has several implications. First, where did the money come from to do it with? Even if Keith claimed he obtained a loan from the bank, the agent would have delved into his credit-worthiness and banking history to see whether such a claim made "economic sense." But Keith claimed the money came from savings. This of course raises the question whether Keith had sufficient net income over the years to amass savings sufficient to fund his project. That would have opened a full spectrum of questions regarding prior years income and spending activities.

The agent also spent time on the support of Nancy's mother and their Florida vacation. These items directly relate to the cost of maintaining the family and supporting their spending patterns.

The big item is that Keith was involved in bartering services in connection with his business. Barter income is taxable, yet most people are unaware this is so. At the same time, many people, especially tradesmen, do exactly that. No doubt the economic reality audit will spell trouble for many if they handle it the way Keith did.

The Components of an Economic Reality Audit

The manual instructs agents to "create an economic profile of the taxpayer." Through the use of such a profile, (read, "dossier") the agency sets out to answer the five broad questions outlined above.

To build the dossier, the agent is to evaluate a person's lifestyle elements. IRS Training Aid 3302-102, entitled, "JOB AID 1, Components of Economic Reality," identifies *forty-seven different aspects* of a person's life as some of the elements of the dossier. Here are just a few:

- Neighborhood
- Home
- Age and number of dependents
- Investment Income
- Number of years in business
- Recreation Vehicles
- Automobiles
- Changes of address
- College Tuition
- Trips
- Club Memberships
- Hobbies
- Weddings of Children
- Legal actions
- Level of Sophistication
- Cultural Background
- Education and Work Experience
- Type of Business
- Insurance coverage/what covered
- Marital history
- Gambling
- Personal Property
- Loan Information, and the like.

Given this, it should come as no surprise the fictional account presented in chapter one pictured an agent following Keith to his boat. Since the IRS is deeply concerned with recreational vehicles, club memberships and hobbies, we can well imagine the agent spying to uncover facts surrounding the boat. It might, after all, reveal some hidden source of unreported income.

As the fictional audit developed, the agent discovered Keith earned barter income by doing remodeling work for the marina in exchange for slip rental. He followed Keith to the boat, then questioned marina employees about slip costs at the facility.

Another piece of the economic reality puzzle is the personal living expenses paid during the years under audit. The "Personal Living Expense (PLE) Checklist" developed by the IRS, JOB AID 3, Training Aid 3302-104, instructs agents to have citizens itemize all personal living expenses paid during the audit years. You might recall that Keith and Nancy worked long into the night to gather and document their living expenses. The agent gave them IRS Form 4822 on which to present the results. Much to their chagrin, they left off items the agent believed essential and he sent them back to the drawing board. These are few of the items you might be called upon to document:

- Food, consumed at home and away from home
- Alcoholic beverages
- All housing expenses
- All utility expenses
- Expenses for household operations
- Housekeeping supplies
- House furnishings and equipment
- Apparel and services
- Entertainment
- Personal care
- Reading
- Education
- Tobacco and smoking supplies, and so on.

Reproduced as exhibit 8-1 on the following page is a copy of IRS Form 4822.

How serious is the IRS about documenting these expenses? To quote the manual, the PLE is "extremely important." Training Aid 3302-127, page 2-11. Personal living expenses are the key to the entire

Exhibit 8-1

Sub.Form 4822 (Rev. 3-72)	Department of the Treasury - Internal Revenue Service STATEMENT OF ANNUAL ESTIMATED PERSONAL AND FAMILY EXPENSES

TAXPAYER'S NAME AND ADDRESS | TAX YEAR

ITEM	BY CASH	BY CHECK	BY CREDIT	REMARKS
Groceries & Outside Meals				
Clothing				
Laundry and dry cleaning				
Barber, beauty shop & cosmetics				
Education (tuition,books,etc)				
Recreation,entertainment,vacat.				
Dues (clubs, lodge, etc)				
Gifts & Allowances				
Life & Accident Insurance				
Federal taxes (Income,FICA,etc)				
Credit Card Payments				
Personal Loan Payments				
Child Support				
Other Personal expense: (list)				
Rent				
Mortgage payments(incl.intrst)				
Utilities(elec,gas,phone,water)				
Domestic Help				
Home Insurance				
Repairs & Improvements				
Other Household expense: (list)				
Gasoline,oil,grease,wash				
Tires, batteries, repairs				
Auto license tags				
Auto Insurance				
Auto Payments(incl.interest)				
Other Auto expenses: (list)				
Contributions				
Medical Insurance				
Prescription Drugs				
Doctor,hospitals, etc.				
Real Estate Taxes				
Personal Property tax				
State Income tax				
Alimony				
Union Dues				
Child Care				
Stocks and bonds				
Furniture, appliances, jewelry				
Loans to Others				
Boat, Recreationl Vehicles				
Other Assets Purchased:(list)				
TOTALS	$	$	$	$

audit. Since they do not appear on a return, the IRS must get the data from you in order to have any idea whether you are living beyond your apparent means. This is why you might be asked to document every nickel you spend and where you spend it:

> Most taxpayers will not intentionally deposit skimmed funds, but will use the cash to increase their standard of living. This will include day-to-day cash expenditures for payment of living expenses, down payments and/or purchases of assets and other investments.
> The more information an examiner can develop, the larger the understatement (of tax). The development of the personal living expenses can be extremely critical in this process. "JOB AID 9, Indirect Methods," Training Aid 3302-110, page 1.

Do you still feel it is implausible for the IRS to follow a person to his boat? Do you believe its "investigative audit" will not seek to explain how the citizen bought the boat in the first place? How much did it cost? Was the purchase financed? How much does it cost to slip the boat? How much fuel is used? How much is spent on maintenance? How much food and beverages are consumed on board? Are the beverages alcoholic or not?

How much was spent on items ancillary to the boat, such as life preservers, ropes, linens, pillows, kitchen utensils, covers, hoses, power cords, batteries, tools, accessories like radio, tape player and TV, lights, cleaning supplies, ladders, spare fuel tank, pumps, maps, bumpers, beverage coolers, binoculars, chairs, rafts, swim toys, personal care items such as shampoo and soap, grill, fire extinguisher, anchor, etc.?

The bigger question pertains to whether these items were purchased with a check or by cash. If by cash, what was the source of the cash? Was the cash properly reported on the return? *PROVE IT!*

Just because you don't have a boat does not mean you will not come under this kind of microscope. Review the elements of economic reality. The forty-seven items (I list only a few) cover every aspect of life. The economic reality investigation is all-encompassing.

Still, the IRS has no intention of relying solely upon your statements. "JOB AID 4, Internal/External Sources of Data," Training Aid 3302-105, offers a host of data sources the agent may pursue. "Internal sources" refer to items found within the IRS' own records, including:

- The tax return
- Prior audits
- Information returns such as Forms W-2 and 1099
- Currency Transaction Reports, IRS Form 4789
- Collection Division information
- Criminal Investigation Division information, etc.

It comes as no surprise that the IRS would rely upon its own data when building its file. What is shocking is the extent to which it intends to develop external sources of data. That is, pursue sources of information not ordinarily available to the IRS. They include:

- Other government agencies such as U.S. Post Office, Department of Motor Vehicles, Social Security Administration, OSHA, Department of Agriculture, Department of Social Services, local law enforcement agencies
- Court records showing divorce, marriage, liens, probate, property records, mortgages, bankruptcy, etc.
- Trade associations
- Credit applications and credit reports
- City Directory
- Banks, credit unions and savings and loans
- Suppliers
- Insurance providers
- Subscriber information such as Dun and Bradstreet, Robert Morris and LEXIS
- Newspaper articles, etc.

Dun and Bradstreet is an information resources company. It gathers financial and other data about businesses, then compiles data bases. *It sells the information* to anyone willing to pay for it. It is used by companies to determine the health and standing of those they may wish to do business with. Such reports often form the basis for ascertaining credit limits, payment requirements, etc. The information is also used by the IRS as a building block in the process of constructing the financial dossier. We might add the Chamber of Commerce and the Better Business Bureau to the list. Beware of doing business with companies who gather data only to pass it on to others.

And the IRS will not stop there. The agency intends to make contacts with third parties who might have information about you. The contacts include:

- Landlords
- Employers
- Employees
- Other business and personal associates
- Ex-spouse
- Neighbors

If these sources do not prove adequate, the agent may develop *"informants."* Training Aid 3302-105, pages 2-3 (emphasis added). In the routine "investigative" audit, the IRS intends to cultivate among American citizens the practice of spying upon one another.

You are probably saying, "Hey, I'm honest. I don't skim. I keep good records. I have nothing to fear." Keith said the same thing and look what happened to him. The reality is, good records and honesty have little or nothing to do with surviving an economic reality audit, for two reasons.

First, as we learned in chapter five, the tax code does not define good records. Citizens struggle to comply with recordkeeping requirements they do not understand. This is the reason the majority of disputes with the IRS involve inadequate recordkeeping. Secondly, even if a person does have legally adequate records, the IRS uses bluff and intimidation to get him to part with his money anyway. Good records are always critical to winning a fight with the IRS, but standing alone, they will not do the job.

Even worse, the IRS is predisposed to disregard the verity of your records. Economic reality manuals discuss at length the process of adding unreported income to a return. The introductory language of one states its purpose is to "get examiners and managers to feel *comfortable"* using various methods of adding income. "JOB AID 9, Indirect Methods," Training Aid 3302-110, page 1 (emphasis added).

The premise is simple. When your records "do not clearly reflect income," the IRS has the legal authority to reconstruct it. There are four circumstances under which, according to the manual, the IRS believes it has the authority to "reconstruct" your income. They are, "when the taxpayers books and records,"

1) are non existent,
2) are not available,
3) are incomplete, and [now get this]
4) "appear to be correct."
Training Aid 3302-110, page 7 (emphasis added).

Not only are good records alone insufficient to defeat the intentions of an economic reality audit, they in fact may be the very reason the IRS adds income to your return. It seems good records are a sign that you set out to throw an unwary investigative auditor off the trail.

Much of what economic reality entails is pointed at small businesses. Business owners have the tendency to dismiss potential threats by the IRS with a somewhat cavalier attitude. "Hey, I'll just have my lawyer or accountant deal with this." Sure, it might cost a few bucks, but that has to be better than dealing with them at your place of business, or trying to answer a million questions about how you earn income and where you spend it. Do not be so sure.

The training manuals put agents through a "brainstorming session" on how businesses might hide income. The opening question is, "What would you do to omit income if you owned a bar or restaurant?" "Facilitator Guide," Training Aid 3302-101, pages 4-3 and 4-4. The manual goes on to list seventeen different ways it might be done. To cope with these potential tactics, agents are instructed to:

- Check with state alcohol authorities to see if you have been investigated for dealing with illegal liquor
- Contact your suppliers to see whether you pay bills in cash
- Contact vending machine owners, including video games and pool tables, to determine how much and in what fashion you are paid
- Observe your party room facilities and activities to determine whether you earn cash income from parties
- Look for payments to subcontractors or unusually large payroll expenses to determine whether you engage in off-premises catering
- Observe your day-to-day operation to determine whether you earn income from betting pools
- Observe your day-to-day operation to determine whether you have cash income from sales of inventory items such as hats, T-shirts, etc.

- Observe what you do with empty containers such as cans and bottles to determine whether you have cash income from re-cycling or bottle refunds
- Observe your day-to-day operations to see whether you accept credit cards in your business, then check bank records to verify credit card deposits
- Observe your day-to-day operations to determine whether you earn cash income by renting space
- Observe your day-to-day activities to determine whether you earn cash income by cashing checks for customers. Ibid, pages 4-5 and 4-6.

The manual goes through a similar exercise for an auto body shop and a vending machine business. In each study, the agent is called upon to "imagine" how such a business might omit income, then develop audit techniques to address the answers. Regarding the body shop, the agent is asked to "look for pictures of special jobs" to see if the owner is earning income from repair or paint jobs for "special customers." Ibid, page 4-10.

Now then, is it so impossible to believe our fictional agent noticed a photo on the wall in Nancy's home, then asked her about it? His training taught him to be aware of how the simple things around him can lead to evidence of unreported income.

Reproduced on the next four pages as Exhibit 8-2, find pages 4-9 through 4-12 of Facilitator Guide 3302-101. These exhibits show the results of "brainstorming" audit techniques for the auto and vending machine business.

This description of business audit techniques should leave you with the clear impression that your books and records, however "good" they may be, are not enough to do the job. Instead, it is clear the agent intends to park himself, perhaps under cover, in your place of business. How else can he "observe" your day-to-day operations to see for himself what is going on?

He also intends to make it clear to every supplier and relevant state and local government agencies that you are a target of an "investigative" audit. What other message is sent when he asks how you pay bills, when, in what amounts, and for what kind of items, etc.? And how might local government agencies react when contacted by IRS examiners to see whether you have been under investigation for any business related illegal activity? My guess is you may have a great deal of explaining to do.

Exhibit 8-2

Suggested
Answers for
Auto Body/
Repair Business

Suggested Answer for Auto Body/Repair Business — Taxpayer's Viewpoint
1. Jobs done for cash by extending discounts to customers who agree to pay cash.
2. Towing and storage fees.
3. Sales of scrap materials and used parts.
4. Exchanges of services for goods or services.
5. Rebuilding and sale of totaled vehicles.
6. Repair and/or paint jobs for special customers.
7. Small welding work for customers for cash.
8. Custom metal fabrication for cash.
9. Insurance fraud, billing for work not done.
10. A related business such as radiator repair or front-end alignment work not reported.
11. Taxpayer runs a car hobby through the business.

Continued on next page

Exhibit 8-2

Suggested Answers for Auto Body/Repair Business — Examiner's Viewpoint	
Ways to Omit Income	**Possible Audit Techniques**
1. Jobs done for cash by extending discounts to customers who agree to pay cash.	Confirmations with selected customers. Sample parts purchase invoices to customer invoices.
2. Towing and storage fees.	Determine if taxpayer owns tow truck and has ample storage space. Contact Auto Club for reimbursement procedures on towing. Ask taxpayer how income is reported for these services.
3. Sales of scrap materials and used parts.	Ask taxpayer.
4. Exchanges of services for goods or services.	Are they a full service shop or do they "farm out" certain work? Note sources of funds for acquisitions of assets.
5. Rebuilding and sale of totaled vehicles.	Check DMV for vehicle transfers. Does taxpayer have a Dealer's License, check DMV.
6. Repair and/or paint jobs for special customers.	Look at what is currently in the shop. Look for pictures of "special jobs."

Continued on next page

Exhibit 8-2

Suggested
Answers for
Auto Body/
Repair Business
(cont.)

Suggested Answers for Auto Body/Repair Business — Examiner's Viewpoint	
Ways to Omit Income	Possible Audit Techniques
7. Small welding work for customers for cash.	Detect use of cash, use Cash T
8. Custom metal fabrication for cash.	Detect use of cash, use Cash T
9. Insurance fraud, billing for work not done. Billing for new parts, but using used parts.	Third party contact with insurance companies. Contact state licensing authorities for pending complaints.
10. A related business such as radiator repair or front-end alignment work not reported.	Inspect business premises, relate "books" to what appears to be going on.
11. Taxpayer runs a car hobby through the business.	Check DMV for owner's cars. Does owner appear to be restoring (repairing valuable cars)?

Suggested
Answers for
Vending
Machine
Business

Suggested Answers for Vending Machine Business — Taxpayer's Viewpoint
1. Cash skimming.
2. Place unregistered machines in various locations. Move machines regularly.
3. Allow bar owners to share in "free play" when introducing new machines.
4. Utilize machines not recorded in inventory.
5. Disengage counters.
6. Perform own repairs.
7. Cash out coins to bills using change machines or sell to laundromat owners.

Exhibit 8-2

Suggested
Answers for
Vending
Machine
Business (cont.)

Suggested Answer for Vending Machine Business — Examiner's Viewpoint	
Ways to Omit Income	**Possible Audit Techniques**
1. Cash skimming — owner collects from machines.	Compare cash collections with inventory of vending machines.
2. Place unregistered machines in various locations — move machines regularly.	Check for schedule of vending machine route service. Check for state/local registration.
3. Allow bar owners to share in "free play" when introducing new machines.	Make sample confirmations with business establishment where machines are located.
4. Utilize machines not recorded in inventory.	Contact suppliers of vending machines and determine the number of vending machines the taxpayer has acquired. Check for insurance coverage.
5. Disengage counters.	Investigate lack of internal controls and test counters on some field machines.
6. Perform own repairs.	Review for outside repair records — Tie parts/supplies to inventory records.
7. Cash out coins to bills using change machines or sell to laundromat owners.	Check banking practices — seek out "local" businesses who might use coins. Query CBRS for cash transactions.

If you think I am over-reacting, that the IRS doesn't really intend to park itself at your business to spy on your operation, consider this. After describing the various ways to determine the unreported income of the hypothetical bar owner, the IRS asks the following question of its agents: (Before I state the question, I want to make it perfectly clear that the use of emphasis in this statement is *not* mine. I restate this sentence exactly as it appears in the manual.)

> • **"Q.   Do the results of the brainstorming give you a clue as to where the audit needs to be conducted?**
> • **"A.   AT THE TAXPAYERS PLACE OF BUSINESS!!!"**
>   Training Aid 3302-101, page 4-8.

The last thing our fictional agent did before leaving Keith and Nancy's home was to engage them in a bit of small talk about a photo hanging on the wall. We already know why he was attuned to stumbling upon such a thing, but what made him use that comfortable, seemingly innocuous conversation style to discover the Florida vacation?

The manual spends a good deal of time training agents in "interview techniques." Job Aid 8, "Interview Techniques," Training Aid 3302-109, lists sixty-one *different tricks and gimmicks* to trip people up during the interview process. These are just a few:

- Put taxpayer at ease
- Read taxpayer's non-verbal language (body language)
- Appear interested
- Be observant
- Feign ignorance when appropriate (act dumb)
- Use appropriate small talk
- Verbally pin down the taxpayer when appropriate
- Maintain composure
- Work to establish rapport
- Maintain an inquisitive mind
- Contain your excitement.

Ibid, at pages JA8-1 through JA8-4.

The Facilitator guide adds to this list, explaining that "successful economic reality examiners" are "street smart," assertive and aggressive, are "risk takers," ask the tough questions, and have sufficient self-confidence to "maintain their position when challenged." Facilitator Guide, Training Aid 3302-101, page 1-12.

The economic reality audit can best be described as a sneak attack. Agents may present themselves as sheep, but they are in reality ravenous wolves intent on devouring those unable to cope with these aggressive and deceptive audit tactics. The chapters to follow specifically address how to keep from falling into the traps that ensnared Keith and Nancy.

Reproduced below as exhibit 8-3 is the chart of attributes of a successful examiner.

Exhibit 8-3

Q. What are the attributes of a successful Economic Reality examiner?

(Suggested Answers) Attributes	
• <u>**Committed to dealing with non-compliance**</u> (key attribute) • "Street smart" • Focused • Inquisitive • Skeptical (healthy) • Innovative • Objective • Observant • Thorough • Analytical • Assertive/aggressive • Comfortable making appropriate confrontation • Have pride in what you're doing • Be an investigator • Identify significant leads • Follow up on significant leads • A good listener • Willing to accept challenge • Not afraid to say "I don't understand."	• People skills (meet and deal ability) • Creative • Seek help if needed • Sense of closure • See the "big picture" • Ask the tough questions • Sufficient self-confidence to maintain their position when challenged • Effective interviewer • Ethical • Focused • Good judgment • Common sense • Decisive • Good communicator • Risk taker • Perseverance • Open minded • Able to read body language • Confident • Willing to make third party contacts

Chapter Nine -
Understanding the Beast's Power
"Knowing the Burden of Proof"

Over the years, I have seen countless audits pointed at income. Virtually every case had these common denominators: 1) an honest citizen with good records, 2) a tax examiner determined to find unreported income, 3) a final audit report claiming the citizen earned income he did not report, and 4) a concomitant demand for taxes, interest and penalties.

On March 25, 1996, Thomas W. Wilson, Acting Assistant IRS Commissioner for Examination issued a memorandum to all compliance officers regarding economic reality audits (referred to as "financial status" audits in the memo). The memo came in response to a series of complaints lodged against the IRS by frustrated tax professionals. The memo extols the virtues of economic reality audits and better than anything I can say, exposes the danger of proceeding through such an ordeal without understanding what is taught here. At page three of the memo Mr. Wilson declares:

> When used appropriately, financial status analysis audit techniques are successful. For example, in 27 cases (involving 65 tax years), examiners found understatements of taxable income averaging over $180,000.

One reason for this difficulty is citizens do not understand their burden of proof in the tax audit. And to make matters worse, the IRS does not tell the truth about it. Our fictional agent left Keith and Nancy with the distinct impression they had to prove they *did not* earn the $20,000 he "discovered" or they would be stuck. You no doubt notice that throughout this discourse, I repeat the axiom that the burden of proof in tax cases lies with the citizen. Expect the IRS to beat you over the head with this rule.

But there are important exceptions I have alluded to already. I shall develop a critical one in this chapter to the end that you cannot be blindsided as Keith and Nancy were. We begin by briefly reviewing the basics.

Burden of Proof Basics

The law requires you to keep such records as are necessary to clearly reflect income and the payment of deductible expenses. If your records do not reflect income, the IRS has the legal authority to "reconstruct" it to obtain a more accurate accounting.

The law places the burden of proof squarely upon the citizen to show that his deductions are proper. This is true both in terms of the amount and legality of the claim. The IRS has no burden with regard to deductions. If it disallows one, it need not support its action. The law places a "presumption of correctness" upon the IRS' determination. The legal presumption is akin to the "presumption of innocence" which cloaks a defendant throughout the course of a criminal prosecution. To defeat the disallowance of your deductions, *you* must overcome the presumption of correctness with credible evidence sufficient to prove your claim.

The Burden of Proving Income

The rules *are not* the same regarding income. True, the IRS may attack income, but it cannot force you into a position of having to prove a negative. We all know that is usually impossible. The agency cannot, for example, say "We believe you had $20,000 worth of income you did not report," then merely rest on the presumption of correctness to see whether you disprove the claim.

It can, however, "test" your claim of income. In other words, it can probe your records to see whether they have been cooked or are otherwise inaccurate. For example, if you report $50,000 of income, it can require you to present a foundation of evidence to support the disclosure. Such proof might come in the form of a W-2 showing wages, coupled with bank statements showing like deposits to your checking account.

Suppose, however, bank records reveal $60,000 of deposits, while the W-2 shows $50,000 of wages. In such a circumstance, the law places the burden of proof on you to explain the $10,000 difference. It may have come from a bank loan. It may have come from an inheritance or gift. It may reflect re-deposits from savings to checking. It may be a non-taxable return of capital from the sale of stocks or bonds. If you cannot offer a suitable explanation, the deposit is considered income.

By offering proof to support your income claim, you build a foundation of evidence to stand upon. Having erected a foundation, the IRS--*not you*--bears the burden to prove you earned income not reported on the return. Hence, your foundation of evidence effectively shifts the burden of proof to the IRS, but only where income is concerned. Now, to support its claim of unreported income, the IRS must present firm, credible evidence that you earned income and did not report it.

Let me illustrate. The IRS uses Bureau of Labor Statistics to "estimate" personal living expenses. Economic reality literature instructs the agents to build a BLS profile of your living expenses even before contacting you. BLS numbers are the yardstick by which to measure the supposed accuracy of your disclosures.

Imagine BLS tables for your area and family size indicate you must spend $20,000 on living expenses. Such expenses do not show up on your tax return simply because they are non-deductible. Suppose further that your tax return shows $15,000 in disposable income. For purposes of this discussion, disposable income is the amount available to spend on discretionary living expenses.

Disposable income is arrived at by subtracting from gross income all payments for state and federal income taxes, social security taxes, and any other expense appearing on your return. That includes mortgage interest, charitable giving, etc.

The IRS refers to this as a "cash transactions" or cash T account. On one side of the ledger the agent lists all known income. The other side is made up of all known expenses. However, the IRS does not know what your personal living expenses are, therefore it guesses using BLS tables as the benchmark.

In our example, it appears from the BLS numbers that you must have spent $5,000 more than you reported. BLS numbers indicate it requires $20,000 to live your lifestyle. However, you have just $15,000 in disposable income on the basis of your tax return disclosures. In such a case, the agent might claim "you must have earned more than you reported" because the BLS tables show you could not live on what you had left after paying all expenses reflected on the return.

Think back to the case of Paul discussed in chapter six. There, the auditor made exactly such a claim. At the end of the audit, she asserted $3,900 in unreported income solely on the basis of her suspicion that he "just couldn't live on what he reported." Her suspicion was driven by BLS numbers for the city in which Paul lived.

Parenthetically, we should note that BLS numbers are merely averages, composites of living costs in a given area. By their nature, they cannot possibly reflect reality in every case. Averages are, after all, a balance between known highs and lows. They are not intended to be an exact measure of what happens in an individual situation.

Can BLS numbers place the burden on you to prove you did not earn the extra income suggested by the data? No, not if your own records provide a foundation of evidence upon which to rest your initial claim. Where you have valid and credible evidence to support your income disclosure, *the IRS must prove its case with a foundation of extrinsic evidence*. Without a strong base of evidence to undergird its assertion, the agency cannot rely upon the presumption of correctness. One example of how it might do so is through credible testimony from customers or clients who paid cash you never deposited to your bank account and failed to report.

Amazingly, economic reality manuals recognize this truth. The instructions are not clear, however, and the IRS colors it to its own liking. As a result, agents in the field hold unwitting citizens to an unrealistic and legally unsupported burden of proof. In the manual entitled, "Indirect Methods," Job Aid 9, Training Aid 3302-110, the IRS discusses procedures for reconstructing a citizen's income when his own books do not "clearly reflect income." It points out that the IRS has the right to "test the reliability of the books." Ibid, page JA9-1. It goes on to note, however, that,

> Before we can challenge the accuracy of the taxpayer's books and records and show by another method of income reconstruction that the records of the taxpayer do not properly reflect income, *we must exercise special care* in testing the validity or accuracy of the taxpayer's records. Ibid, page JA9-2; emphasis added.

That same manual goes on to point out that the IRS "has a special responsibility of thoroughness" in reconstructing income. Citing the warning given it by the Supreme Court in *Holland v. United States*, 348 U.S. 121 (1954), the IRS observes that it carries the burden to 1) "prove a likely source of unreported income," 2) negate "all possible non-taxable sources," and 3) check and negate all leads furnished by the citizen "with respect to likely sources of non-taxable receipts." Ibid, page JA9-4.

The IRS is not free to summarily reject your records and testimony in favor of its own income reconstruction if it cannot prove them unreliable. In sum, BLS numbers or any other form of reconstruction the IRS may employ are without moment when clear evidence to back them up is lacking.

How the Courts Rule

There are two reasons the IRS ignores these facts. The first is people do not understand the rules. As a result, they can be bluffed into believing they carry the burden of proving a negative fact and cannot meet the challenge. Secondly, the burden of proof rules vis-a-vis income *are not delineated in the Internal Revenue code!* As hard as that is to imagine, it is nevertheless true. For that reason, we cannot expect poorly trained revenue agents motivated only to "get the money" to turn up rules of law crafted to favor the citizen. Expect agents to merely regurgitate the "presumption of correctness" doctrine as though it is the alpha and the omega.

For a true grasp of these rules, we must examine court authority on the matter.

Case Study No. One — *Portillo v. Commissioner*, 91-1 USTC 50,304 (5th Cir. 1991).

Ramon Portillo was a self-employed painter from El Paso. He contracted with builders to paint residential and commercial projects. General contractors paid him on a weekly basis so he could pay crews doing the work. Each payment was carefully recorded in his ledger at the time he received a check. That way, his records were contemporaneous in nature.

Ramon did not have a bank account. Consequently, after recording the contractor's check in his ledger, he cashed it. He used the proceeds to pay his employees and to purchase supplies. All payroll records were maintained by Ramon in a separate ledger.

At the end of each year, Ramon used Forms 1099 issued by the various contractors to confirm the gross receipts shown in his ledger. He then handed them to a preparer to complete income and employment tax returns. In 1984, however, the preparer did not have a 1099 from a particular contractor when preparing the return because it was not filed on time. Thus, he determined receipts from that contractor strictly from Ramon's own ledger.

In mid 1985, that contractor filed a Form 1099 with the IRS. In 1987, Ramon was audited for tax year 1984. When the agent reviewed the form and cross-checked it with Ramon's tax return, he discovered an important discrepancy. Checks paid to and cashed by Ramon totaled $13,925. However, the contractor's Form 1099 said he paid Ramon $35,305, a difference of $21,380.

Ramon denied receiving any more from the contractor than his own records reflected. The agent in turn questioned the contractor, asking him to provide records of his payments. The contractor was able to produce checks showing payments of $13,925, exactly as Ramon claimed. The contractor claimed the difference was due to cash payments, but had no evidence to verify his claim.

What do you suppose the agent concluded with respect to Ramon's income? He asserted $21,380 in unreported income. The agent prepared his report accordingly and presented it to an IRS reviewer. The reviewer was concerned about the discrepancy in the contractor's statements. The reviewer explained that there were "several ways" to "follow up," to check if Ramon indeed received cash. The auditor refused, saying "it was Portillo's burden to prove that he did not get the payments." The auditor concluded the 1099 was "presumed correct" and shrugged off the reviewer's concerns. The final audit determination held Ramon responsible for tax, penalties and interest on the alleged unreported income.

Ramon appealed. On appeal, he testified he did not receive $35,000 from the contractor in question. He presented his ledgers showing what he actually received. This established the factual premise that the Form 1099 was false. In addition, the contractor produced his records showing payments of just $13,925. No proof existed for anything else.

Ramon challenged the IRS' decision using the burden of proof rules presented above. The burden of proof rests with the IRS to establish a foundation of evidence upon which the determination of unreported income can securely rest. Without such a foundation, the courts have universally held such a determination is "naked" and does not enjoy the presumption of correctness. "Several courts, including this one," reads the decision in Ramon's favor, "have noted that a court need not give effect to the presumption of correctness in a case involving unreported income if the Commissioner cannot present some predicate evidence supporting its determination."

The court laid an affirmative duty at the feet of the IRS. The agency must support its claim with hard evidence. The court demanded the IRS "engage in one final foray for truth in order to provide the court with some indicia that the taxpayer received unreported income." In the court's mind, the "final foray for truth" translates to the responsibility to investigate the facts and determine whether indeed the citizen received the income he is accused of earning.

Here, the IRS found no records to prove anything beyond what Ramon reported. That should have told the agency the contractor either made an error or deliberately falsified the 1099. Apparently, the obvious conclusion never entered the auditor's mind. Then again, such a conclusion would have made the agency no money! Consequently, the IRS charged ahead, lacking any credible evidence. It made no further effort to engage in the final foray of truth required to support its claim. In the final analysis, Ramon was not put into the position of having to prove a negative.

Case Study No. Two — *Krause v. Commissioner*, T.C. Memo 1992-270 (May 11, 1992).

One example of how the IRS uses statistics to make otherwise naked assertions of unreported income occurred in Atlantic City during 1984 and 1985. Agents of the Criminal Investigation Division conducted surveillance of all local gaming casinos. The Atlantic City Tip Project was specifically designed to uncover tip income earned by casino employees. The project focused on waitresses, bartenders and gaming dealers.

After completing the surveillance, the IRS audited a targeted group of employees. On the average, the IRS claimed employees earned tip income of about 13 percent. If that amount were not reported, the IRS added it to the employee's return.

In the Atlantic City project, teams of two IRS agents observed cocktail servers for periods of thirty minutes at a time. The agents went to locations chosen at random by computer and observed the tips given to a server. They were instructed to make certain conservative assumptions during the operation. For example, if they could not clearly see a bill, they were to assume it was a dollar. If they could not clearly see a coin, they were to assume it was a quarter.

During 1984 and 1985, there were sixty-three half-hour periods of surveillance conducted at each of the ten gaming casinos in Atlantic City. In 1987 and 1988, forty-two half-hour spying sessions took place at each of the now twelve casinos. IRS statisticians in turn developed a formula said to represent average tip income. These figures varied according to work shift. The evening shift, for example, was said to earn more tips per hour than the day shift.

In case after case, the IRS hit casino employees with tax on unreported tip income. The determinations were based solely on the statistical analysis. The Tax Court approved the IRS' ruling because the citizens were without a foundation of evidence to support their claim.

Judy was a bartender at the Sands hotel. She was swept up in the dragnet and ended up in court for 1985. She lost. The Court found that what few records she bothered to keep did not "clearly reflect" tip income. It approved the IRS' reconstruction alleging tips equal to $6.77 per hour on the strength of the surveillance evidence.

Judy learned a valuable lesson from her bitter experience. She began keeping contemporaneous, detailed records of her tips using a log. She carried a small notebook to work with her every day. In it, she entered the amount of tips earned that day, either immediately after work or when she arrived home the same evening. At the end of each pay period, she reported total tips to her employer. The tip income was then included on her weekly pay stub and the appropriate income and social security tax withheld. On Form W-2, those tips were in turn reported to the IRS.

When the IRS took another crack at Judy, she was ready. Judy claimed $6,473 in tip income in 1986. According to IRS statistics, she should have claimed $12,324. The IRS asserted unreported income of $5,852. While this is precisely the problem she faced in 1985, this time she had a foundation of evidence beneath her.

At trial, Judy presented her contemporaneous log. She testified about her habit of carrying the log with her to work each day and recording her tips. She also explained she made a report to her employer so the tips were included in Form W-2. This way, she provided for income and social security tax withholding.

The IRS, on the other hand, argued that their statistical analysis showed Judy "must have" earned $12,300. The agency hung its case solely on the analysis. It tried to box her into the cage of having to prove a negative.

However carefully the IRS may have observed the casino employees, and however scientific its analysis may have been, it does not change the fact the IRS did nothing more than guess at Judy's tips. They had no way to know what those tips were.

This time around, the court agreed with Judy. It specifically found the IRS' otherwise valid statistics "do not reflect (Judy's) income in tax year 1986 as accurately as her own daily records." By presenting the foundation of evidence to establish the validity of her income claim, the burden shifted to the IRS to present clear evidence to contradict it. The evidence of its spying operation was not enough to outweigh Judy's documentation.

Case Study No. Three - *Senter v. Commissioner*, T.C. Memo 1995-311 (July 13, 1995).

The IRS claimed Chuck failed to file tax returns for years 1987-1990. An auditor mailed him a letter saying that because there was no record of his filing, he should either mail copies of the returns or appear at an appointed date to allow the agent to review his records. She was going to determine whether he was required to file.

Chuck responded saying he could not provide any information without counsel, and because he could not afford a lawyer, he would not attend the meeting. After another failed attempt to get records from Chuck, the IRS mailed a notice of deficiency claiming tax liabilities for all the years. It determined his income and tax due using the Consumer Price Index (CPI) for each of the years. Just as I illustrated in chapter five, the IRS took the income from Chuck's most recent return, 1986, then merely applied the CPI to each of the succeeding years to project his income.

Chuck petitioned the Tax Court contesting the proposed deficiency. During the proceeding, he made a bold move, one which I do not recommend. He presented *no evidence* whatsoever concerning the IRS' claim. Rather, he sat back and challenged the IRS to prove he received any income. Naturally, the agency could do no such thing.

Instead, the IRS hauled out the thread-bare argument that Chuck had the burden of proof. It asserted its deficiency determination enjoyed the "presumption of correctness." The Tax Court, fresh from the teachings of *Portillo v. Commissioner*, refused to countenance the argument.

Acknowledging that the general rule is the citizen bears the burden of proof and the IRS' determination is presumed correct, the court noted,

> However, an exception to this general rule is recognized by several courts of appeals for situations where the Commissioner determines that the taxpayer received income that was not reported on the taxpayer's return. The rationale for this exception is based on the recognized difficulty that the taxpayer bears in proving the non-receipt of income. Citing *Portillo*, supra, *Sealy Power, Ltd. v. Commissioner*, 46 F.3d 382 (5th Cir. 1995), and *Anastasato v. Commissioner*, 749 F.2d 884 (3rd Cir. 1986).

In *Portillo*, you will recall, the IRS hung its hat on an erroneous Form 1099. The Fifth Circuit said that was not good enough. In this case, the IRS "provided no predicate EVIDENCE" whatsoever to support its conclusion that Chuck earned any income during those years. (Emphasis in original.) The court therefore easily concluded the IRS' determination was "arbitrary and erroneous" and struck it down.

What Chuck did in presenting no records was extremely risky. The approach taken by Judy and Ramon is more advisable. It is better to establish *your* foundation of evidence to shift the burden to the IRS. This is done with affirmative proof that your income declaration is correct. Having done that, it is unquestionable the IRS has the burden to prove its claims of unreported income.

Provided you are not an outright tax cheat who indeed failed to report income, the IRS can likely have no success attempting to reconstruct your income in the economic reality environment. Furthermore, if it ignores these rules (which through arrogance it often does), it runs a growing risk. For example, Ramon was able to extract an award against the IRS for the fees and costs he incurred fighting its determination. *Portillo v. Commissioner*, 988 F.2d 27, (5th Cir. 1993). In my book, *How to Fire the IRS*, I have a chapter illustrating how to make a successful claim to recover fees and costs from the IRS.

Other Case Studies. My analysis of the burden of proof is not novel. An early case on the subject is *Helvering v. Taylor*, 293 U.S. 507 (Supreme Court 1935), dating back more than sixty years. However, as the IRS has grown more brazen with its approaches to reconstructing income, there have been more cases slamming the door on its efforts. Another is that of *Carson v. Commissioner*, 560 F.2d 693 (5th Cir. 1977), in which the court said, "The tax collector's presumption of correctness has a herculean muscularity of Goliath-like reach, but we strike at the Achilles' heel when we find no muscles, no tendons, no ligaments of fact."

The "New Burden of Proof" Law

Erroneous information returns are the source of a great many problems with the IRS. Over one billion are filed every year and cross-checked with more than 116 million individual tax returns. It is unquestionable there are errors in the preparation, filing, and processing of such a mountain of data. When errors arise, the IRS smugly asserts the "presumption of correctness" and errantly puts the burden on the citizen to prove a negative.

The Taxpayers' Bill of Rights Act 2, passed on July 30, 1996, contained a provision said to correct this problem. Intended as a direct response to the *Portillo* case, the law was to put the burden on the IRS to make a "reasonable investigation" into the facts where a citizen disputes an information return. If the IRS failed to make such an inquiry, it would carry the burden of proof on the matter.

What came out of the Congressional wringer was not what went in. New code section 6201(d) reads as follows:

> In any court proceeding, if a taxpayer asserts a reasonable dispute with respect to any item of income reported on an information return filed with the Secretary under subpart B or C of part III of subchapter A of chapter 61 by a third party and the taxpayer has fully cooperated with the Secretary (including providing, within a reasonable period of time, access to and inspection of all witnesses, information, and documents within the control of the taxpayer as reasonably requested by the Secretary), the Secretary shall have the burden of producing reasonable and probative information concerning such deficiency in addition to such information return.

As you can see, this law does not plainly put any "burden of proof" on the IRS, though that is what its original authors intended. In fact, the only burden is to present "information" (is that the same as evidence?) which is "reasonable and probative" of its determination.

That is certainly not the same as requiring the IRS to prove its case *a la* the language of the Tax Court in *Senter*.

The law does, however, require the IRS to support its claim with something more than just an information return. It can no longer rely merely on a 1099 or W-2 to support a deficiency, where the citizen disputes it and cooperates to set the record straight. The problem is, there is no clear directive to the IRS to shoulder the burden of proof.

I fear this provision will do little to help the burden of proof problems we face. It remains imperative to grasp the rules expressed above in order to hold the IRS' feet to the fire on the law.

Chapter Ten -
Controlling the Beast
"Neutralizing the Economic Reality Audit"

Recognizing the Economic Reality Audit

Keith and Nancy never knew what hit them. Before they had any idea *why* the agent was asking, they were spending sleepless nights gathering records to show purchases of toothpaste and plastic water toys. When they were told their many hours of work were not sufficient and had to go back for even more, Keith sheepishly responded, "Sure." The agent's every request was met with nothing more than a cross look.

In the end, every bit of data was somehow used against them. This is entirely consistent with the IRS' teaching. In "JOB AID 9, Indirect Methods," the manual states, "The more information an examiner can develop, the larger the understatement (of tax). The development of the personal living expenses can be extremely critical in this process." Training Aid 3302-110, page 1. It is for this reason the IRS might ask for documents regarding every purchase imaginable, *including* the kitchen sink. It is also this very characteristic that betrays the identity of the economic reality audit.

Three items portend an economic reality audit. The first we already addressed. It is IRS Form 4822, the Personal Living Expense Statement. See Exhibit 8-1. The second is Form 4564, Information Document Request (IDR). Do not misunderstand. Virtually every audit involves an IDR. It is the manner by which the IRS requests data. However, in an economic reality audit, the IDR is *very broad* and effectively all-inclusive. By contrast, an IDR in an non-economic reality matter involves documents relating to one or more deductions or very specific items of income, such as a stock sale.

Reproduced on the next page as Exhibit 10-1, please find a sample IDR. This one comes from the IRS' Facilitator Guide, Training Aid 3302-101, page AK1-7.

Notice that much of the requested information has nothing to do with tax return claims. Item 2, for example, seeks "all books and records" relative to income "and expenses." It does not confine itself to documents relative to deductible expenses, but rather, asks for data on "all expenses."

Item 9 seeks information about the purchase of personal assets, such as "automobiles, boats, or motorcycles." This is an illustration of how the IRS intends to "sneak up" on people. In the hypothetical case portrayed by the IRS, a citizen purchased a boat with cash. The IRS learned of it through Form 8300. You may recall from chapter two that Form 8300 is used to report cash transactions in excess of $10,000. The IRS' description of its sample IDR states,

> Notice how the IDR is prepared asking for information about the boat. Because a Form 8300 has been filed indicating an *unusual method of payment for a business person*, the question about the boat is included with questions about an automobile and motorcycle. The IDR *does not indicate* the requester knows about a boat purchased with cash or cash equivalent. That information may be of the type that if the taxpayer knew you were aware of the transaction, *they may be unwilling to talk to you*. This type of transaction, that which *may produce an unwanted action* on the part of the taxpayer, could be referred to as *volatile information*. Facilitator Guide, Training Aid 3302-101, page AK1-8; emphasis added.

The various presumptions implicit in this statement indicate the IRS' predisposition. First, it presumes legitimate business people do not pay cash for personal assets, as though cash is used only by criminals or in a criminal context. Next, it assumes it must hide the fact that it knows about the purchase. That itself seems curious because the citizen had to provide information to the seller to complete Form 8300 in the first place. Why would any reasonable person believe the IRS does *not know* about a transaction expressly reported to it? Third, the IRS assumes the citizen will lie or refuse to talk about the boat when asked. As a result, it feels necessary to orchestrate a sneak attack.

The third badge of an economic reality audit is the type of questions an auditor may ask. Certain questions indicate the direction the agent

Exhibit 10-1

EXERCISE 2-7

Form 4564 Rev.Jun.1988	Department of the Treasury Internal Revenue Service INFORMATION DOCUMENT REQUEST	Request Number 1

TO: (Name of Taxpayer and Co. Div.or Branch) | Subject
                                              | 1993 Federal Tax Exam

Gordon & Marian Harris
21 Lincoln St. | SAIN No. | Submitted to:
Anywhere, USA 99999 | |

Please return with listed documents | Dates of Previous Requests
to requester listed below. |

Description of Documents Requested

1. Reconciled beginning and ending bank balances for all accounts for the year 1993. Business and personal bank records including cancelled checks, deposit tickets, and monthly statements for all bank accounts for the period 1993, include your 12/31/92 and 01/31/94 statements.

2. All books and records concerning your income and expenses.

3. Copy of divorce decree.

4. All monthly broker statements for 1993.

5. Records of any loans obtained in 1993 including credit applications and financial statements.

6. Records of any loans paid off or reduced in principle amount for 1993.

7. All purchase documents relative to your new house including copies of credit applications, financial statements, closing documents and method of downpayment.

8. Records, including invoices for business assets purchased in 1993.

9. Records including method of payment for any personal assets purchased in 1993 such as automobiles, boats, or motorcycles.

10. Records and amounts for any non-taxable income received in 1993 such as cash gifts received, inheritances, loans from friends or relatives and the amounts of any money not kept in a bank account.

11. Copies of all forms W-2s, W-3s, 1099s, 940 and 941s for 1993.

12. Invoices or cash register tapes for sales, invoices for business expenses and inventory purchases. Ending inventory records including count sheets and sources of values used for ending inventory.

13. Accountant's workpapers used to prepare the tax return and detailed depreciation schedules.

From:	Name and Title of Requester	Date
	Office Location	Telephone

Answer Key
Solution, Exercise 2-7
Page 1 of 3

is moving. Please think back to the probing personal questions asked of Keith and Nancy. They included, among other things, 1) the use of their boat, 2) the improvements made to their home, and 3) how they spent their family vacation. Exploring these and other highly personal areas of your life indicate an attempt to illustrate a pattern of spending not justifiable on your reported income.

The auditor may ask "How much cash did you have on hand on January 1, 1994?" The typical response is, "Well, I don't know. Not very much I guess." Believing it is best to keep the amount low, when pinned down they may say something like, "just a few hundred dollars."

The purpose of that question, which the auditor will *never tell you*, is to prevent you from later asserting a "cash hoard" claim. A cash hoard is a stash of money that generally does not appear in a bank account. The citizen claims it was earned and saved over the years. By asking you how much cash you have on hand at the beginning of the year, and anticipating a small amount in response, you are later foreclosed from defending an unreported income claim by saying, "We saved cash over a long period of time."

Now that you know whether you are in an economic reality audit, let us address specific techniques for controlling it.

Diffusing the Economic Reality Audit

To diffuse an economic reality audit and keep from being victimized as Keith and Nancy were, you must understand the legal limits of your responsibility. You have the burden to prove your tax return is correct. I have said this time and again. Here is one area where that truth becomes critical. You *do not* have the responsibility either to keep or produce records if they have no bearing upon the correctness of your return. Much of what is asked for in connection with the income probe has *nothing whatsoever* to do with the return.

In his March 25, 1996 memo to all Regional Chief Compliance Officers, Acting Assistant Commissioner for Examination Thomas Wilson described circumstances under which the economic reality audit is *not* appropriate. Page two of the memo reads,

> For the average wage earner, the IRS is able to verify virtually all income and most deductions by matching information returns (Forms W-2 and 1099) with the individual income tax return. Thus, these audit techniques are generally not

appropriate in an examination of a wage earner unless there is an indication of income not subject to information reporting.

Turning his attention to the business owner, the memo goes on to state,

> However, examiners are not to assume that an audit of a business or self-employed taxpayer automatically means that there is unreported income and therefore use in-depth income probes on every audit. Examiners must evaluate the facts and circumstances of each case and apply judgment. It is not an efficient use of resources to have examiners perform in-depth income probes and ask questions about personal assets and personal expenditures when there is no reasonable indication of unreported income. *The more in-depth probes should only be employed when there is a reasonable indication of unreported income* (emphasis added).

Prior to that, Mr. L.E. Carlow, the sitting Assistant Commissioner for Examination issued a memo of his own. It came in direct response to my radio shows blasting the audits. The memo is dated August 8, 1995 and went to all Regional Chief Compliance Officers. In it, Mr. Carlow states,

> I want to emphasize that examiners must assess the facts and apply sound judgment in determining the scope [of an audit] on a case by case basis. We have been alerted to instances where in-depth initial interviews were routinely used to explore a taxpayer's financial situation when there was not (sic) indication of such a need. This may not be appropriate.

While these statements are not the world's clearest and most binding guidance on the matter, they constitute guidance nonetheless. You can be sure if I had not been on the radio talking about these audits there would be no guidance whatsoever. It would be a mere audit free-for-all. As it happens, the IRS had to tone down its approach, at least on paper. We can now use these statements to limit economic reality audits.

Agents *are not* to use these sweeping techniques in every case. In fact, they are to use them only where there is a "reasonable indication" of unreported income. Without something concrete to suggest you are cheating, there is no reason you should be subjected to the kind of treatment meted out to Keith and Nancy.

The unfortunate part of these memos is the instruction that tax auditors are to evaluate the facts and apply "sound judgment." The sad reality is the job of the auditor is to get the money--period. When you mix that directive with the fact that too many do not possess sound judgment, you arrive at a recipe for trouble, *unless* you use these techniques aggressively to limit the audit.

In combination with the burden of proof teachings of chapter nine, the memos above provide the formula needed to dissuade a full-scale economic reality probe. There are two things you must do to accomplish it. I address them here.

Step One: Provide affirmative proof of income. The burden of proof law teaches that if you establish a foundation of evidence upon which to support your income claim, the IRS cannot put you into the unenviable position of having to prove a negative. The memos suggest economic reality audits are improper where there is no indication of unreported income. This is especially true in the case of W-2 wage earners whose income is reported by their employers.

Therefore, step one is to provide affirmative proof that your income is correctly reported on the return. I recommend this be done with an affidavit, accompanied by bank records, income logs and other materials which tend to confirm your claim. Let us consider the example of the W-2 wage earner.

A wage earner receives a W-2 showing income paid by his employer. However, it does not address what might have been paid by others, or what might have been earned through self-employment activities. Therefore, the wage earner must address those potential questions head on. The affidavit should state that the W-2 represents "all income earned" during the year in question. It should also state that "there was no other source of income" other than that shown on the W-2.

Suppose the W-2 shows $40,000 in wages and there is no other source of income. Suppose the paychecks were deposited to a checking account. In that case, the checking account should reflect deposits about equal to the wages. The affidavit should clearly describe these facts. You should also provide copies of the bank statements and illustrate the fact that bank deposits match wages.

Now let us suppose there are substantial differences in the deposits versus wages. Those differences *must be explained* in the first instance. Do not wait to see if the auditor "discovers" them. Assume he will and explain them on the front end. This eliminates the potential negative inference the agent might otherwise draw and will likely keep the matter from mutating into a full-scale life-style audit.

Let me illustrate this. Suppose your bank account shows $50,000 in deposits, but the W-2 shows $40,000 in wages. You received $5,000 from Uncle Ed's estate when he died and borrowed $5,000 from your sister to pay off credit card debt. On the bank statements reflecting the deposit of this money, use a marker to highlight the deposits. In your affidavit, specifically refer to the deposits and explain why they do not constitute income. In this example, inheritances are not taxed and loan proceeds are not considered income.

In the event a deposit is taxable, you should point to the line on the return where it is claimed as income. Suppose the $10,000 came from a stock sale. Specifically describe in your affidavit what was sold and point out that the profit was reported in Schedule D, Capital Gains and Losses. In turn, provide records to support the facts surrounding the purchase and sale of the stock.

This is important because taxable profit from a sale is likely quite different from the amount deposited. If you sold one thousand shares of the ABC Company for $5 per share, the deposit will be $5,000. However, if you bought the stock for $4.75 per share, the taxable profit is just $250.

Self-employed persons use a variation of the same process. Many self-employed persons operate as independent contractors. As such, they receive Forms 1099. Describe in your affidavit who you perform work for and expressly declare that all income is shown on the 1099s provided by those companies. You should use your own ledgers to confirm 1099 amounts the way Ramon did as illustrated in the previous chapter. In turn, confirm the ledgers and 1099s with your own bank statements. When these three items substantially match the income reported, you have successfully established a firm foundation supporting your claim.

The income of many self-employed people is not reported on 1099s. Those in retail operations are prime examples. They sell goods and services to the public and in most cases, no reporting requirements attach to the transactions. These people are more susceptible to being dragged into the economic reality audit because they are less able to confirm their income through third parties.

If you are such a person, it is fundamentally important to have a good income log or journal. The log must reflect all payments to you and their nature. In some cases, small business people use only their business checking account as an income log. Deposits show up on the bank statement each month making a clear record of income. This is fine, but it is critical that your affidavit expressly state that "all income is deposited to the account" and therefore "bank statements reflect 100 percent of income earned."

Just as we did with the W-2 wage earner, substantial differences between bank deposits or log entries versus income on the return must be identified, pointed out and *explained*. Those found by the auditor will be looked upon in an extremely negative light. If you point them out, it portends honesty and thoroughness.

I strongly recommend both wage earners and self-employed persons develop and use income logs. This is the best way to establish the foundation of evidence needed to support your income claim. My book *How to Fire the IRS* has a chapter showing you exactly how to do it.

Step Two: Establish sound reporting and return preparation techniques. Once you have clearly established the amount and source of your income, you must illustrate that you exercise strong, consistent controls over your recordkeeping. This is critical to showing that your records are reliable. In reviewing the language of the two memos above, we find that *the lack* of hard evidence of unreported income, combined *with affirmative evidence* of strong controls over the recordkeeping and reporting processes, add up to a return *not subject* to an economic reality audit.

To establish that you exercise controls leading to accurate records, describe in an affidavit exactly how you record your income. For wage earners, this process is very simple. You might simply record the income figures from your check stubs, and indicate deductions for taxes and other withholding.

Next, show that all checks are deposited to your bank account. The bank statements therefore "clearly show 100 percent of the wage income earned." You might include a statement in your affidavit declaring that "each paycheck earned during the year was deposited to the bank account." This establishes the fact that your income logs and bank statements accurately reflect income.

If you work more than one job, you would do well to have an income log for each job. Paychecks from each job are then recorded in their respective logs before being deposited to the account.

Lastly, the affidavit must declare that "the income reported on the return was determined on the basis" of these records. If you prepare your own return, it is a simple matter of explaining the act of taking income numbers from your W-2 and income logs, and entering them on the return. If you employ a tax pro, specifically declare that you provide the preparer with the W-2 and income logs so the pro can "accurately report all income."

By following this example, you illustrate that your W-2 is tied directly to checks, which are tied to the income log, which is finally tied to bank account deposits. This creates a chain of evidence plainly showing strong controls over the accounting process and in turn, buttressing the reliability of your records.

The process for self-employed persons is the same. Whether we are talking about 1099s or W-2s, they must be tied to your own income logs and bank deposits as shown above.

In cases where there are no 1099s, you must by necessity concentrate on your income logs. The IRS' question in this case is, "How do we know all income is recorded in the log?" This is where testimony about your recordkeeping practices is essential.

Describe the process by which you record income. Explain, for example, that when paid by a customer or client, the payment is "always recorded in an income log." Note that such payments are recorded "whether by cash or check." This establishes the fact that no cash is left "off the books." You might even point to bank records showing cash depoits to the account.

Then explain that periodically, deposits are made to the bank, and that bank deposits are reconciled with log entries. In this way, you illustrate control over the receipt of income and the performance of practices ensuring completeness of income logs and bank statements.

The task is to show consistency between your income logs, bank statements and tax return declarations. Just as I explained to the W-2 wage earner, the self-employed person must make this connection. If you prepare your own return, simply declare that your "income logs and bank statements provide the basis of the income claim." If you use a tax pro, state that he is provided with the income logs and bank statements to enable him to correctly report your income.

Take the initiative with regard to these two steps if the IRS gives the slightest indication of questioning your income. Such an indication is plain if you receive a Form 4822, or the IDR betrays a curiosity over your earnings. Do not wait until the agent is asking you to document the number of video tapes you rent. By following these two steps, you likely avoid all of that.

Details on drafting affidavits are presented in my book, *41 Ways to Lick the IRS with a Postage Stamp.*

Avoid the Personal Living Expense Statement

Dale Carnegie is famous for his advice on building professional relationships, salesmanship, public speaking, etc. His advice about how to win an argument is profound. He says simply, "Do not get into one."

This is precisely how to avoid the pitfalls of the Personal Living Expense (PLE) statement. Do not panic when I suggest refusing to complete the PLE. The IRS itself recognizes it does not have the legal authority to force you to complete one. In the Facilitator Guide, the IRS states that "no specific authority exists to require the taxpayer to fill out a PLE." Training Aid 3302-101, at page 3-11.

This issue was addressed by Assistant Commissioner Carlow in his letter dated October 27, 1995. The letter was mailed to Mr. Willis Williams, CPA, of Kansas City, Kansas. Mr. Williams is a member of the Tax Freedom Institute, which is a national association of tax professionals of which I am Executive Director. He expressed his concerns to the IRS over the economic reality audit. In the response letter, Mr. Carlow says, "A taxpayer does not have to answer an agent's questions, including those being asked to determine monies expended for personal assets and support."

Apart from the fact there is no legal obligation to complete a PLE or to answer a myriad of questions about your toilet paper consumption, such information is unreliable. Keep in mind that all of the expenses, with few exceptions, are for items that are not legally tax deductible. As a result, you have no legal obligation to keep records of such items, and very few people do. In fact, why would anybody in his right mind keep track of expenditures for "personal care items?"

As a result, it is impossible to accurately state what you spend on these items. Therefore, the process of completing the PLE is reduced to guessing what was "likely" spent. To complicate matters, remember that you are being audited for a *prior year*. If the audit is conducted *during* 1997, it is probably examining *tax year* 1994 or 1995. That means you are guessing *in 1997* at what you spent on haircuts and soda pop *in 1994*. I want somebody to tell me how that can be done in a way that gets you even remotely close to reality.

In short, asking you to guess at what you spent on these items is no more reliable than using BLS tables to find a number. The only thing that is reliable are hard records showing hard numbers. In nearly every case I have seen, those attempting to scale the PLE precipice end up with high estimates. The IRS then uses their *own statements* against them to support a claim of unreported income.

So while you should not get caught in the quagmire of the PLE, you must establish your foundation of evidence with hard records showing hard numbers. This is done using affidavits and the two-step process outlined above.

Should the agent press the issue of the PLE, ask the question, "It is important to establish my income using reliable records, isn't it?" What do you suppose his response will be? Then ask, "Shouldn't the information I provide *accurately* reflect *all* my income?" Guess at his answer. Finally, point out that, "The PLE is unreliable because it cannot be based upon actual records. I do not keep records of what I cannot claim as a deduction on my return. However, I have true, accurate and *reliable* records of income which I have already provided and which do show that my return is correct. I opt to stand by those."

How can he argue?

Keeping the IRS Out of Your Home

I can think of nothing more intimidating and outrageous, or more offensive to the notion of personal liberty, than an agent of the Internal Revenue Service sitting in your home taking inventory of your family photos, suits and dresses, and rummaging through your underwear drawer looking for the twenty bucks he thinks you stashed there.

Just as is the case with the PLE, the IRS has no legal authority to unilaterally gain access to your private residence. Often the IRS cites the regulation regarding the "site visit" as its "authority" to enter one's home. It is Revenue Regulation section 301.7605-1(d)(3)(iii). Let us examine it carefully:

> Regardless of where an examination takes place, the Service may visit the taxpayer's place of business or residence to establish facts that can *only be established* by direct visit, such as inventory or asset verification. The Service generally will visit for these purposes on a normal workday of the Service during the Service's normal duty hours (emphasis added).

As you can see, there is no language compelling you to allow an auditor into your home. The regulation says the agent "*may visit*" your residence. What it does not say is that he must have your *express permission* to *enter* the residence unless he has a court order signed by a judge authorizing such entry.

The circumstances under which the IRS may obtain either a Writ of Entry or a search warrant authorizing entry to a private residence are very narrow. Generally, search warrants issue only in criminal investigations, and then only when an agent can specifically testify under oath that he has probable cause to believe the premises contain evidence of a specific tax crime.

The Writ of Entry is used to enter private premises for the purpose of affecting tax collection. Do not confuse a tax audit with tax collection. The audit is nothing more than the process of determining the correctness of the return. The collection process is engaged after a tax is assessed, and only then after the citizen fails or refuses to pay it. To obtain the writ, the revenue officer must testify before a court that he has reasonable cause to believe there are items within the premises that can be used to satisfy the liability. *G.M. Leasing Corp. v. United States*, 429 U.S. 338 (Supreme Court 1977).

The Supreme Court was quite clear in its ruling in the *G.M. Leasing* case. Without court authorization obtained in strict compliance with the dictates of due process, the IRS has no right to enter the private property of a citizen. Where a business open to the public is concerned, the IRS may enter the otherwise public areas without a warrant. It cannot, however, access the private ones without consent.

For example, suppose you operate a restaurant. The business consists of a dining room where patrons eat, a kitchen where food is prepared, two restrooms, a private party room, a store room, and a small office. The public has unfettered access to just the dining room and the restrooms. Unless advanced arrangements are made and rent paid, the party room is not used. All other areas are off limits to the public. As a result, an agent may not have access to those private areas without your consent or a court order. He does, however, have access to the public areas.

Let us again turn our attention to the regulation. Even if this regulation did impart the lawful authority for an agent to view your home, such authority is *conditional*. The regulation provides for a site visit to "establish facts that can *only be established* by direct visit."

I would like you to point out the facts relevant to your tax return that can only be verified by a direct visit of your home. The answer is, *there are none!*

Even in the case of the home office deduction, where the IRS may argue a site visit is necessary to verify the existence of the office, there are at least four alternatives. The office can be verified by photos, drawings, video tape, or oral testimony of witnesses. Clearly, not even that is an issue which can be verified by "only a direct visit."

There is no legal or tactical reason an IRS agent should ever be in your home. As a matter of fact, under ideal circumstances, the entire audit should be conducted through the correspondence process to avoid the pitfalls of a face-to-face confrontation.

PART IV - TAMING THE BEAST

Beasts prey on the innocent
The silence weighs the cost
Ravaged children search for truth
While sanctity is lost

Hungered villains laud their heights
As trampled victims sigh
Voices shout their disbelief
The victors wonder why

Truth dismembers righteousness
And virtues cloud the air
When wisdom holds its sanity
Strength rises from despair

Echoes carry lost refrains
The mindful hear the song
Beasts and dragons lose their hold
Salvation comes along

P. L. Engstrom

Chapter Eleven -
Challenging the Beast's Power
"Appealing Tax Audit Decisions"

Why You Must Appeal

The tax auditor's decision is never final. Too many people believe it is and end up paying taxes they do not owe. To obtain a review of the audit, the IRS has established a division known as the Appeals Office. Its express function is to negotiate settlements with citizens who disagreed with auditors.

In chapter four we learned that 89 percent of all returns audited are found to owe money. The average tax debt generated by the process is about $4,000. However, in 1995, only about 3 percent of those audited appealed their case. Internal Revenue Service 1995 Data Book, Table 31. This testifies to the degree to which the IRS has the public convinced it cannot win when challenging an audit.

Ironically, on appeal, more than 84 percent of all cases are settled satisfactorily. Ibid. And the magnitude of the errors found by the Appeals Division is *shocking*, even to me.

In a 1994 report on Appeals Office work, the GAO tracked the breadth of examination changes made by Appeals during 1992 and 1993. The report examined tax disputes involving the fourteen most common code sections. Among them are sections 61, 162, 167 and 311.

Code section 61 defines "gross income." It is the touchstone from which all income tax debt flows. If an item is not considered income, it is not taxed. When the IRS makes a claim of unreported income, it cites code section 61 for its authority.

In 1992, the Examination Division made adjustments to income in the amount of $3.784 billion under code section 61. On appeal, those adjustments were reduced to $1.664 billion, a cut of about 57 percent. Similar results appear for 1991 audits. Very simply, the Appeals Office cut by more than fifty cents on the dollar every income determination appealed by citizens. *Unfortunately, the vast majority did not appeal.* General Accounting Office, "Recurring Tax Issues Tracked by IRS' Office of Appeals," GAO/GGD-93-101, May 1993, page 17.

Code section 162 allows a deduction to businesses for all expenses incurred in earning income. If the expense is "ordinary and necessary," it is allowed. During 1992, the Appeals Office considered cases involving $2.517 billion in section 162 adjustments. On appeal, those adjustments were cut to $743 million, a *71 percent reduction.* Ibid, page 15.

Depreciation expenses under code section 167 is another recurring issue tracked by GAO. In 1991, the Appeals Office considered cases in which Examination proposed adjustments to income of $1.696 billion based upon disallowed depreciation expenses. On appeal, those adjustments were cut to just $155 million, a reduction of *more than 99 percent!* Ibid, page 19.

Still another recurring issue arises under code section 311, relating to the taxability of corporate distributions. During 1991, the Examination Division proposed adjustments of $533 million under section 311. On appeal, those adjustments were reduced to *zero, a cut of 100 percent!* Ibid, page 31.

Let me reemphasize that these cuts occurred only for those who *appealed the decision.* The majority of citizens *do not* appeal their case. These facts should make it clear to even the most casual observer why so many are able to reach an amicable settlement with Appeals whereas they cannot with Examination.

What can possibly account for this wild spread in the results between the two? For starters, never lose sight of the fact that the function of the Examination Division is to *"get the money."* The function of the Appeals Office, however, is much different. It is best expressed by the language of Revenue Regulation section 601.106(f), which sets forth the rules of procedure for Appeals Officers. Rule I states:

> An exaction by the U.S. Government, which is not based upon law, statutory or otherwise, is a taking of property without due process of law, in violation of the Fifth Amendment to the U.S. Constitution. Accordingly, an Appeals representative in his or her conclusions of fact or application of the law, shall hew to the law and the recognized standards of legal construction. It shall be his or her duty to determine the *correct amount of the tax*, with strict impartiality as between the taxpayer and the Government, and without favoritism or discrimination as between taxpayers. Regulation section 601.106(f)(1), Rule I; emphasis added.

As you can plainly see, the Appeals Officer is under strict regulatory guidance regarding the settlement of cases. He is not driven by the need to "get the money." Rather, his function is to determine the true facts and correctly apply the law to those facts. This leads to a correct determination, not a falsely inflated one designed only to fill the Treasury's coffers.

For this reason, I often say that the purpose of the Examination Division is to cause problems with citizens, while the purpose of Appeals is to solve them. With which would you rather deal?

Too often, citizens fail to appeal because they believe it will only make matters worse. They believe the Appeals Officer might reopen issues previously accepted or not reviewed by the auditor, or worse, may start another audit. However, Revenue Regulation section

601.106(d) stipulates that while the case is under consideration, the Appeals Officer is not to either "reopen an issue" agreed on at the audit level, or to "raise a new issue." Unless a serious mistake is made at the audit level which will have substantial impact on the tax liability, Appeals action is limited to reviewing the decision of the tax examiner.

How to Appeal

In any income tax audit, the citizen is vested with the right to appeal an "unagreed" case. Revenue Regulation section 601.103(c)(1). It is done by filing a timely protest letter. While not all cases require the protest be in writing, I submit that it is *always best* to make your request in writing for two reasons. First, the procedure is very simple. And second, it *eliminates* the potential for miscommunication.

The time for making the appeal is set by Revenue Regulation section 601.105(d)(1)(iv). It provides that when an examination is complete, the revenue agent must communicate his findings to the citizen in the form of a "revenue agent's report" (RAR). The RAR states the basis of the proposed adjustments and must be accompanied by a thirty-day letter. The regulation describes the thirty-day letter as, "a form letter which states the determination *proposed* to be made." Ibid; emphasis added.

Notice that the thirty-day letter is *not* a final assessment. Rather, it is the process of communicating the reasons why the agent believes you owe more tax. The thirty-day letter must also inform you "of appeal rights available if [you] disagree with the proposed determination." Ibid.

The thirty-day letter asks you to agree with the auditor's findings and sign the waiver included. The waiver is Form 870. You have no legal obligation to sign it and the IRS cannot punish you if you refuse. If you do sign it, the IRS assesses the tax and proceeds to collection. Your right of appeal is not lost, but the manner of execution is significantly altered. In the meantime, the IRS can and will try to collect.

If you disagree, you are usually presented with three options. The first is to submit additional information relevant to the agent's findings. If you have additional data that has not been presented, by all means do it. The second is to request a meeting with the agent's supervisor. This too can be helpful and should be considered. The final choice is to submit the protest letter asking for an appeal. If you have exhausted all possible remedies at the Examination level, this is the course to pursue.

You have thirty days from the date of the cover letter in which to submit your written protest. Drafting the protest letter is tremendously simple. To be effective, you must follow the guidance of IRS Publication 5, "Appeal Rights and Preparation of Protests for Unagreed Cases." According to Publication 5, the protest letter must contain these specific claims:

1) your name and address,

2) a statement that you want to appeal the examination findings to ` the Appeals Office,

3) the date and symbols from the letter showing the proposed changes and findings you disagree with,

4) the tax periods or years involved,

5) an itemized schedule of the changes with which you disagree,

6) a statement of facts supporting your position on any issue with which you disagree, and

7) a statement of the law or other authority on which you rely.

You must declare that the statement of facts under paragraph six is true under penalties of perjury. Do this by adding the following signed declaration:

> Under the penalties of perjury, I declare that I have examined the statement of facts presented in this protest and in any accompanying schedules and, to the best of my knowledge and belief, it is true, correct, and complete.

Without such a declaration, your protest is considered inadequate. In fact, if you fail to include a statement under any of the points above, your protest is considered inadequate. On the other hand, it is not necessary to submit a "legal brief" to support your case. It is enough merely to state the code or regulation section upon which you rely.

For example, suppose you challenge the disallowance of business expense deductions. Your statement of the law under item seven could be as simple as, "Code section 162 allows a deduction for any 'ordinary and necessary' expense incurred for the 'purpose of earning income.'" Be careful to state facts which allow the reader to conclude that the disputed expenses qualify as deductions under section 162. This puts the issue before the Appeals Office where you have the right to present any and all evidence and authority necessary to support your case.

Mail the letter via certified mail, return receipt requested, to the "person to contact" as shown in the thirty-day letter.

The Appeals Conference

After lodging your protest letter, an Appeals Officer is assigned to determine your case. He notifies you in writing of the Appeals conference. The conference is an informal meeting between the parties where you may present evidence, argument, legal authority or other support for your position.

Appeals Officers are markedly different in their approach to matters as compared to auditors. First, they are generally more knowledgeable about the tax law. Second, they have a far better capacity to apply the facts of your case to the applicable law in order to reach a proper conclusion. Third, they are more inclined to consider the hazards of litigation, i.e., the government's risk of losing a case should it maintain its posture. And lastly, they are not under the same pressure to produce revenue. All this adds up to a person better able to determine the *correct* tax, versus one trying only to *collect* tax.

At the Appeals conference, be prepared to take the Officer by the hand through the RAR pointing out specific errors the agent made in calculating your tax. Present facts in the form of documents and affidavits. Argue the law from specific sections of the code, regulations or other authority supporting your claim. Be prepared to make or consider an offer of settlement based on what you present.

Handling the Belligerent Agent

The vast majority of tax auditors conduct themselves in a professional and polite manner. That is not to say they are inclined to do you any favors or lose sight of their goal; they merely do not act like thugs in the process. Occasionally, however, you do run across one who watches too many movies.

Such a person may make unreasonable demands for records. He may ask you to perform accounting tasks unnecessary to determine your correct tax. He may make multiple demands for information either already submitted or wholly irrelevant.

Such a person is generally arrogant and unwilling to recognize the limitations of his office. Indeed, such a person often believes, or at least tries to imply, *there are* no limitations to his office. He may threaten to increase penalties for "failure to cooperate." He may suggest the IRS can "seize everything you have" if you do not cooperate. He may even go so far as to claim you could "go to jail" for the perceived malefaction.

There are two things you must never do when presented with such a beast-like attack. First, *do not* argue or otherwise contend with the agent. Second, *do not* succumb to the threats and intimidation.

Arguing gets you nowhere. It may only play to his attempt to frustrate you and emphasize your apparent lack of power. At the same time, his resolve is strengthened by your inability to intellectually push him off the point.

But that is not to say you should concede either. The single most effective way to deal with unreasonable, belligerent agents is to kindly point out the improper nature of the request, establish that what you have done to that point is all that is necessary to prove the accuracy of your return, and ask that he rescind his demand. If he does not, explain that as far as you are concerned, the audit is *over*. Ask him to prepare a final report *at once* based on the information submitted and to transmit it to you without delay. Explain you will in turn exercise your absolute right of appeal.

Expect the agent to respond in one of two ways. The first is to explain in a huff that all your deductions will be "disallowed." "If that happens," he may assert, "you will owe substantial additional tax, interest and penalties." That is not, however, accurate. The thirty-day letter transmitting the RAR is subject to the right of appeal. The assessment is never final until *after* your appeal is considered.

The second, and more likely reaction is he will be overcome by a spirit of quiescence. It suddenly becomes unnecessary to push those issues and demands which, just moments ago, were dispositive of the entire matter. You can now move toward a reasonable resolution of the case.

The Right of Tax Court Review

Though a great many cases are resolved favorably at the Appeals level, not every case can be settled satisfactorily. This is true for a number of reasons. First, the Appeals Officer may be unimpressed with the validity of your proof. Second, the law may be such that the Appeals Officer believes you are not entitled to the benefits you claim. Third, and least likely, is the Appeals Officer is really a tax auditor with a face-lift and is just trying to get more money.

The Appeals Office is not the final arbiter on whether you owe taxes. The Appeals Office makes the final *administrative* determination on the matter, but that is subject to review by the United States Tax Court. If you cannot reach an agreement with Appeals, the IRS must mail what is called a Notice of Deficiency (NOD). The NOD is the letter transmitting the Appeals Office determination on the case.

The NOD is often referred to as a "ninety-day letter" since it provides ninety days from the date of issuance to submit a Petition for Redetermination in the Tax Court. Code section 6213. This deadline is solidly fixed by law and *cannot* be extended. Therefore, to appeal to the Tax Court, submit your petition *within ninety days*. In counting the time, include Saturdays, Sundays and legal holidays. Please note that the time period is *not* three months, but rather, *ninety days*. Therefore, take into consideration the fact that some months have thirty-one days while others have thirty.

Once mailing the NOD, the IRS is effectively estopped from assessing any tax while the ninety-day waiting period is pending. Code section 6213(a). If a petition is filed within the deadline, it cannot assess until the Tax Court's judgment becomes final. If no petition is filed within the deadline, the IRS can and will assess the tax shown in the NOD.

The Tax Court advantage is two-fold. First, the case is reassigned to the Appeals Office for settlement consideration. The difference between the first Appeals trip and the second is significant. The second time through involves a *docketed court case* where the IRS is under pressure to settle.

Second, filing the Tax Court petition brings the IRS' Office of District Counsel into things. These are the lawyers who represent the IRS in Tax Court. They have absolute settlement authority over cases pending in the Tax Court and have the power to override Appeals Office recommendations to settle cases on terms they deem suitable. A Tax Court case therefore provides two bites of the settlement apple. Of course, if you are unable to reach an agreement with District Counsel, you have the right to present your case to a Tax Court judge.

In chapter four of my book, *Taxpayers' Ultimate Defense Manual*, I provide step-by-step guidance in drafting a Tax Court petition and walking a case through the court.

Reopening a Prior Audit

I say throughout this discourse that too many people do not understand or are misled concerning their right to appeal audit decisions. As a result, the vast majority of those audited face assessments they do not legally owe. This begs the question, "What can I do if I have been so victimized?" The answer is found in the audit reconsideration. That is the procedure whereby closed cases may be re-opened. Let me illustrate.

Steve received a notice from the IRS that his return was selected for audit. He promptly took the notice to his preparer for help. He left his preparer's office with the assurance she "would handle everything." Confident she was capable of fulfilling her promise, Steve forgot all about the audit.

In the following months, he received a few more letters and each time he took the same action. He took it to the preparer's office and placed it in her care. Each time, she offered assurances regarding the progress of the case. The unflinching representations left him with every reason to believe all was "under control."

One year later, Steve received a bill demanding full and immediate payment of $4,915.25. How could this be? The preparer was handling everything. Her repeated assurances indicated that the matter was under control. Obviously, this was not the case.

After confronting the preparer, Steve learned she had done nothing. The notices he forwarded to her were duly filed and ignored. She did not attend the audit conference, submitted no letter of explanation or proof on Steve's claims.

When the thirty-day letter was issued, Steve did not avail himself of his appeal rights as he was unaware of them. The preparer ignored the paperwork. Next came the NOD which also was ignored. As a result, taxes were eventually assessed and that is when Steve faced enforced collection. By reason of the preparer's incompetence, Steve was deprived of both his right to present evidence and to appeal the auditor's decision.

The audit reconsideration is available in any circumstance where "the assessment is excessive in amount." Internal Revenue Manual Supplement 41G-154, section 4, citing Revenue Regulation 301.6404-1. Under such circumstances, the IRS has the discretionary authority to abate any assessment "if it is in excess of the taxpayer's correct tax liability." Ibid.

The manual lists three general reasons why it will entertain the reconsideration:

1) the request is based upon information "not previously considered" but which if timely submitted, "would have resulted in a change to the assessment,"

2) an original return is filed by the citizen after an assessment was made by the IRS under the Substitute for Return (SFR) Program, or

3) there was an "IRS computational or processing error in adjusting the tax." Ibid.

In Steve's case, he possessed proof of the validity of his deductions that was never submitted because of the incompetence of his preparer. Clearly, he is entitled to reconsideration under this manual guideline.

Another common situation is where one files no return and the IRS prepares a return for him. This is done under the authority of code section 6020(b) and is known as a substitute for return (SFR). The SFR becomes the basis of the assessment though it does not consider the deductions, exemptions, credits, etc., against the tax.

The manual clearly provides that the audit reconsideration must be made in writing. The request must seek abatement of the excessive tax. Specifically explain why you were deprived of the ability to submit data or appeal the original audit decision. Illustrate how the data would have reduced your tax if presented at the time of audit. Point out the language of Manual Supplement 41G-154, section 3, which says,

> The mission of the Service is to collect the proper amount of tax. To require payment of erroneous assessments leads to poor customer relations and overinflates our Accounts Receivable Dollar Inventory.

Include the following material with your letter:

1) identification of the prior audit issues and the reasons for the abatement request,

2) a copy of the tax return in question,

3) a copy of the original examination report if available,

4) documents supporting your claim, and

5) if you never filed a return, you must submit an original return and documents to support it. Manual Supplement 41G-154, section 5.

When the evidence indicates the underlying assessment is in error, the case is to be assigned to an auditor for reconsideration. The auditor is to review the evidence and make the necessary adjustments. Because the reconsideration is discretionary, there is no appeal right from the auditor's decision. You may, however, "request a conference with the examiner's manager" to discuss the matter. Manual Supplement 41G-154, section 15.

By following this procedure, erroneous assessments can be corrected even though the ink on the examination report has long since dried.

The Offer in Compromise (OIC)

Section 7122 of the code affords the IRS the authority to "compromise" any outstanding tax liability. There are two reasons why a liability may be compromised. The first is where there is doubt as to "collectibility" of the tax. That is shown by proving you cannot pay the amount assessed. The second is where there is doubt as to tax "liability." That is shown by proving the tax assessment is erroneous.

The OIC can be an effective way of dealing with closed tax cases. Provided there has been no Appeals Office or Tax Court determination of your liability, the OIC affords a potentially effective avenue of review.

Whether to proceed with an OIC or audit reconsideration is a delicate question requiring careful balance of the competing interests. The audit reconsideration is a simple process. The IRS must look at your case when you meet the various criteria set out above. However, there is no appeal right from an adverse decision.

The OIC, on the other hand, is more complicated. While it implies the same documentation needed to prove an erroneous audit, the paperwork necessary to pull it off can be more cumbersome. What is more, the OIC takes longer to process and review because of Collection Division case loads. In addition, when you file an OIC, the statute of limitations governing the IRS' right to collect from you is stayed during the period of time the OIC is pending, plus one year. On balance, however, you have a right to appeal an adverse OIC decision. That puts the question of your liability before the Appeals Office.

The OIC is beyond the scope of this work. However, I address in great detail both aspects of the OIC as well as the collection statute of limitations in my book, *How to Get Tax Amnesty*. Review it carefully before submitting an OIC.

Chapter Twelve -
Spying on the Beast
"Staying Ahead of the IRS"

Protecting Future Returns

It is possible to take what we have learned about 1) how returns are selected for audit, 2) tax audit defense techniques, 3) your responsibility to make and keep records which "clearly reflect income," and 4) the IRS' burden of proof, then blend them into an elixir that prevents audits in the first place. Not only do we prevent the damaging results of audits in the general sense, but we avoid altogether the trauma of the economic reality audit.

The process starts with recognizing the reason so many have inadequate records of income. About 87 percent of Americans work for an employer, receiving W-2 forms at the end of the year reporting wages and withholding. These workers generally do not keep independent records of their income. Instead, they rely on the employer to provide accurate W-2s.

For a number of reasons, this is a critical error. For starters, employers make mistakes. Usually the errors are inadvertent, but they nevertheless cause serious problems. Look at what happened to Ramon in chapter nine when a contractor filed an errant 1099. Without independent income records, it is more difficult to correct mistakes.

Do not believe that errant W-2s and 1099s are isolated problems. In fact, they are so pervasive that Congress considered as part of the Taxpayers' Bill of Rights Act 2, requiring all payers to put their telephone numbers on information returns to better enable citizens to contact them when disputes arise. On April 1, 1996, the IRS issued a notice asking payers to voluntarily begin the practice effective with date of the notice. IRS Announcement 96-5, April 1, 1996.

The second concern is that a few people file fraudulent information returns in a deliberate effort to get others in trouble. This too is more widespread than you might think. It caused Congress to add a provision to the law as part of the Taxpayers' Bill of Rights Act 2 allowing those harmed by such documents to sue the perpetrator. New code section 7434 allows one to sue for damages when harmed by a fraudulent information return.

The third problem is companies can go out of business, then fail to issue information returns. If you do not have independent records of your income, you may never notice the missing return, especially if you have changed jobs often. However, the IRS often does notice if it obtains your bank records or discovers the data by auditing the company in question.

The fourth and most compelling reason to make independent records of your income is simple. A Form W-2, however accurate it may be, *does not* speak to what you earned *elsewhere*. It addresses only what you earned from the company making the report. An agent may say, "Sure, the W-2 proves you earned X amount of dollars from the ABC company, but it does not address what you earned working on the side." This is an attempt to box you into proving a negative. You cannot prove you did not work a second job by merely producing a W-2 issued by your principle employer.

On the other hand, independent income logs, such as those made by Judy and Ramon which we analyzed in chapter nine, give you just such an advantage. All information returns must be tied to income logs which in turn must be tied to bank records. Finally, they must be supported with an affidavit declaring that income earned from all sources is accurately reflected in the logs and bank records.

When you accomplish that, you have an airtight package of documentation that can defeat any unfounded claim of unreported income. My strongest recommendation therefore, is you begin now, for all future returns, to document your income through your own independent logs.

My book *How to Fire the IRS*, takes you by the hand to illustrate just how such logs are created and maintained. With the expenditure of very little time and effort *and no expense*, you can put yourself into an elite category of American taxpayers: those who cannot be taken advantage of in a tax audit.

Audit-Proofing and Penalty-Proofing

Having created income logs throughout the course of the year, you are now ready to take the next step, i.e. using them to audit-proof and penalty-proof your tax return.

Recall from our earlier discussion how returns are selected for examination. For the most part, returns are flagged on the basis of the Discriminate Function (DIF) scoring process. Each line of your return is compared to averages for persons in your same income bracket, location and profession. If any line of your return is at variance with the averages, the difference is scored. The higher the score, the greater the chances of audit.

My audit-proofing techniques are based upon that procedure. To audit-proof a return, provide information *with the return* sufficient to answer any potential questions raised *in the return*. To audit-proof your income claim, provide copies of your independent logs and an affidavit to support them.

The audit-proofing process is neatly tied together with IRS Form 8275, Disclosure Statement. The Disclosure Statement is specifically designed for this purpose. It notifies the agency regarding a return claim it may question, then you provide the answers with the return. This avoids the need of a lengthy and costly examination and keeps you out of the beast's cauldron.

Moreover, you give yourself two clear advantages. First, we know the IRS has nowhere near the manpower to audit everybody. That is one reason the agency is pushing so hard for a flat tax. Under such a system, most of the variables are removed and the IRS is better able to scrutinize vastly more returns.

As a result, the audit process must *and does* focus upon those returns with the most promise. The IRS refers to this as "potential for change." Those with little potential for change are not disturbed. Those with significant potential for change are introduced to a tax examiner, beginning the quest for revenue.

Using Form 8275 in combination with providing information answering potential questions in the return sends the clear message that your return holds little promise of increased revenue for the IRS. It will be forced to cast its bread upon other waters.

The second advantage is equally impressive. In the event you do make an error (people can make honest mistakes), you avoid penalties by making full disclosure of the facts at the time of filing. Penalties are pointed at those who are "willfully negligent" in complying with the law. Those who deliberately overlook their duties or knowingly take improper liberties face the wrath of over 140 different penalty provisions.

Penalties are not intended for those who do their level best to comply with code, but through no fault of their own, make an honest mistake. Penalties cannot apply to those who act in good faith and based upon a reasonable cause for their actions. Using Form 8275 evidences good faith and reasonable cause on the front end. More details on audit-proofing and penalty-proofing tax returns are presented in *How to Fire the IRS*. I discuss penalties in more detail in chapter thirteen of this book.

Keeping an Eye on the IRS

What would it be worth to you to know in advance whether your return was selected for audit? We know that forewarned is forearmed. That kind of advanced knowledge gives you a world of advantages, not the least of which is the ability to prepare an airtight package of documents necessary to prove income long before being contacted. The best part is it does not take a brother-in-law working for the IRS to get it done.

The IRS maintains a file on every tax return, both business and individual. It is known as a Master File. For 1040 filers, the file is an Individual Master File (IMF). Business tax return information is organized in a Business Master File (BMF). Each file is a computerized statement of account and record of all relevant activity. The date of filing your return is shown in the IMF for a given year, as is the tax assessment date, amount of tax assessed, whether interest and penalties are added and in what amounts, the notices sent regarding the account, etc.

All activity is reported using what the IRS calls transaction codes. Each three digit code represents a given transaction. For example, the filing of a return and corresponding assessment is shown with a TC 150.

When a return is flagged at the service center for review and potential examination, a TC 420 shows up in the master file. If, after review, it is found that the return has no potential for change, a TC 421 is entered, reversing the TC 420. That ends the matter. If the return is handed off to the district office for examination, the master file shows a TC 424.

Generally speaking, it takes several months for the first review process to take place before a decision is made on passing the case to the district office. From that point, it takes several more months before the case is assigned to an examiner. In turn, it takes a few more months before the examiner sends a notice informing you of the good news about your audit. In the meantime, however, the various notations are placed in the IMF. When you know how to obtain it, you have wonderful advanced warning of the gathering storm.

In addition to the IMF and BMF, the IRS maintains a similar computer file for information returns. It is known as the Information Returns Master File (IRMF). This is the file that is cross-checked with Master File records to see whether citizens receiving Forms 1099 and W-2 timely file their returns reporting all income reflected in those forms.

The IRMF is a fruitful source of data for those needing to confirm the information returns that are filed. Monitoring the IRMF helps to avoid costly confrontations should an errant W-2 or 1099 appear in the system. Please recall that citizens have the burden to "fully cooperate" with the IRS in cases of errant information returns. Code section 6201(d), discussed in chapter nine. When you do cooperate, the IRS bears an affirmative duty to present "reasonable and probative information" relative to the document. It cannot rely upon it blindly.

Accessing data in IRMF puts you into a commanding position with regard to that duty. Keep track of the information returns submitted on you and be aggressive about correcting them long before the IRS comes knocking on your door. This may be one of the surest ways to keep the burden on the IRS regarding errant information returns.

How to Get Into IRS Files

The Freedom of Information Act (FOIA) provides access to all these IRS files, and more. Under the FOIA, you have the right to receive any material the IRS has compiled with regard to your personal tax matters. There are some narrow exceptions for records relating to national security and ongoing law enforcement matters. However, all of the master file records are clearly and quite simply obtainable under the FOIA.

Moreover, records generated by an auditor in connection with your case are likewise obtainable. These include workpapers, activity reports, examination reports, information obtained from third parties, etc. Such material often proves tremendously valuable when defending an audit. The IRS will not, however, release informant statements or identities.

To obtain master file records, make a written request under the FOIA to the Disclosure Officer at the Service Center where you file returns. You must establish your identity and right to receive the material. Do that by submitting an affidavit attesting to your identity and provide a photocopy of a picture ID bearing your signature. A drivers license works well.

The request must be specific as to the documents sought. Identify master file records by tax period and type of return. For example, to obtain your IMF for 1994, request the "Individual Master File Statement of Account relative to Form 1040, for tax year 1994." A business master file may use different tax periods than an IMF. For example, when requesting the BMF relative to employment tax returns for 1994, you must specify all four quarters since each quarterly return is subject to a separate BMF record. A business income tax return is also recorded in a separate BMF.

Obtain records relevant to an ongoing audit by writing to the Disclosure Officer at the local district office. Use care in specifying the documents sought. The FOIA does not require the IRS to guess at what you are after, but to provide specific documents not otherwise exempt under the law. What is more, the FOIA does not require the IRS to answer questions. If you are seeking data relative to a particular issue, phrase your request in terms of producing *documents*, rather than stating a *question*.

For example, suppose you need information relative to the filing date of your return. Do not ask the IRS, "What is the date of filing my 1994 income tax return?" Instead, ask the agency to "Produce documents which reflect the filing date of my 1994 income tax return."

The FOIA is stringent about how the request is styled. I discuss the process at length in the book, *Taxpayers' Ultimate Defense Manual*, chapter three. The guidelines say the request must:

1) be in writing and signed,

2) state that it is made under the FOIA,

3) be addressed to the IRS' Disclosure Officer,

4) reasonably describe the records you are seeking. When you know what you are after, as in a master file, state your request with precise clarity. When you do not know the specific document, give as much detail as possible,

5) establish your identity and right to receive the material,

6) give an address where you can be contacted,

7) state whether you wish to view the documents in person or have them mailed, and

8) agree to pay the costs of searching for and reproducing the documents, though the first 100 pages are provided free.

When making a master file request, ask the IRS to provide a copy of Document 5576, ADP (Automated Data Processing) Transaction Codes. It shows the translation of the transaction codes used to signify account activity. Without it, you will be lost in interpreting the IMF or BMF.

By keeping close tabs on your master file, you can always be one step ahead of the IRS.

Chapter Thirteen - De-Clawing the Beast

"Thirteen Bluffs and Intimidations and How to Counter"

In testimony before the Senate Finance Committee in 1969, former Senator Henry Bellmon of Oklahoma told his colleagues,

> In a recent conversation with an official of the IRS, I was amazed when he told me, "If the taxpayers of this country ever discover that the Internal Revenue Service operates on 90 percent bluff, the entire system will collapse.

The art of bluff and intimidation is an integral part of IRS training and practice, though its employees and manuals never admit it. History speaks plainly, however. It is clear that without the bluff, in many cases, the IRS just would not collect money.

Sometimes the bluffs are subtle. In one case, an IRS agent explained that he would hate to see the citizen "run up all kinds of legal fees fighting a case he couldn't win." By not taking the bait the citizen did fight, and did win--without running up "all kinds of legal fees."

Other times the bluffs are not so subtle, unless you think a train wreck is subtle. An example is a doctor who was harassed to within an inch of his life by the IRS. After the auditor made literally hundreds of thousands of dollars in mistakes and lost the doctor's receipts, the case went into collection. The IRS demanded he pay $55,000 in back taxes, "now." After listening to the doctor's explanation that he did not have the money to pay "now" and pleas for time to allow him to raise the funds, the revenue officer told him, "Our experience with doctors who say they don't have the money is, if we just squeeze them hard enough, the money they don't have just seems to come from someplace."

Whether subtle or bold, the success of the bluff is dependent upon two things. First is the hope that the individual cannot recognize it as a bluff. Secondly, is that his own lack of confidence moves him off his position and into an emotional state necessary to accept the "bad news."

Throughout this treatise, we discuss ways the IRS uses these tactics to get money that is not owed. In this chapter, I clearly identify the more common ones. That way, if you end up paying money, is because you owe it, not because you were bluffed. Please also review chapter seven for more on your rights in an audit.

Bluffs Used in the Audit

1. The Bluff: *"You must appear at the audit when told."* In chapter seven, under the heading, *"The time and place of the audit,"* I discuss your rights under section 7605 to set a "reasonable" time and place of your audit. I shall not restate my case here, but must emphasize a few points.

This law is clear that you cannot be pushed into attending an audit for which you are ill-prepared. Since the burden of proof is on you, fundamental fairness mandates you be afforded reasonable time to prepare. This includes time necessary to gather, organize and if required, reconstruct records.

Often an agent presses the issue by claiming that if you are not in attendance by "X date" or if records are not produced by "X date," all your deductions will be disallowed. However, agents have no unilateral authority to disallow your deductions. The agent can only *propose* disallowance. His proposal, or thirty-day letter, is subject to your right of appeal. See chapter eleven for more on appeal rights.

2. The Bluff: *"You must submit to a 'line audit'."* For years, the IRS has used the highly invasive, costly and cumbersome Taxpayer Compliance Measurement Program (TCMP) audit to build its statistical data base. In turn, that data base is used to select the majority of returns audited. In chapter four, under the heading, *"How returns are selected for audit,"* I explain the process. I also explain that due to my testimony to Congress, the planned TCMP sweep for 1995 and 1996 was de-funded. But while the TCMP is temporarily quieted, the issue is not dead. Congress may choose to resurrect it at any time.

The TCMP audit concentrates on the entire tax return--one line at a time. They are wholly arbitrary in the manner of selecting returns. They are, in the truest sense of the phrase, a "fishing expedition."

While TCMP is designed as a research tool, it is unquestionable that the IRS uses it to get more money. Because citizens lack notice of which items are in question, the agent is free to create problems as the audit develops. The citizen must react to on the spot demands and questions, something that most people find difficult to do. Combine that with unreasonable time constraints on producing data and you have a recipe for abuse.

The TCMP audit can be neutralized with a little forethought and the understanding of your right to appeal audit decisions. Whereas, the auditor's function is to cause problems, the Appeals Office solves them. Let me put this into perspective.

In the ordinary audit, a person produces his records and, if the IRS has its way, ends up with a tax bill. The Appeals review is *limited* to whether the examiner correctly computed the tax under all of the facts of the case.

Now let us can work this knowledge to our advantage. Suppose you do not produce records in a TCMP audit. What would be your reasons for not doing so? What would be the IRS' likely reaction to your stance? And what would be the consequences? The following hypothetical dialogue answers these questions.

AUDITOR: Good morning, Mr. Smith. My name is Jim Henderson. Thank you for coming this morning. Let's get right down to business. Did you bring all of your books and records for 1996? I would like to go through them.

MR. SMITH: Well, Jim, before we go in to any of that, tell me, what part of my return is in question?

AUDITOR: The entire return. This is a TCMP audit. We look at each item.

MR. SMITH: Why?

AUDITOR: To see if the return is correct and to help the IRS keep accurate statistics for future audits.

MR. SMITH: Is there a specific entry that caused this audit?

AUDITOR: Well, no, not exactly. We want to look at each item.

MR. SMITH: Are you saying there is no one particular entry that caused my return to be kicked out?

AUDITOR: No. Your return was selected at random just to review it. That helps us make adjustments to our data base and to more accurately select other returns for audits in the future.

MR. SMITH: Why should I go to all this hassle if there is nothing wrong with my return?

AUDITOR: You have to. When your return is called into question, you have to verify all items claimed.

MR. SMITH: You just said there's nothing on my return that has been called into question. You said this audit is arbitrary to help you build your data base.

AUDITOR: Look, if you don't want to produce your records, I will just have to disallow all your deductions. Then you will have a bill to pay, with interest and penalties!

MR. SMITH: Are you saying I don't have any right to have your decision reviewed? Are you the one and only person I'll ever deal with here?

AUDITOR: Of course not. But if you don't produce records, the Appeals Office will uphold my decision every time.

MR. SMITH: I am perfectly happy to verify anything you feel may be out of line. But I am not going to waste my time going through this hassle just so you can beef up your computer system. Just tell me the item you think is out of line and we'll talk about it.

AUDITOR: I just explained I must look at each item. We can take them one at a time if you like but I must have proof for each item. If you don't want to cooperate, I'll just disallow your deductions and you can go from there.

MR. SMITH: I just told you I'm willing to verify my return if there is something wrong with it. But you keep saying there's nothing wrong with it. Then, in the next breath, you tell me I have to produce every scrap of paper I own to prove it. That doesn't make sense. So unless you just tell me what's wrong, I guess I will take it to Appeals.

Later on, at the Appeals level:

APPEALS OFFICER: Mr. Smith, we are here to review the determination made by Examination that you owe additional taxes. It appears from the file your deductions were disallowed because you refused to cooperate. Apparently, you refused to turn over your records. What is your contention here?

MR. SMITH: First of all, I didn't refuse to cooperate. I told the agent again and again I would produce any records he asked for if he would just tell me what was wrong with my return. He wouldn't — so I didn't.

OFFICER: Well, my job is to decide whether the determination is correct. It appears to me that it's just a matter of verifying what you've claimed. If you're willing to cooperate, it'll be just a simple matter. If not, there's nothing I can do. In the absence of records, we just can't allow any deductions. Are you willing to do that?

MR. SMITH: Yes. I was willing to do it at the audit, but the examiner would not cooperate with me. Let's just take the items one at a time. We can begin with . . .

What do you accomplish? The case is transferred to the Appeals Division, responsible for *solving* problems, and away from the Examination Division, responsible for *creating* them. You may ask, "How have I helped myself? I still have to produce my records. Why didn't I just give them to the auditor and be done with it?"

The auditor's job is to find ways to collect more money. In a wide open TCMP audit, he could have found any number of ways to do that. By contrast, the Appeals officer only determines whether the auditor's actions are justified. At that point, it is simply a matter of *verifying* deductions by producing records. Since the auditor made a blanket disallowance, the resulting tax bill is overcome by records production at the Appeals level. Appeals changes the environment radically and the advantage swings to the citizen's favor.

You should note, however, auditors enjoy the right to summons records under code section 7602. This power is not often used to procure records from the individual, but is used to obtain them from third parties such as banks and employers. If the agency uses the summons against the citizen, the law generally requires you provide the records.

3. The Bluff: *"Your proof for this deduction is not sufficient."* The most common audit bluff is for the examiner to attack your form or method of proving deductions. Agents claim canceled checks are no good. They often ignore receipts. And even year-end statements are said to be ineffective. Of course, most agents never accept testimony despite the rules we teach in this book.

The "Your Proof is No Good" bluff works under just one condition, if you believe you have no recourse to contest the auditor's decision. However, when your proof meets one or more of the criteria set out in chapter six, there is no need to fall victim to this bluff.

4. The Bluff: *"No witnesses are allowed in the conference."* It is not unusual to desire the presence of witnesses at an audit conference. Usually, the witness is needed to present relevant evidence on a claimed deduction. One example is the case of Paul who claimed travel expense deductions for a trip to California. He brought a friend with him. The two traveled to California to research a possible investment the second man was considering in Paul's business.

The audit called into question the propriety of these deductions. To establish the business purpose of the trip, I intended to bring Paul's travel companion to a follow up conference. I intended to present his testimony regarding the purpose, length, and nature of the trip.

Upon walking in the door with our witness, we were met with immediate opposition from the revenue agent. "These conferences are confidential," she said. "I cannot permit unauthorized persons to be present." I explained that the man's presence was for the limited purpose of offering testimony on the travel expenses. Once that is concluded, the witness could be excused. That way, he would not be privy to anything else.

"I'm sorry," she responded. "The law is quite clear and I just can't allow it."

The law is code section 6103. It forbids the IRS from releasing any confidential "tax returns or return information" to any "unauthorized person." The intent of this law is certainly noble. However, auditors deliberately use it as a sword, not a shield. Without the testimony of Paul's witness, we could have been at a decided disadvantage. The agent knew this and that is exactly why she flexed the section 6103 muscle.

However, I anticipated the objection. To counter her power play, we prepared in advance IRS Form 8821, Tax Information Authorization. Its purpose is to permit the citizen to give his consent, in writing, to the IRS so it may release otherwise confidential information.

With Form 8821 in hand, the agent had no legitimate cause to exclude our witness and his important testimony. See chapter seven, under the heading, **"The right to present evidence,"** for more on Form 8821.

5. The Bluff: *"You must sign this waiver."* At the conclusion of the audit, the agent presents the RAR. If tax is owed, the citizen is asked to sign Form 870, Waiver. Form 870 permits the IRS to assess the tax and begin collection.

Signing the form is, of course, not mandatory. What is more, the IRS is powerless to force a signature. If you do sign, however, your only appeals recourse is to pay the tax in full, then file a claim for refund. To talk with the IRS, though, you would believe that unless you sign the form, "bad things will happen."

Years ago, Bud came into my office looking for help with his audit. He already went through several conferences with the auditor, his lawyer and accountant. The IRS questioned the sale of some real estate in 1984. However, due to a mistake, the sale was not reported on the '84 tax return. The agent analyzed the sale, made some adjustments and computed a new tax. The agent presented Bud with a bill for about $14,000, before interest. Bud was told he must pay it. The agent also demanded, rather rashly, that Bud sign Form 870.

But Bud did not agree with the figures and had no intention of paying the tax if he could help it. The agent gave Bud no alternative. "Sign it," he said. "If you don't, I'm going to write it up just the way it is." Exactly what he meant by, "I'm going to write it up" was never explained. The implications were left solely to Bud's imagination.

Bud turned to his lawyer and accountant for help. The accountant's advice was profound. "We've done all we can do. Looks like you're gonna have to pay."

The lawyer's observation was even more compelling. "You haven't paid much taxes in the past four years anyway--might as well just give 'em the money." Great advice, don't you agree? The best part is Bud paid for it!

Now let us understand something important before we go any further. The agent's computation was dead wrong. He computed some important aspects of the sale improperly and overlooked several thousand dollars in deductible expenses. In addition, he asserted a penalty that was totally out of line. I pointed the errors out to Bud and sent him back into the beast's cauldron with the new ammo.

Bud returned just two days later. He got nowhere. He sadly reported that the agent just repeated his demands or he would "close the case." The bold, unmistakable impression left by the ultimatum was if Bud did not voluntarily sign the waiver, the IRS would just collect the tax anyway.

I explained to Bud his appeal rights, a fact ignored by the agent. "Hey Bud," I said, "If you don't agree, let him 'write it up.' All it means is you have the chance to take the case to Appeals and then to the Tax Court. You have a right to trial before you have to pay 'em a dime. If he won't bend, that's fine. Go over his head."

"No kidding," replied Bud, in wide-eyed disbelief, "he never said I could do that."

"Of course not," I observed, "you might take him up on it."

Bud asked for another meeting and the agent agreed to look at the evidence more carefully. Bud attended the meeting but was discouraged by the report. The agent remained unimpressed. Again he demanded Bud sign the 870 or he would "write it up." Now that Bud knew what "write it up" meant, he challenged the agent. "Fine, write it up," he said. "I will just appeal."

Rather astonished, the agent replied, "Appeal? You will appeal?"

"That's right," pushed Bud, more confident now. "I disagree with your figures and I have made a counter-offer that is correct. And if you don't accept it, I'm going to appeal!"

Apparently pushed into a corner, the agent said, "Fine. Appeal it. I'll issue the notice."

Bud left the office. Not more than three hours later the agent called Bud at home. It seemed he reconsidered. It seemed the case was not worth hassling over any longer. It seemed his computations indeed overlooked several items and he was willing to settle the case as Bud proposed.

"Great!" said Bud, "I'll write it up!"

That saved Bud over $8,000. And all it really took was the intestinal fortitude to say "no" and stick to it. With just a little information, Bud was not bluffed into paying thousands in taxes and penalties he did not owe.

Chapter eleven explains how to exercise the right of appeal.

Bluffs Used in the Appeal

1. The Bluff: *"If you pre-pay the tax, you can avoid interest."* At the conclusion of an audit or appeal, expect the IRS to ask for payment of the additional tax owed. The pitch generally is, "if you pre-pay the tax, you can stop the interest from running and save yourself a lot of money. You can maintain your objections, but at least the interest stops."

Like a broken clock, this statement is both correct and incorrect. Pre-paying a tax liability does indeed stop interest from running, a major consideration when fighting the IRS. However, often misleading is the claim that after paying, you can "continue to object."

Again, this is a true statement, but if taken out of context, it creates a false impression. Under ordinary circumstances, the IRS cannot collect a dime without an assessment. It cannot obtain an assessment without issuing a Notice of Deficiency. Upon receiving an NOD, you have the right to petition the Tax Court before paying the tax. See chapter eleven for details.

The IRS mails an NOD only if there is an "underpayment" of tax. Code section 6211(a) states that a deficiency is *reduced* by the amount of tax collected by the IRS. Consequently, if the IRS determines that a $2,000 deficiency exists, and you pay $2,000, it *will not mail an NOD*. Consequently, you *will not* have an opportunity to petition the Tax Court for redetermination of the bill.

After paying the tax, the only method of continuing the battle is to file an administrative claim for refund. But the IRS does not explain that legal nuance when making request for pre-payment. Believing he will be notified by the IRS, the citizen writes his check then goes home to await the next letter. The next letter, however, never comes. The reason is the burden is now on the citizen to file a claim for refund, something he either does not know or does not know how to do. The result is the IRS gets more money with less fight.

Before making a decision to pre-pay taxes, carefully and objectively weigh the chances of success. Do that by considering all the facts of the case and the governing law. More information on that topic is presented later in this chapter.

Next, if you decide to pre-pay, do it in such a way as to preserve all possible avenues of pursuit. Designate the payment *in writing* as a "deposit in the nature of a cash bond." Never say you are "paying the tax." The deposit not only stops the interest but ensures you will be mailed a notice of deficiency preserving the right of a Tax Court appeal.

2. The Bluff: *"All bets are off!"*

The Appeals conference involves a process of give and take designed to reach an agreement. As you move through the points of contention, the goal is to narrow the scope of the dispute as much as possible. If a trial becomes necessary, it encompasses as few issues as possible. Narrowing the disputed issues is the underlying purpose of any pre-trial negotiation. This is desirable for a number of reasons. Most notably, you reduce the inherent risk of litigation and greatly reduce your burden should the case go to trial.

The process of a give and take negotiation eventually leads to one party making an offer of settlement. Suppose your audit involves the following issues:

1) $1,500 in travel expenses disallowed,
2) $2,500 in home office expenses disallowed,
3) $1,000 in charitable contributions disallowed, and
4) 25 percent in penalties added to the bill.

After reviewing your evidence, the Appeals officer makes this offer, "I will allow all the contributions. I will give you $1,000 in travel expenses. And, I will allow one half of the office-in-home expenses." He makes no specific mention of penalties. Thus, as far as he is concerned, the penalties remain in the case as part of the deal.

You respond, "I don't like it. I want the penalties out of there. I believe the facts justify removing them."

The Appeals officer is firm on his position. "I don't think you have shown the good faith required to kill the penalties."

Unwilling to budge, you are now faced with a decision. Either you take the deal offered, or you litigate the issue of the penalties. Comfortable with the figures offered on the remaining issues, you state, "I am willing to settle on the basis of the deductions offered, but I want the penalties out. If you are not willing to bend, I'll litigate the penalties."

The Appeals officer responds with the bluff. "Okay, then all bets are off. I will withdraw my offer to settle the deductions, and you will have to litigate *everything*. The offer I made is to settle the case. If you don't want to settle the case, I withdraw it."

Your blood runs cold. With the offer you have a bird in the hand. If it is withdrawn and you are forced to try each issue in court, you stand to lose that bird in the hand. What to do?

I follow a two step process. The first is rather simple. Elicit an admission that his offer of settlement is based upon the proof that you provided. You could ask, "You would agree, wouldn't you, that the reason you are allowing $1,000 in travel expenses is because I proved $1,000 in travel expenses?" When he says, "yes," ask the same question as to each issue. After eliciting affirmative responses each time, proceed to the second step.

Step two is to make reference to Appeals practice Rule I. I quote it in chapter eleven, under the heading, *Why You Must Appeal*. Please recall that Rule I prohibits any settlement not based on the law and facts of the case. Rule I contains a stiff admonition against making or withdrawing offers solely on the basis of discouraging litigation on a legitimate issue.

Moreover Rule II provides that Appeals officers are to give serious consideration to any taxpayer proposal which,

> [F]airly reflects the relative merits of the opposing views in light of the hazards which would exist if the case were litigated. However, no settlement will be made based upon nuisance value of the case to either party. If the taxpayer makes an unacceptable proposal of settlement under circumstances indicating a good-faith attempt to reach an agreed disposition of the case on a basis fair to both the Government and the taxpayer, the Appeals official generally should give an evaluation of the case in such a manner as to enable the taxpayer to ascertain the kind of settlement that would be recommended for acceptance. Revenue Regulation section 601.106(f)(2), Rule II.

I approach the matter with three carefully worded questions.

1. "You of course recognize your obligation to resolve this case on the basis of the law and facts as they exist in the case, do you not?" Do you think he will say no? Next question.

2. "And the offer you made to settle the deductions is based entirely on the law as you understand it and the facts as they exist, isn't it?" What do you think his answer will be? Next question.

3. "So if you withdraw your offer and force me to litigate issues which you have already agreed have been proven, your case is no longer based on the law and facts, is it?" What can he possibly say? And when he agrees with you, he is finished!

Using this technique allows you to carve problem issues out of the case yet remain strong on those where the law and facts are behind you. At the same time, you have substantially reduced the "hazards of litigation."

Merely recognizing the bluff does not guarantee success overcoming it. You must be sure the law and facts support your stance before you can taste success.

3. The Bluff: *"Just file an offer."*

This is a last resort plea to induce a settlement in a case involving big numbers. Of course, one of the major indices used to determine whether a settlement is acceptable is the bottom line. "How much will I owe if I accept this offer?" You must ask this question or you are cheating yourself. After all, tax disputes are about money.

The bluff refers to the Offer in Compromise (OIC) provided for by Code section 7122. I mention it in chapter eleven. The OIC allows the IRS to reduce a tax bill if you either do not legally owe it or cannot pay it.

If your liability is determined by Appeals, you eliminate one ground upon which the OIC can be based. The IRS will not consider an OIC based on liability when that question is previously determined. Internal Revenue Manual Chapter 5700, part 57(10)7.43; *How to Get Tax Amnesty*, chapter eight.

On the other hand, an OIC based upon doubt as to collectibility involves a lengthy and detailed income and asset investigation. The IRS wants to ensure you are unable (not just unwilling) to pay the debt. If you have the income and assets to satisfy the bill, regardless of how excessive it may seem, you are expected to pay it. Your OIC will therefore be rejected. Ibid.

Do not fall into the trap of accepting an otherwise unacceptable proposal simply because the OIC carrot is dangled under your nose.

4. The Bluff: *"We will add a $25,000 penalty if you litigate."* This common bluff is often used when one is determined to take an issue to trial in the Tax Court. The IRS threatens to apply for an award of the $25,000 penalty provided for under code section 6673. The idea behind the bluff is that if one loses a case in Tax Court, not only is he required to pay the tax, but he is responsible for an additional $25,000 penalty to boot. This of course, is very dissuading to the would-be litigant. The penalty is not, however, automatic.

Under the law, the Tax Court has three reasons to impose a penalty of up to $25,000. They are, 1) if your legal position is "frivolous or groundless," 2) if the proceeding was instituted "primarily for delay," or 3) if you unreasonably failed to pursue "available administrative remedies."

The penalty is avoided if, 1) your legal claim has not been specifically rejected by the Tax Court in previous cases, and 2) if found in your favor, the claim would reduce the tax deficiency. When these conditions are met, you face very little risk of incurring the $25,000 penalty. As long as you act in good faith and for the purpose of resolving the dispute, not delaying the inevitable, the penalty does not apply. The penalty is to punish those who abuse the system, not those who use it to legitimately redress improper IRS decisions.

The third condition of the statute was added by the Tax Reform Act of 1986. It makes it imperative that you do all you can to properly exhaust administrative remedies before petitioning the Tax Court. The 1986 act added another section relating directly to this issue. It is section 6213(d). It gives the IRS the authority to "rescind" a notice of deficiency mailed in error, eliminating the need to file a Tax Court petition.

To implement section 6213(d), the IRS created Form 8626, "Agreement to Rescind Notice of Deficiency." Once the form is signed by both the citizen and the IRS, the NOD is treated as though it never existed. If the agreement is not accepted, you must petition the Tax Court within the ninety-day grace period. Please see *Taxpayers' Ultimate Defense Manual*, chapter four, for a full discussion of Form 8626.

5. The Bluff: *"There is a 90 percent chance we will win the case."* After all other inducements to settle have failed, expect the Appeals Officer or District Counsel attorney to inform you of your chances of prevailing on the merits of the case. Glibly, he claims the government's chances of prevailing are high, perhaps as high as 90 percent. "There really isn't much sense in going forward," he reports. "I can tell you what the court is going to say about this. There is a 90 percent chance this is going to go our way. I don't see what you have to gain by pursuing this."

Anybody with any experience in trial work can tell you that the only thing certain is the outcome is uncertain. The one aspect of litigation universally recognized by trial lawyers is the risks are high. For that reason, our judicial system has been almost completely transformed into a forum for arbitration and settlement. Maybe that is good, maybe it is not. The point is, very seldom can anybody accurately predict the outcome of a trial. IRS lawyers, while they often pretend to be capable, are no exception.

It is true that certain cases contain attributes making them more or less likely to meet with success. An example is the so-called "tax protester" cases. Over the years, people have challenged the constitutionality of the tax laws on several grounds. Almost without exception, the courts reject the claims as meritless. *How to Fire the IRS*, chapter four. But not every tax issue has a record paved with the defeats of predecessor cases. And without some case history to go on, an attempt to place odds on the chances of success or failure on the merits of a given case is, at best, a shot in the dark.

I once dealt with a District Counsel attorney in negotiating a settlement. The issue involved the deduction of $12,000 of fees paid to a return preparer and business manager. The IRS offered to allow just $4,000.

Our position was that as a business manager, the preparer performed services in an ongoing capacity. These services were essential to maintaining the profitability of the company. In addition, a portion of the services were attributed directly to tax return preparation and bookkeeping services which are absolutely deductible expenses. Code section 212.

Early in the negotiations, the IRS held firm on its offer. Despite my protestations, the attorney and Appeals officer were both convinced the IRS had a "95 percent chance" they would be successful if we litigated the question.

I phoned the attorney to discuss the matter. "Mike," I asked, "on what do you base your statement that there is a 95 percent chance the IRS will be successful on this point?" He answered quickly, "You haven't shown that all of the consultant's work was directed at earning income for your clients."

Pointing to the evidence we submitted, I countered, "All of the consultant's time sheets detail with particularity the work he did. You heard the testimony of my client concerning his work. Surely this evidence does satisfy the requirement."

Mike's only retort was, "Well, I don't think it does."

There was no question that the attorney was firm in his position, but I also knew he had no tangible legal authority to back him up. So rather than attack his position, my tactic was to make him *argue* his position, in as strong of terms as he could. Knowing his stance was weak, I believed the most effective way to convince him of that was to allow him to convince himself.

I asked, "Mike, I want you to talk me out of litigating this case. What do you have in the way of case authority to dissuade me from taking this any further?" He responded flatly, "I don't have any."

Not surprised, I asked, "Well then what specific facts are you going to rely on to support the notion that we are not entitled to the whole deduction?" Smelling my approach, he got defensive. "Hey, he snapped, "you have the burden of proof. I don't have to prove anything."

"That's true," I replied calmly, "and my proof consists of the testimony of my client and that of the consultant himself. You heard what each had to say. You are not saying these people are liars, are you?"

More reserved now, he said, "Of course not."

Pushing a little more, I asked, "In fact, Mike, you would have to agree that they are both quite believable people, wouldn't you?"

The attorney was no dummy and knew exactly what I was doing. He just could not prevent it. He said, "If you are asking me whether I think the court will find them to be believable, yes, it probably would."

My last question spelled the end of the fight. "Well then," I said, what is there in your case that justifies your hard-line position on this issue?" In light of all the previous admissions, he was forced to come to grips with the weaknesses and surrender.

The bluff works when the citizen has no idea what the prevailing state of the law is on the issue. When you have a grip on reality, the bluff means nothing.

Bluffs Used in Collection

1. **The Bluff:** *"You owe penalties."* The tax code contains over 140 different penalty provisions the IRS uses with reckless abandon. The citizen has the burden to prove the penalty *does not* apply. Therefore, the IRS asserts them without regard to the facts and often, without even an investigation. This happens not only in the audit, but as an integral part of the IRS' computer notice program. As we learned earlier, the IRS mails millions of notices each year. In 1995 alone, it assessed about 34 million penalties against individuals and businesses, most through the mail. The notice simply declares you owe a penalty and demands payment. If you do not pay, it threatens "enforced collection action."

Every penalty provision contains a good faith or reasonable cause provision. It means simply that a penalty does not apply when the citizen acts in good faith and based on a reasonable cause for his actions. This is to ensure penalties are issued only against the deliberately negligent citizen, he who takes affirmative steps to improperly avoid paying the correct tax.

Examples of good faith, reasonable cause include, *but are not limited* to:

1) adverse financial conditions brought on by circumstances over which you had no control,

2) medical factors leading to the inability to meet your tax obligations,

3) reliance upon the advice of qualified counsel, *or the IRS*, which turned out to be in error,

4) reliance upon IRS statements or publications which turned out to be in error, or

5) simple ignorance of the law or requirements in a particular area, where you demonstrate you made at least minimal efforts to ascertain your responsibilities.

These ideas are not intended to be exhaustive. The concept of good faith is entirely subjective and turns on the facts of a given situation. What may seem reasonable to one person may not to another. Therefore, present your good faith argument based upon what you knew or believed, not on what somebody else knew or believed.

Most penalties are assessed at the Service Center and communicated by letter. Often those trying to deal with them are told by IRS employees, "The penalty is automatic. You just have to pay it." Nothing could be further from the truth. You have the right to cancel any penalty on the premise of good faith when you prove your case.

To meet the burden, make a written request for abatement of the penalty. Support it with a sworn statement to establish all the facts. Provide copies of all relevant documents such as medical records, etc. Offer sufficient detail to support the contention that you acted in good faith and based upon a reasonable cause for your actions. Failure to provide detail is the most common error in penalty cancellation requests. The facts should contradict the legal presumption that the penalty applies. Mail your request to the office that issued the penalty using certified mail, return receipt requested. In the context of the tax audit, the same rules apply, though you merely present your request to the auditor.

Historically, the IRS has used penalties both as a means of raising revenue and to pressure citizens to accept audit findings they did not otherwise agree with. Agents often threaten to load more penalties onto the bill if their unreasonable demands are not met.

In 1992, the IRS adopted a Policy Statement expressly agreeing to *abandon* this practice. It declares it will use penalties only for their "proper purpose," that is, when citizens deliberately disregard or disobey the law. The policy is intended to ensure that penalties are not used "as bargaining points in the development or processing of cases." IRS Policy Statement P-1-18, May 19, 1992. Use this to prevent the auditor from threatening penalties if you do not accept an erroneous determination.

Chapter six of my book, *41 Ways to Lick the IRS with a Postage Stamp* is probably the most thorough, definitive discussion ever written to the public on techniques for winning abatement of penalties. Because of that exhaustive analysis, I elect to be more brief here. Anyone setting out to challenge tax penalties does himself a disservice if he does not read that discussion.

2. The Bluff: *"You owe more taxes."* Part of the IRS' 1984 Strategic Plan was to increase "computer-generated contacts." Since then, the IRS has orchestrated a blizzard of computer notices claiming unsuspecting citizens make mistakes on their returns and owe more tax. In 1993, the IRS mailed 60 million notices affecting about $190 billion of taxpayer accounts.

IRS calls most of the notices "mathematical recomputations." I call them "arbitrary notices." Often with no explanation, the notice claims an amount is due. Just like the penalty letter, it states that unless you make immediate payment, "enforcement action" will be taken.

In 1991, former IRS Commissioner Shirley Peterson reported that "service center account adjustments alone accounted for 10 million notices." Internal Revenue Service "Highlights," Annual Report, 1991. This correction program is responsible for generating billions in additional revenue each year. Just how many people pay these illegitimate notices is unknown. The Annual Report does not include a column entitled, "Number of idiots who took the bait."

However, we do know from repeated GAO studies that IRS computer notices are wrong about half the time. From the IRS' own data, we know its audit results are wrong *at least* half the time. This tells us people pay a fortune in taxes they do not owe. The plot unfolds this way. After receiving an arbitrary notice, the innocent victim phones the toll free "assistance" line and talks to an IRS representative.

"I got this notice today," he says. "It claims I made a mistake on my return and I owe $650. I don't understand. It doesn't say what the mistake was. I asked my accountant and he is sure the return was prepared correctly."

The friendly voice says, "I'll bring up the file. What is your social security number, please?" After giving the number, the caller hears the sound of computer keys being skillfully punched. Soon the voice says, "Yes, here it is. Your return was corrected due to an error. You owe $650."

"I know that," the caller chirps. "But why?! My accountant says the return was done correctly." Responding abruptly, the voice says, "I don't have that information in my computer. The file only shows an assessment. When may we expect payment?"

Frustrated, the caller barks, "I don't even know if I owe this and you can't tell me why. Why should I pay it?"

Firm now, the voice threatens, "Sir, if you don't pay promptly, we can take enforcement action. That includes filing tax liens and levying your wages, salary and bank accounts."

Anybody with sense enough to write with his inquiries gets a form letter in response. It reads,

> We are giving special attention to your inquiry about the tax account identified above. We will write you again within forty-five days to let you know the action we are taking.

After some time, the next communication is the levy or lien mentioned by the Voice. By then, it is just a matter of biting the bullet and paying the tax.

The bluff is successful if one does not respond to the initial letter properly. Code section 6213(b) allows the IRS to correct "mathematical" and certain other tax return "errors." But the law also expressly states the citizen,

> [M]ay file with the Secretary within 60 days after notice is sent . . . a request for an abatement of any assessment specified in such notice, and upon receipt of such request, the Secretary *shall abate the assessment*. Section 6213(b)(2)(A); emphasis added.

Provided you respond timely and properly, the IRS has no choice but to abate the tax. Moreover, if convinced the assessment is correct, it must mail a Notice of Deficiency in accordance with section 6213(a). That gives you a right to be heard in Tax Court before paying a dime. See chapter eleven.

Any response which is, 1) not in writing, 2) does not demand immediate abatement of the tax under section 6213(b)(2)(A), and 3) is not made within sixty days, renders the tax subject to enforced collection action. I provide details on the abatement process and other computer notices in *41 Ways to Lick the IRS with a Postage Stamp*.

The Unspoken Bluff - "You will go to jail!"

One of the most heinous elements of the 1984 Strategic Plan is that calling for the IRS to "create and maintain a sense of presence" in all America in order to "encourage and achieve the highest degree of voluntary compliance" possible. There is little doubt the IRS aspires to be the American Gestapo.

Ask anyone you see on the street what will happen if you cheat on your taxes. The answer is always, "You will go to jail." To ensure this attitude prevails, the IRS does its best to prosecute a token number of misfortunates each year. Is it mere coincidence that the majority of the prosecutions take place in the spring, on the threshold of the tax return filing deadline? After being convicted of tax fraud, Leona Helmsley was ordered to report to prison on April 15. The New York judge who sentenced her said he did it to "send a message."

Elsewhere, newspaper headlines shout, "Man Charged With Tax Fraud - Faces 15 Years."

"Fifteen years?! *Good Heavens!* Why didn't the idiot just pay the stupid tax?"

Americans bombarded with the propaganda not only have the poor stooge convicted even before a trial, but are themselves convinced that when you mess with the IRS, you can look forward to exactly the same fate. One appalling thing is an incredible portion of the population believes you run a risk of jail just by *speaking out* against the IRS.

What has the IRS become if it commands that kind of respect? More importantly, what has it done to *earn* that kind of respect?

I believe it is high time we end the *myth* about jail. The reality is that not all so-called tax cheaters go to jail. And as hard as the IRS strives to achieve ubiquitous power, it is not there yet.

The criminal investigation and prosecution statistics tell the real story. According to the Internal Revenue Service's 1995 Data Book, Table 20, there were 5,000 total criminal investigations undertaken that year. About 26 percent (1,302) involved narcotics. Right out of the chute your chances of being implicated in a tax crime are automatically reduced *26 percent* if you are *not* a drug dealer.

Please also keep in mind that in 1995, about 116 million individual income tax returns were filed. When that figure is compared to five thousand criminal investigations, you quickly realize that you have a better chance of being eaten by a shark than you do of being implicated in a criminal tax investigation.

Also note that while five thousand investigations were undertaken in 1995, only 3,386 ran their full course resulting in a criminal prosecution. So, just 68 percent of the criminal investigations ever progressed into actual, full scale, liberty threatening criminal prosecutions. Even at that, just 2,229 citizens were sent to prison. The highest majority of those actually sentenced to jail were involved in *narcotics crimes*.

Just 1,387 citizens were sentenced to jail time in 1995 as a result of non-drug related tax crimes. When you divide that number by 116 million, the number of individual returns filed, you find the true statistical probability that any one citizen will ever do time as a result of a tax crime. It computes to about *1/100th of a percent*. Honestly, who is kidding whom?

The reality is, even with all its computers and everybody-on-the-block-is-a-spy attitude, the IRS is not capable of prosecuting every person who fails to dot an "i" or cross a "t." I do not say this to encourage cheating. On the contrary. The point is, people *need not* be terrified simply because a few tax cheaters are convicted each year. People need not be afraid to speak out against IRS abuses or unjust collection practices on the vague threat of jail.

In *How to Get Tax Amnesty*, chapter three, I explain in detail the IRS' burden of proof in criminal cases. It is much different than in the civil context.

When is the IRS NOT Bluffing?

The foundation of wisdom is the recognition of not only what is a bluff, but what *is not* a bluff. Even though many IRS demands have no legal basis, some threats are backed with awesome power.

Make no mistake about it. The IRS' Collection Division has staggering powers and too often, a twitchy trigger finger. Its lien, levy and seizure arsenal make it the most powerful federal agency. And this fact is exploited by the IRS. It cleverly uses publicity generated by its own, sometimes tyrannical collection practices to create a condition of fear. This helps keep people whipped into shape. The IRS calls this "encouraging voluntary compliance." It goes hand-in-hand with criminal prosecutions.

Everybody has heard an IRS horror story. It is the kind of story that makes your blood run cold. There have been countless books, articles, and news accounts of how the IRS seizes businesses, homes, bank accounts and autos with almost indiscriminate abandon. The impact of such accounts is profound. People become convinced that if you do not turn out your pockets when asked, your house will be seized or worse, you will go to jail. The stories have emasculated the public. An overwhelming fear of our own government causes many to seek refuge in blind obedience to every demand, regardless of its legality.

In 1995, we saw the largest single-year increase in delinquent collection accounts since I have been paying attention. In that one year, the IRS faced more than 5.7 *million* delinquent citizens. In 1994, it handled 5 million. To collect, it issued more than 2.7 million wage and bank levies and filed nearly 800,000 tax lien notices. Over 11,000 people lost homes and businesses.

Tax delinquencies are growing fast and the IRS enforces collection in the most oppressive ways. To make matters worse, the Collection Division has the *least* in the way of objective guidelines to control its actions. Most enforced collection practices are employed without supervisory approval.

The bottom line is simple. The Collection Division does not bluff. When it states that "enforced collection action will be taken," that is exactly what it means. Enforced collection means liens, levies and seizures of property. Any correspondence from Collection must be taken seriously and dealt with promptly. Anyone facing a back tax debt must consult my book *How to Get Tax Amnesty*. Since its release in 1992, it has helped tens of thousands of people settle delinquent tax debts they might never have otherwise settled.

Chapter Fourteen -
Speaking the Beast's Language
"Secrets to Effective Communication"

Much of the confusion swirling around the IRS involves communication. IRS regularly mails hundreds of letters. It routinely makes phone calls and yes, even house calls. In the majority of cases, tax problems begin with *mis*communication.

It starts with a letter the recipient does not understand. He stumbles along with no information or misinformation. That is the catalyst for a series of events that go from bad to worse. He first tries to settle the matter with a phone call to the IRS. This does nothing but illustrate that the left hand does not know what the right hand is doing.

The reason is there is no *central* office controlling or monitoring cases within a district. The IRS is quite decentralized. Its cases are controlled by the *division* responsible for it. For example, the Examination Division has no knowledge of a case handled by the Collection Division. While there are exceptions to this general rule, the first key to effective communication is to recognize this reality.

This chapter contains specific techniques for communicating with the IRS while your case is in various stages.

1. Maintain a Current Mailing Address

This may seem simple, but it is often overlooked. You cannot solve problems you are unaware of and cannot be made aware of them if the IRS is unable to reach you. The IRS' legal burden is to notify you at your "last known address." That is the address shown on your most recently filed tax return. *Abeles v. Commissioner*, 91 T.C. 1019 (Tax

Court 1988). If you move and do not notify the IRS, you may miss important communications.

Consider the case of the man who moved three times in five months. Mike originally lived in New Brighton, Minnesota. In April 1985, the IRS mailed an NOD to him. The NOD demanded over $3,400. Before its mailing, Mike moved to Los Angeles. The IRS was informed of the move by the Post Office so it remailed the letter to Los Angeles. Before it reached him, he moved again, this time to a suburb of L.A. Then for good measure, he moved to Florida. IRS gave up by the time Mike headed for Florida.

By November 1986, Mike relocated to St. Paul, Minnesota and started a new job. The IRS traced him through his social security number. Soon he began receiving notices and demands for payment of the tax. Prior to that, Mike had no idea the IRS attempted to contact him. You can imagine his chagrin when it levied his bank account. By the time the IRS did catch up, interest and penalties escalated the bill to over $8,000.

Such movement is not unusual for many Americans. Therefore, you must take steps to ensure the IRS has your correct address. This is vitally important because an NOD or notice of levy mailed to the "last known address" is valid whether or not you receive it. However, if IRS knows or has reason to know that such address is incorrect, the notice is invalid. *Gibson v. Commissioner*, 761 F.Supp. 685 (C.D. Cal. 1991). As a result, you have the burden to provide the IRS with notice of a new address.

After years of chasing citizens and finally clobbering them with collection matters such as happened with Mike, the IRS created a change of address form. It did so as a result of my complaining that such a form did not exist. Complete IRS Form 8822, Change of Address, to communicate your new address to the agency. The form can be used for either individuals or businesses. Form 8822 should be sent by certified mail to the address shown in the instructions.

Running from the tax collector does not solve problems. It can only escalate them.

2. *Take Delivery of all Certified Letters*

I know people whose only defense to IRS claims is that they refused to accept the IRS' certified mail. Hiding from the IRS cannot solve the problem and neither can ignoring its mail. In fact, ignoring the mail only means losing your available defenses.

When you ignore letters, especially certified letters, you often risk a default tax assessment as we saw in Mike's case. Assessments lead to enforced collection.

3. Respond in a Timely Manner

Nearly every IRS communication requires a response within a certain period of time. Only by responding within the time established by law can your rights be preserved. These are the most common errors:

1) failure to petition the United States Tax Court within ninety days of receiving an NOD--code section 6213(a),

2) failure to respond to an auditor's RAR within thirty days-- revenue regulation section 601.103(c),

3) failure to demand abatement within sixty days of a tax assessment made under the mathematical recomputation rules--code section 6213(b)(2), and

4) failure to respond within thirty days to a notice and demand for payment of assessed taxes--code section 6331.

Notices and procedures regarding tax collection are handled in *How to Get Tax Amnesty*.

4. Respond to the Appropriate Office

The IRS is a decentralized bureaucracy. As a case progresses from stage to stage, the file changes hands from one office to another. No division of the IRS necessarily knows or cares what the others are doing. If your case is in the Appeals Division, a response directed to the Examination Division falls on deaf ears.

IRS communications are usually on letterhead stationery disclosing the particular division handling the case. Knowing that enables you to do two important things. First, it tells you where your case is within the system. Secondly, you are able to commence or continue negotiations under procedures appropriate to that division.

If a communication does not identify the division handling the case, the signature on the letter often provides the title of the person writing the letter. The typical titles and the division they correspond to are as follows:

Title	Division
Revenue Agent	Examination
Revenue Officer	Collection

Appeals Officer	Appeals
Special Agent	Criminal Investigation
Attorney	District Counsel
SPS Advisor	Special Procedures
Researcher	Automated Collection
Taxpayer Assistance	Service Center

On the IRS' letterhead you find a pre-printed portion containing information about the communication. It tells you, 1) the year in question, 2) the date of the letter, 3) an entry next to a heading, "Person to Contact." You also generally see a "mail stop" or "room number" next to this person's name. Initial responses should go to that person.

5. Make all Communications in Writing

All communications should be in writing. You must be able to refer to the date you said what to whom. There is no better way of keeping such a record.

Mail all letters via certified mail with a return receipt requested. Maintain a photocopy of the letter in your personal file. Attach to the photocopy the Post Office receipt for certified mail and the return card bearing the signature of the recipient. This constitutes proof that the letter you claim was mailed was indeed received by the IRS. That can be very important in many situations such as when the date of filing a Tax Court petition is called into controversy.

6. Do not Respond to Verbal Contacts

It is not unusual for the IRS to initiate contacts via the phone or through personal visits. For example, two revenue officers appeared at the office of a local business. They barged into the room and demanded the secretary point them to the file cabinet where they might find copies of federal tax returns. One agent flashed some kind of badge but was so quick about it the secretary was unable make it out.

The boss was out of the office but just happened to phone at the instant this transpired. "Who are they? What do they want?" These questions bounced off the terrified secretary like rubber balls. Either the agents did not make themselves very clear (possible) or the secretary was too shook up to make sense of it (probable). Her boss said simply, "Send them away and have them put whatever it is they want in writing. I will respond to them promptly." The fear-stricken secretary carried out the instructions. The agents' saber-rattling and grandstanding had the secretary so spooked she could barely remember her name.

To write a response to the visit, I later questioned the secretary. "What were their names?" I asked.

"I don't know," she said. "They didn't say."

Surprised, I said, "Didn't you ask?"

"No. They just said they wanted to see the files."

"What files were they talking about?"

"I don't know," she said. "The one lady just kept saying something about tax returns."

"What type of returns she was talking about?" I queried.

"I don't know. She just kept telling me that the forms had to be mailed to her right away."

"Did you ask for her address?"

"No."

When I asked why such a basic question was not asked, she squeaked defensively, "I didn't know I was supposed to ask for one. I didn't know what to do."

It is very easy to become scared and disoriented when IRS personnel appear unexpectedly and begin making demands. For this reason, it is wise to know in advance how to handle it.

Since there was no tangible information upon which to base a reply, we decided to do nothing. What do you say when you have no idea who appeared or even why they appeared at your door? I felt that if the contact were genuine, the IRS itself would follow up with a letter.

A few days later, a letter appeared at the office. After calmly reading it, we saw the IRS somehow misfiled the company's employment tax returns under an erroneous identification number and had no record of them. All that was necessary to settle the dispute was to supply copies of the requested documents with an affidavit verifying they were filed timely.

In retrospect, it was good the boss was not present. He may have provided all kinds of documents not having any idea where the inquisition was heading. The presence of mind to send the agents away with a request that they put their demands in writing helped in many valuable ways. First, and perhaps most significantly, it eliminated the tension of the moment. It allowed everybody involved, particularly the poor secretary, to catch their breath and actually think before reacting out of pure fear.

Secondly, it put the onus on the IRS to make a specific demand rather than permit it to continue the shotgun approach. That way, the IRS would not have unchecked access to "the file cabinet." Lastly, upon receiving the written demand, we were able to analyze the request in light of the history of the company and its filing practices. We could then determine the best, most effective and least risky way to settle the dispute. None of this is possible when responding spontaneously to verbal demands made without prior warning.

I once asked a special agent why they make it their routine practice to call upon targets of criminal investigations *without* prior warning. For example, the special agents arrive at the home at 7:30AM, just as the man is getting out the shower. After reading a Miranda warning they begin asking one question after the other about what took place three, maybe four years ago. "Why?" I asked. "Where is the sense of fair play in this type of tactic?"

The agent's response was that an unannounced interview "encourages spontaneity" and that "spontaneous answers tend to be more accurate." That answer may be sound impressive but my experience shows there is an ulterior motive.

Consider this scenario. You have been surprised by a special agent quite early in the morning. Before hand, you had no idea the IRS was even interested in you, much less concerned about potential criminal conduct. After hearing a Miranda warning at 7:00AM, you are bombarded with questions concerning transactions and events occurring years ago.

You have not given a moment's thought to any of the events since they occurred. You are confused. You are scared. You do not know why the IRS is asking you these questions. When you try to get a little information, the agents sandbag you. "We can't tell you that," they say. "We are asking the questions here."

The result is you make statements and give information which *is not* accurate. No other result could reasonably be anticipated under the circumstances. Later, after having a chance to review your records and consult counsel, you find the statements were indeed wrong. The difficulty is that you can never *change* information previously given to the IRS. All you can do is *supplement* it with information you believe is correct. Remember the old saying, *you cannot unring the bell.*

What is important is *not* that the latter material is indeed accurate. But, rather, that it *contradicts* your initial responses. Contradictions do not bode well with the IRS. I have therefore concluded that this tactic is deliberate and carefully calculated, *not to obtain correct information*, but to cause the citizen to make *contradictory* statements.

For these reasons, I insist that all correspondence be in writing. If the initial contact is made via phone or in person, politely send the agents away asking that they follow up with a written request. At the same time, it is good practice to make careful notes of conversations you do have. The notes should be in the "I said — he said" format. They should also bear the time and date of the conversation together with the names of the parties involved. These types of notes, referred to as Memoranda of Interview, are *always* kept by the IRS. Your notes can then form the basis of, 1) a follow up letter summarizing the points of the conversation, and 2) a reference from which to reconstruct obligations made and agreements reached during the course the conversation. They also serve to contradict inaccurate IRS statements about the substance of the conversation.

7. *Take Careful Notes During Face-to-Face Discussions*

Unless you are an extremely unusual person, it is difficult or impossible to recall all the points raised during an audit. This handicap is overcome through the exercise of the skill mentioned above--take copious notes!

For example, agents regularly request additional information or further proof of certain items. One audit involved several issues where follow up documentation was necessary. We needed additional proof of business miles, uniform deductions, and rental property expenses. I did two things to protect the citizen's interests. First, I took careful notes, recording the items verified and those needing additional documentation. Secondly, I asked the agent to provide an Information Document Request.

I compared the agent's IDR with my own notes. This allowed me to not only verify the items needing more proof, but also allowed me to verify those we did prove. When mailing the supplemental proof, I sent a cover letter itemizing the documents contained in the package. Based upon my own notes and the IDR, I itemized the issues *already proven*. This prevented the agent from later saying those items were still in question.

8. *Be Sure You Are Always Dealing With a Person*

It is very common for the IRS to send computerized notices lacking a person's signature. Although I have mastered the microwave, I have not yet been able to negotiate successfully with a computer. The problem is computer notices are inflexible and present no apparent alternative to the written demand.

Respond to unsigned communications promptly but ask that an agent, that is, a living person, be assigned to handle your case. I worked with a man in Memphis who received a letter from the local IRS office. The letter requested he appear for audit on a certain date, "between the hours of 8:30AM and 4:30AM." There was no name on the letter. He was to see the "appointment clerk."

I wrote a letter with a simple request, "Please assign an agent so that pre-conference discussions might resolve as many issues ahead of time as possible." In a subsequent conversation with the appointment clerk, she said, "We will not be assigning an agent until the taxpayer comes in to the office."

"You may have misunderstood my letter," I replied. "We won't be coming into the office until an agent is assigned."

Rather huffy, she explained, "Our policy here is not to assign an agent until the taxpayer arrives."

"I have several good reasons why an agent should be assigned now," I stated. "For example, the audit notice does not indicate which specific items are in question. I must speak with an agent to see what proof we need to prepare before our meeting. Secondly, it is my policy to at least talk with the agent before the meeting to establish the ground rules under which the audit will take place. I will not be coming into the office before the assignment of an agent with whom I can discuss these matters."

She agreed to consider my request. I wrote a follow up letter based upon my notes of the conversation. In the letter, I summarized the facts and restated my reasons. I repeated my specific request for an agent and informed the clerk that we would not be appearing without one.

Eventually I received a phone call from a revenue agent who had been assigned to the case. We discussed the audit and agreed on the procedures for handling the case. Again, I followed up the conversation with a letter to verify the agreements reached.

It is even more important to have an agent assigned when you deal with one of IRS' Automated Collection Sites (ACS). ACS is charged with collecting delinquent accounts. It is done through computer generated payment demands and liens and levies.

Resist the temptation to ask questions about such notices. Whether you write a letter laced with questions or phone the 800 number, you likely will get no satisfaction. "I'm sorry, Mr. Jones," will be the refrain. "The computer shows your account is past due for 1996 income taxes. You owe $4,593. You have to pay that amount."

ACS personnel are humorless people. An ACS representative once phoned me seeking payment from my clients. "Mr. Pilla," she sighed, "we have here an outstanding balance for your clients in the amount of $854,837.54. When may we expect payment?"

When may we expect payment? As if we could send them a check for $800,000 just like that! "Ah, honey? Have you made the deposit yet? We have an unexpected bill this month!"

I quickly responded by saying, "I'm sorry. My client cannot make that payment. He only has $854,800 in his account!" There was dead silence on her end of the phone. Sarcastic humor is not one of their strong points.

The lady was not interested in my explanations. Before I could expect any real progress in the matter, the case would have to be transferred to the local Collection office. There, I could talk with a revenue officer to ensure the case was handled in the most beneficial manner. Without a transfer, collection is fully automated and insensitive to the problems and particularities of the individual.

If you face a collection situation, you must consult my book *How to Get Tax Amnesty*. I have two chapters dealing expressly with collection in general and ACS in particular. They take you a step at a time through the process.

9. Establish Ground Rules Before Your Meeting

Another common error is to walk into an IRS meeting blind. The advantage is decidedly with the IRS if you are ignorant as to the purpose of the meeting. For your own good, establish the ground rules for the meeting before hand.

Here are three specific examples. The first involves an audit raising complex questions surrounding equipment purchases and installation. The IRS contended the equipment did not qualify for certain business deductions and credits. During the audit, we intended to do two things the IRS generally looks upon with disfavor. We intended to bring witnesses to testify about the nature and use of the equipment and we intended to tape record the audit so the testimony could be used later if necessary.

The IRS does not like "unauthorized persons" present during audits. I explain this both in chapters seven and thirteen. My "ground rules" letter informed the IRS we would present witnesses. I informed the agent that we would have IRS Form 8821, Tax Information Authorization, for each witness.

Since it was our intention to tape the audit, the law requires notification at least ten days in advance. Chapter seven, under the heading, *The Right to Record the Audit.*

The third example grows out of a case involving a tax return preparer who came under attack by the Criminal Investigation Division. In an effort to build a case against the preparer, the IRS targeted each of his clients for audit.

Some went well beyond the scope of the typical audit. Rather than focusing upon the correctness of the tax return, the auditor asked a myriad of questions relating to the preparer. Obviously, the IRS was using the audit as a means of gathering evidence and information to use against the preparer. The client I worked with had no intention of being used as an unwitting source of information. Our ground rules letter informed the agent ahead of time of the issues we would and would not discuss.

Specific items that may be addressed in a ground rules letter include:

- The time and place of the meeting
- The presence of witnesses
- The specific issues in question
- What will and will not be discussed
- The nature of evidence for and against you
- Disclosure of appeal rights
- Use of tape recording devices
- Representation by counsel
- The probable result of failure to cooperate
- The IRS' legal authority to demand the meeting, and
- How the information they obtain from you can be used.

This list is not exhaustive. It varies depending upon the facts and circumstances of each case. Be aware of your right to establish basic rules for your face-to-face meetings to accomplish two very important goals. First, you eliminate unknown aspects of the conference. You learn the exact reason for the meeting and the circumstances under which it will be conducted. And, you learn, indeed help to establish, the latitude each party is permitted.

Secondly, by setting ground rules, you communicate the message that you are an informed citizen, fully cognizant of your rights. As such, the IRS is less likely to attempt to take advantage of you.

10. Do Not Ask Questions, Make Demands

The IRS is quite effective at dealing with requests. The answer is generally pretty simple--"No!" For that reason, I have long since abandoned the idea of making *requests*. Rather, I have found it more effective to make specific *demands*, politely and professionally. For one thing, there is no question about what you want when you affirmatively state your position. When your stand is not clearly defined, it is more difficult for the IRS to understand your needs.

The most flagrant example of where the "request" operates to your disadvantage is with the "mathematical recomputation." Under section 6213(b), the IRS is allowed to recalculate your tax bill if there is a math error in the return. But, if you object in writing within sixty days of receiving the notice, the IRS is obligated to abate its assessment.

The typical response, however, is to write the IRS and *inquire* as to the nature of the bill. "Please tell me what error I made. I do not understand why you penalized me." This is not a specific demand and the IRS is not obligated to take any action.

This is more effective, "I have reviewed your bill and I disagree with the amount you claim I owe. Please abate the tax immediately. If you feel I owe it, I demand a hearing." This very specific statement is impossible to misunderstand.

As long as your request does not expressly depart from settled statutory principles, you are entitled to have that request honored. I refer back to the case of the harassed tax preparer. Recall that I sent a ground rules letter to the agent informing her we would not discuss the preparer. During the meeting, the agent adamantly insisted we do. I repeated our position. "We are here to prove the correctness of the return," I said. "That is where this meeting will begin and end." After some heated discussion, the audit proceeded on the issue of the tax return. We did not answer other questions and regardless of her snarling, we could not be forced to.

11. Focus on Agreements, Not Disagreements

An Appeals officer once told me that, "If we can agree on the major issues, the small ones have a way of falling through the cracks." He is saying that some issues are "litigation points" and others are "bargaining chips." Litigation points are the issues neither party wishes to concede. Bargaining chips are those one is willing to give up to prevail on a litigation issue.

Litigation points are those most profoundly affecting the pocketbook where the law and facts are clearly on your side. It is with respect to these issues you want to remain most tenacious. At the same time, it is possible to reduce the number of issues sacrificed as bargaining chips. In the ideal negotiation, *none* of your issues are surrendered. In the realistic negotiation, some (but not all) are surrendered in exchange for success on the litigation points. The extent to which you are successful depends largely on technique.

The best way to bring about overall consensus in a tax dispute is to start by discussing the agreements that already exist on the minor points. This has a profound psychological benefit and many practical ones.

Psychologically, the audit environment is quite adversarial. When the typical person walks into an IRS office, he is usually raving about the ridiculous bill he received or the arbitrary way he was treated in an audit. Although some may doubt this, IRS agents are human and human tendency is to defend one's actions, right or wrong, in the face of an all-out, frontal assault.

Consequently, when you begin negotiations with such an attack, all defense mechanisms are immediately summoned and your adversary goes to "red alert, battle stations." You are faced with a bitter fight on each and every point. Before you know it, you stand to lose on all issues.

On the other hand, if one begins with a less acrimonious attitude, he is less likely to meet with resistance. He creates a less adversarial environment. It naturally becomes much easier to reach agreement on critical issues. I am not saying to be milquetoast or allow yourself to be swept away in the current created by the IRS representative. On the contrary. My formula *creates* circumstances dictating the overall direction of the negotiations, rather than reacting to them.

I begin by identifying all the issues in question. This simple technique prevents you from overlooking important elements of the case. Review the issues by reference to your ground rules letter, the audit notice or the RAR. Now proceed issue by issue seeking the agent's assent to the proposition that such point is an issue in the case. By the time you reach the end, you have not only gotten the agent to agree with you several times (creating a positive atmosphere), you accomplish the important task of fixing the points you must now address one at a time.

Starting with the first issue, begin by discussing the aspects of the issue to which there is or can be no reasonable disagreement. Focus upon the agreements, not disagreements. Let me give you an example of how it works in practice.

I once helped Marilyn remove a federal tax lien from a home she and her husband were selling. The IRS had obtained a large tax judgment against her husband. However, the assessment was not against Marilyn. She owed the IRS nothing.

The revenue officer was quite belligerent, not allowing the sale to close without full payment. The tax exceeded $22,000 and the equity was just $18,000, half of which belonged to Marilyn. The revenue officer convinced the closing company the entire lien had to be paid.

Marilyn's position was that the most the IRS could get was one-half the equity. Marilyn's interest in the home could not be touched since she owed no tax. Furthermore, her money could not legally be seized to satisfy her husband's debt. But all of the pleadings of her attorney fell on deaf ears.

When I contacted the revenue officer, her opening words were, "What do you want from me?" It did not take a prophet to know she was uninterested in resolving the problem. After a couple of minutes I determined this "hard case" would have to be taken very slowly and deliberately. I began to focus on the most basic points on which I knew we could agree.

I took a deep breath and began. "Pat, I said, "you will agree with me, won't you, that there is no assessment against Marilyn?" She did.

"And you will agree, won't you, that without an assessment, the IRS cannot file a lien against Marilyn?" She did.

"And you will also agree, won't you, that without a valid assessment, the IRS cannot collect any money from Marilyn?" She did.

"And you will also agree, won't you Pat, that before the IRS can get an assessment, certain administrative procedures have to be followed?" She did.

"Now Pat, you will follow all established IRS administrative procedures with regard to Marilyn, won't you?" Of course, she agreed!

"Then you must also agree that you cannot legally seize any of Marilyn's money from the sale of the house, don't you?" She did.

Having gotten her agreement on the basic underlying facts, I moved the revenue officer into a position where it was impossible for her to disagree with me on the ultimate issue. The next question I asked was, "Then there is no legal reason not to lift the lien and allow the home to be sold, is there?" She was forced, based upon the previous agreements, to accept this premise. I followed up the conversation with a letter and the house sale went ahead as scheduled. Marilyn got her full share of the money and the buyers got a clear title.

It is usually not necessary to resort to such basic statements of fact in order to get an agreement from the IRS. What is necessary is that you begin with the simpler issues, moving up to the more difficult or controversial issues. Proceeding in this fashion enables you to, 1) obtain as many agreements as possible before reaching the pivotal issues, and 2) having reached the litigation issues, you surrender as few bargaining chips as possible.

By moving backwards, the agent has the ability to negotiate your litigation issue by cashing in some of your bargaining chips. Since I do not like to surrender points, I do not move backwards. Also, by moving from lesser points to litigation issues, it becomes more difficult for the agent to retract a previous agreement in order to negotiate a litigation point. He becomes more or less committed to previous concessions.

Let me illustrate. Rowena was involved in several farm-related businesses. One concerned a mechanical heating system that enabled farmers to capture body heat from animals and actually heat barns with it. My client purchased the system from the manufacturer and leased it to several veal producers.

Rowena received an NOD covering the years the business operated. Many of the points raised in NOD were nuisance items, but a major issue revolved around the leases. The IRS took the position that Rowena purchased *paper* (written lease contracts) from the manufacturer. Rowena insisted that she purchased *equipment*, not paper, then leased it to farmers. The difference is substantial. If the IRS prevailed, Rowena would be denied over $10,000 in investment tax credits since they applied to equipment only.

In negotiations, the IRS Appeals officer made it clear he was willing to surrender on several of the lesser issues in exchange for the major lease question. Having foreseen this, I determined to head it off at the pass. Just as I described above, I presented proof to the IRS attorney and the Appeals officer on each of the minor points. One at a time, we offered canceled checks, receipts, and testimony to their satisfaction. After presenting proof on an individual item, I was careful to receive agreement that such proof was sufficient to eliminate the point as an issue. If there were further questions, they were resolved before moving on. This went on until I reached the lease issue.

As I anticipated, we could not reach an agreement on the question. The IRS held to its view and we stuck to ours. The result was an impasse and each party threatened to go to Tax Court. As is its wont, the IRS lawyer announced, "All bets are off if you litigate." Expecting this ploy, I pointed out that he *just agreed* we were entitled to those items! "You cannot, in good faith," I asserted, "litigate issues you already agreed have been proven."

After some bantering, he agreed that if we were to litigate, the only point of the trial would be the matter of the leases. This worked to carve tens of thousands of dollars worth of bargaining chips out of the case allowing Rowena to make the decision to litigate based solely upon the probability of success on the key issue alone and not risk losing the lesser issues.

12. Negotiate the Deduction, Not the Tax

One of the biggest mistakes a person can make is to attempt to negotiate *non-negotiable* points. After receiving a bill for $1,700, a man once asked me if he could, "offer 'em $850 to settle the whole thing?" The Examination and Appeals Divisions do not concern themselves with paying taxes. Their function is to determine the *correct tax*. Therefore, they are unimpressed with offers to settle a case "for half what you say I owe."

But this gives us a major clue as to *how* to approach them. As I said, their job is to determine *liability*. They do it by considering total income and all applicable deductions, credits and exemptions. If income is increased or a deduction, credit or exemption is deceased, the final tax liability goes up. The process is that simple.

So rather than negotiating the bottom line *liability*, negotiate the *deduction* that created it. For example, suppose you claim a $5,000 charitable contribution deduction. Suppose the agent disallows the entire deduction. When presented with the bill, you are asked to pay $1,500 in taxes, penalties and interest.

To negotiate the deduction, you might approach the problem this way. "Mr. IRS Agent, I claimed $5,000 on the return. You disallowed the entire amount. But surely my receipts prove I gave $2,500 to charity. I feel this evidence entitles me to at least half the deduction, or $2,500." Provided you prove at least $2,500 in contributions using one or more of the techniques we discuss in chapter six, the agent must oblige. The result is the ultimate tax is cut in half!

13. Do Not Negotiate Based on "Nuisance" Value

Litigation is expensive, both for the government and private citizens. In cases not involving the government, attorneys routinely settle cases based upon their "nuisance" value. The nuisance value is the cost a party faces if the case goes to trial, whether or not he wins.

Citizens have a tendency to bring nuisance values into tax negotiations believing the IRS is interested in keeping its costs down. The IRS does not consider settlement offers based on a case's nuisance value. Appeals Rule II, Revenue Regulation section 601.106(f)(2); chapter thirteen.

Settlement offers must be based upon the law and facts of the case. They must represent a good faith effort to settle the case in a manner that fairly represents the interests of both parties. For this reason, any offer of settlement must be buttressed with solid references to the facts and applicable law.

14. Always Ask for a Hearing Date

It is a good practice to always demand a face-to-face meeting, or hearing, on the merits of your claims. An example is where you submit a written protest letter in response to a thirty-day letter. Chapter eleven. The hearing allows you to present evidence and testimony to prove your case. Absent a request for a hearing, your case may not be assigned for one.

15. Enlist the Aid of Outside Offices

In stalled negotiations, the lines of communication can sometimes be re-established by appealing to one of two "outside" offices. The first is the Problems Resolution Office (PRO). PRO is charged with the duty of getting to the bottom of and sorting out disputes when normal channels fail. PRO operates under the authority of the Taxpayer Advocate, a position created by the Taxpayers' Bill of Rights Act 2. Code section 7802.

PRO helped in a case where a citizen filed a claim for refund. The revenue officer to whom the claim was submitted sent it to the Service Center for processing. Thereafter, nobody in either the district office or the Service Center could find it.

After several months of waiting, we wrote a letter to PRO asking assistance in tracking it down. Within a matter of days, PRO located the refund claim. Once we knew where it was, we were able to correspond directly with the persons responsible for making a decision.

PRO also has the authority to *stop* the IRS from taking action which may result in causing "significant hardship." Code section 7811. This generally involves enforced collection action. An Application for Taxpayer Assistance Order is filed using Form 911. More details on this process are provided in *How to Get Tax Amnesty*, chapter five.

The second outside office that can be of valuable assistance is that of your Senator or Congressman. In some circumstances, determined prodding by a conscientious Representative may lead to favorable results.

One problem that hampers Congressional inquiries is the IRS is forbidden to release tax return or return information to unauthorized persons. Senators and Congressmen are no exception. To avoid the problem, sign and submit to the Congressman IRS Form 8821, Tax Information Authorization. He can then submit it to the IRS together with the request for help or action.

Not all Congressional inquiries obtain results. To increase your changes, follow this process:

First, always submit a written description of the legal problem, citing code sections and where appropriate, case authorities. This eliminates the need to do any of research on the legal aspect of the problem. If such information is not provided, I do not believe you can expect your Congressman to seek it out.

Next, prepare a detailed written procedural history of the case. This evidences that all administrative remedies have been pursued and exhausted without satisfaction.

This kind of file communicates the fact that you have done your homework and your Congressman will not be made a fool of after shooting his mouth off in your favor.

Once a Congressional inquiry begins, the IRS responds in writing to any letters and generally sends a copy to the citizen. In the final analysis, the effectiveness of this appeal is directly related to your ability to provide ammunition from the background. Remember, it is your case and you, not the Representative, know all the facts and must live with the results. Therefore, quickly respond to IRS letters. This gives the Representative something tangible with which to fight.